Confronting Injustice

Livingston Armytage

Confronting Injustice

A Lawyer's Journey from Law to Justice

Springer

Livingston Armytage
Centre for Judicial Studies and The University of Sydney
Sydney, NSW, Australia

ISBN 978-981-95-3572-9 ISBN 978-981-95-3573-6 (eBook)
https://doi.org/10.1007/978-981-95-3573-6

This Springer imprint is published by the registered company Springer Nature Singapore Pte Ltd.
The registered company address is: 152 Beach Road, #21-01/04 Gateway East, Singapore 189721, Singapore

To my grandchildren
Rafael, Matilda and Atticus

Foreword

This book is a terrific read, engaging, eye-opening and entertaining. And beautifully written.

Livingston Armytage is one of those rare individuals who manages to straddle the academy and legal practice with skill and aplomb in both. I've known him for more than two decades and have worked with him in the field, the classroom and the rarefied air of scholarly research and writing, and have always harboured admiration for the way in which he slips seamlessly from one space to another while taking care to cultivate the common ground between them. This book is a testimony to these efforts and expertise.

At the book's core is a cornucopia of the author's experiences in reforming the law courts to deliver better justice in some of the most difficult and dangerous places on Earth, each one aptly flagged by his elegant and artful chapter titles. He lays bare the extraordinary difficulties he and his colleagues faced while trying to reform judicial systems in Afghanistan, when only one-fifth of the judges had law degrees (most were graduates in Sharia Studies); in Cambodia, when only seven judges survived Pol Pot's crazed barbarism and where the kleptocracy of the government that replaced him is so brazenly opposed to any notion of reform; in Papua New Guinea, where ancient tribalism and endemic violence subvert and regularly replace the country's political and legal systems; in Palestine, where mundane program details are negotiated across desks with drawers stuffed full of high denomination US dollar bills and against which Kalashnikovs and AK-47s are casually propped; and in Pakistan, when faced with the bizarre-cum-menacing problem of how to manage his program funding, suddenly increasing four-fold to $350 million while at the same time having to dodge truck bombs in downtown Islamabad.

Strikingly, the author interlaces these tales with prescient and fascinating potted histories of the countries he has worked in, alongside touching observations of life that surrounded him and how he handled it, whether with fear, doubt, sadness, hope or wonderment. He brings you with him when describing the panoramic star-strewn night sky of Australia's Central Desert; the nobility and bravery of some of the judges he worked with, the craven supplication of others and the pettiness of officials and others in uniforms; the astonishing stoicism of local fellow travellers when planes plummet, jeeps careen and trucks teeter on the edges of precipitous ravines; the happy throngs of uniformed schoolgirls in a (briefly) Taliban-free Kabul street; the stark and harsh beauty of the Hindu Kush; and the sinister secret of millions of tonnes of radioactive dirt buried beneath the apparently pristine atolls and sapphire blue waters of the Pacific islands. He relates stories of being robbed while freezing atop a truck travelling through the Khyber Pass, and again by deft pickpockets in Jerusalem, only later to get his wallet back (minus the cash) once the police realise who he is working for. He also tells the story of how Kevin, a young indigenous man who had spent more of his life inside prison than outside, brought judges to tears when he described his life and how, shockingly (I gasped), his life ended far too early.

And in all this, Livingston also delights us with turns of phrase that arrest us as much by their poignancy as by their insight. "Aid at the barrel of another invader's gun. I felt tired before even starting", he says of the law reform in Afghanistan post 9/11, and later, while reflecting on his time there, he talks of reaching some understanding that "both beauty and loss can co-exist". And in Nepal, echoing something of a theme that he admits courses through much of his career in the field, he notes with a sigh that "our ambition exceeded our budget and timeframe".

This collection of work-related reflections and insights is reason enough to commend the book, but what it offers in addition burnishes its demands to be read. Livingston bookends his experiences in the field with a clutch of opening chapters on his upbringing, education and training that led him to become the roving international development lawyer that he is and, at the end, some revelatory analyses of what it means to him or might mean to the reader. Together these existential moments turn what is otherwise a fine professional memoir into one that is also, engagingly, personal.

We see how the young Livingston responds to the earliest of life's rude lessons with self-imposed discipline and respect for learning, as well as nurturing a well-honed sense of fairness—attributes that became hallmarks of career. He shows us how he was drawn to law by the social role it plays in both exercising and controlling power, and why running marathons is not just good for the body and brain, but also the soul. The author is frank about his experiences of the competing values of legal practice—especially in corporate law—where personal rewards (pecuniary as well as intellectual) are often pitted against existential questions of the point of it all. Indeed, Livingston's "is that all there is" question, that he asks himself at the very moment he reaches the pinnacle of partnership in a law firm, is not only pivotal in his journey, but it is also one that will resonate with many readers. For Livingston, it precipitated his abandoning the partnership and heading down the path less trodden that populates most of the pages in this book.

The book's closing chapters comprise a forthright examination of the meaning of this alternative career. The author looks back along the path, distilling his in-country experiences in ways that are both revelatory and heartfelt, as well as intellectually stimulating. It's no surprise that here we see him return to the theme of fairness, and most especially how he might serve what he describes as "my vocation to leave the world a fairer place than I found it by helping the courts to administer better justice". His candid reflections on how difficult it was (and is) to serve such a calling are intriguing. His dawning realisation that "the ideals of justice are routinely subverted in most countries", is realistic, to be sure, but it is also awkward for someone trying valiantly to turn hope into expectation. Corruption, elite capture, poverty and entrenched inequities seem to stand in his way at every turn, often leading, he admits, to despair. Yet, true to form, Livingston takes on the challenge, giving rein to optimism over pessimism. He describes how he found solace and support in hitting the books again, embarking on a PhD that gave him both the time and the opportunity to see how others dealt with the abiding challenges of promoting justice. He draws on the greats of philosophy, both ancient and modern, as well as policy wonks in the fields of development, law and justice. But also, importantly, he draws on the innate and visceral incantations of what's fair and what's not that he'd often heard from the people he'd encountered while actually doing law and justice work.

These academic reflections, built on such deep foundations of practical experience, are what make this book such an education as well as a pleasure to read. Livingston's journey is not only captivating, it is also openly self-critical in the sense of always asking the why, what for and how questions. It's also surprising. In one chapter, he dips into his love of photography and we get glimpses of his skill in taking the many and often extraordinary opportunities his work afforded him to capture striking images. And in his penultimate chapter, he explores the satisfaction he gains from teaching. Though perhaps this is not all that surprising, not only because he is such a fine exponent of the art in formal settings of classrooms and lecture halls, but also because it is, in effect, what much of his career has been based on—an eternal cycle of learning, listening, showing and telling that must be valued for the journey as much as for its destination. The task of addressing the never-ending contest of unfairness may indeed be "a Sisyphean quest" as Livingston puts it, but it is also one in which it is possible to find "contentment, peace and even beauty".

Sydney Law School
Sydney, NSW, Australia

David Kinley

Acknowledgments

This narration began as an endeavour to make some sense of my life. Once started, it became a celebration of my community of companions who have joined me along this journey. As these pages reveal, I am fortunate to have shared and learned so much with you. Thank you for walking through these pages, lending me your voices and guiding my hand to tell these stories. And thank you, Professor David Kinley, for proposing that I share them:—

Mareva Bentham-Annadale, Judge Jazeela Aslam, Professor Carl Baar, Margaret Barron, Kirsten Bishop, Appeal Justice Dr Ananda Mohan Bhattarai, Gilles Blanchi, Helen Burrows, Professor Amnon Carmi, Wade Channell, Dr Bidhya Chapagain, Huma Chughtai, Kenneth B Clark, Rob Clemente, Robert Clifton-Steele, Dr Maureen Connor, Dr Diane Cowdery, Gary Creighton, Phyllis Cox, Natalie David, Professor Sinclair Dinnen, Mary Fran Edwards, Chief Justice Dame Sian Elias, Laima Etemadi, Justice Dame Susan Glazebrook, Professor Neil Gold, Ahmad Gorchiyev, Dr Carolyn Graydon, Dr Linn Hammergren, Rolly Hassall, Bob Holland, Professor John Hudzik, Erik Jensen, Ingrid Kabua, Hamidul H Khan, Judge Dr Rai M Khan, Senior Advocate Satish Karel, Jakhongir Khaydarov, Justice Michael Kirby, John Lipton, Florence Lo, Chief Justice Sir Anthony Mason, Dr Abby Mcleod, Lorenz Metzner, Steve Miller, Stephen Mokis, Chief Justice Debbie Mortimer, Judge Muhammad Amir Munir, Chief Justice Sir John Muria, Justice Vui Clarence Nelson, Chief Justice Arthur Ngirakelsong, Sara Ferrer Olivella, Mitsu Parikh, Cao Xuan Phong, Justice Hari Phuyal, Kerin Pillans, Kepas Poan, Dr Doug J Porter, Kystle Praestlin, Justice Shafi'ur Rahman, Judge Sayedur Rahman, Prem Chandra Rai, Wendy Raptigh, Frederick Rawski, Chris Roper, Jackson Ross, Scott and Rosslyn Rough-sleepers, Vin Ryan, Chief Justice Sir Gibuma Salika, Justice Sathavy Kim, Joseph Sawyer, Hamid Sharif, Dr Donna Spears, Professor Ramaswamy Sudarshan, Dr Bobbi Sykes, Darren Tohovaka, Christy Tull, John Tyynela, Imran Vittachi, Aumua Ming Leung Wai, Justice Clifford Wallace, Judge Tom Wallitsch and Irwan F Wyllie.

My elder brother Harry, who was always present in my earliest memories; my sister Lydia, whom I tied to a tree in the orchard before absconding for lunch, and my younger brother Stephen, who spurred me finally to start this book. My hugely impressive daughters Rosita and Danika—now both older than my mother when she first cradled me in her arms—who are ever re-educating me on the changing ways of this world. And Miyako, the woman of my life, best friend, patient listener and dedicated editor of my sometimes outlandish expression, who reveals ever new layers of her nature, becoming more thoughtful, strong and elegant as each year passes.

Thank you all for accompanying me.

Competing Interests The author has no competing interests to declare that are relevant to the content of this manuscript.

About this Book

Livingston is an international development lawyer who works to build fairer societies by helping the courts to deliver better justice in some of the world's most dangerous places. In this memoir, he takes the reader on an extraordinary journey far beyond the tourist path to share his encounters with injustice in the legacies of history, empire, atomic testing and natural disaster.

This journey takes us onto the red dust of the Central Desert to confront the massive over-incarceration of Indigenous Australians; into the squatter settlements of Port Moresby to loosen the murderous grip of the "*raskols*" over the night; across the killing fields of Cambodia to end the impunity of the Khmer Rouge for genocide; up to the Hindu Kush to restore the Afghan judiciary degraded by decades of war, onto the flatlands of the Nepali Terai to open the courts to Dalit women; and finally out to the Marshall Islands to witness the aftermath of US nuclear testing that killed and exiled its inhabitants with scant reparation. In each place, he encounters the resilience of the human spirit in the face of harrowing injustices.

This journey is rich in fascinating political and historical insights into exotic places. Along the way, he addresses two core questions: *what is justice,* and *what has he learned about making the world a fairer place*?

Livingston argues that justice is core to human dignity and well-being and, in its essence, is all about fairness. While there may be no universally agreed definition of justice, it is readily identified in its absence. Every 4-year-old child recognises unfair treatment from her parents and knows when justice is denied. This understanding is visceral, transcultural and indeed universal. Yet there are many different paths to justice. Trained as an Australian lawyer grounded in the thinking of Greek philosophers, Roman principles of law, Enlightenment notions of liberalism and Christian values of morality and ethics, Livingston soon discovers the Islamic, Confucian, Hindu and indigenous traditions of justice. Each is foundationally diverse, enriching his understanding of the nature of justice.

Along this personal and professional journey, Livingston learns to trust his inner voice, listen to the fears that warn him of dangers to be avoided, and value the lessons learned from his mistakes. This journey is filled with a sense of the wonders and mystery of life that give us all opportunities to attain our destinies. We can each leave the world a little better than we found it, he concludes. This is how history builds its path behind each of our steps, however small they might sometimes seem to be.

Contents

About the Author

Livingston Armytage practised law as a litigation specialist in Melbourne, before launching his consulting practice to work with the UN, World Bank and others in more than 50 developing countries around the world. He holds a PhD in law and has presented on justice at Harvard, Oxford, Cambridge and Berkeley. Livingston is Director of the Centre for Judicial Studies, and was Adjunct Professor of Law at the University of Sydney. He now lives with his wife, Miyako, overlooking Sydney Harbour. In 2019, he was awarded the Order of Australia for significant service to justice nationally and internationally.

https://www.centreforjudicialstudies.com

Books

Livingston has published six other books on justice, including two collections of photographs.

Reforming Justice: a Journey to Fairness in Asia, Cambridge University Press 2012.
Searching for Success in Judicial Reform, Oxford University Press, (ed.) 2009.
Educating Judges: Towards Improving Justice, Brill Nijhoff, (2nd Ed.), Leiden 2015.
Homeless: Hidden in Plain Sight—Photographs, Chatwin Books, Seattle 2022.
Unseen Faces; Unheard Voices—Portraits of Injustice, IBC, Tokyo 2018.
Educating Judges: Towards a New Model of Judicial Learning, Kluwer, Hague 1996.

He has also presented papers at numerous international conferences, and published many articles in peer-reviewed international legal journals.

Audience

This book is for readers interested in the idea of justice including lawyers, legal scholars and students, law and justice reform practitioners, international development professionals, judges and people curious about the world around them.

Royalties

*All **royalties** from this book go to charities supporting education of disadvantaged girls.

Prologue: Afghanistan—1978

It was winter when I left Peshawar to travel through the Khyber Pass sitting on the roof of a truck bound for Kabul. The clouds were grey, the wind was fiercely cold, and my clothes were hopelessly inadequate. On the journey through the steep rocky ravines beneath abandoned fortresses, I was robbed by a man with a knife and rolling eyes.

The Khyber Pass had been used by traders and invaders as the gateway to India since Alexander the Great had crossed through the mountains in the third century BCE. During the nineteenth century, as part of '*the great game*' for territory and resources, soldiers of the British Empire defended the Pass in the Anglo-Afghan wars, building a road and later a railway passage. Even to this day, the lands to either side remain beyond the reach of any government. Indeed, the CIA speculated that Bin Laden had lived and commanded al Qaeda from this lawless region. After 9/11, the Pass proved its continuing strategic value as a supply route for coalition forces during America's 'War on Terror', when their conveys were regularly ambushed and torched by the Taliban.

Back in 1978, aged 26, I had taken a break from practising the law and travelled to Europe overland through Asia. My journey through the Pass took the whole day, pausing at Landi Kotal which was bustling with mysterious turbaned traders among the gunsmith stalls. When I arrived in Kabul, cold and exhausted, I saw young women wearing bright clothes and skirts above the knees. There were also Soviet 'advisers' lounging in badly tailored suits. Two days later, I hurried west to Kandahar, revitalised with cups of scalding sweet tea. The journey was dramatic even then. Bands of bearded men carrying guns stopped the draughty bus to demand 'taxes.' Sometimes they removed passengers. Snow-covered mountain peaks to the north glowered silently above us hour after hour. Then onwards, I dozed sporadically through the night until the Iranian border. Here the bus passed military vehicles still smouldering at the roadside. Bearded students in jeans directed traffic carrying M16s from Shah Pahlavi's looted armouries. I clutched a note hand-written in Farsi:—

L. Armytage, *Confronting Injustice*,
https://doi.org/10.1007/978-981-95-3573-6_1

'I am AUSTRALIAN, not American.'

A geopolitical pendulum had just swung. This was a time of profound change after the American defeat in Vietnam, the Islamic Revolution in Iran, and the communist overthrow of Mohammad Daoud Khan in Kabul. It was just months before the Soviet military invasion of Afghanistan.

The notion of Afghanistan is an historical misnomer. It has never existed as a sustainable unitary state; rather it was a space whose function was to buffer the jostling empires of Russia, China, India and Persia. The highlands of the rugged Hindu Kush form a cross that has always separated these empires. This geographic partition explains the disunity that characterises the four main peoples of Afghanistan with their diverse ethnicities, cultures and alliances. In the north-east nearest to China are the Hazaras and Nuristanis; in the south-east nearest to India are the Pashtuns; in the south-west nearest to Persia are the Balochis; and in the north-west nearest to Russia are the Tajiks, Turkmens and Uzbeks—each being quite foreign to the others.

Afghanistan has long been the graveyard of infidel invaders. In the first Anglo-Afghan war in 1842, the British were routed at Gandamak by Afghan tribesmen. The entire British Imperial Army of 16,000 troops, as well as accompanying families and civilians, were slaughtered in a grisly bloodbath. One lone survivor was permitted to escape to report on this carnage as a warning to others. This rout prompted Britain's imperial retreat—just one humiliation among many others. Next came the Russians and then, most recently, the Americans—each to their identical fate.

The human toll of the Soviet invasion was catastrophic. Some six million Afghans—a half of the total population—were displaced between 1979 and 1989. Many people were forced to flee their homes to Pakistan and Iran. Of those, over two million still remained refugees, only some of whom had returned a decade later.

In 2001, I photographed those refugees who were still languishing in the Jalozai Camp outside Peshawar in the North West Frontier Province (now: Khyber Pakhtunkhwa or KP) of Pakistan.[1] They were living in a dust bowl that no one else wanted. Their homes were UNHCR plastic tents that flapped in the scouring westerly winds from the Arabian Gulf. It is hard to describe the sweltering heat on those barren, treeless plains. Routinely, it was over 50 °C—so hot, that I could photograph for 90 minutes only at a time. After that, my viewfinder would fog, and the camera became too slippery from sweat to hold. Drenched and dehydrated, I would then retreat from that wretched camp for shelter and cups of scalding sweet tea served in chipped white china cups in the village outside. After 9/11, it became impossible to ever return for security reasons.

Given the history of other nations' defeats in Afghanistan, the US displayed extraordinary arrogance, or astonishing myopia, to once again invade in 2001, just 20 years after the Soviet retreat, and then imperial hubris in presuming to teach the Afghans how to fight.

In 2005, I returned to Kabul to work on a project to help rebuild the courts. By then, Afghanistan had been in continuous war for 25 years. An entire generation of children had never known peace and, since then, a second. Our goal was to deliver a segment of the much vaunted 'democracy dividend' by supporting the degraded courts to restore what international aid donors liked to call the 'rule of law.'

On the flight from Delhi, the plane flew north-west alongside the ramparts of the majestic Himalayas which glittered above the clouds. As usual in my work, there were no tourists on board. The cabin was noisy with the chatter of Dari, Pashto, Hindi, Urdu and Mandarin. On final approach, the plane crested the peaks and dipped seemingly a stone's throw from rock-strewn outcrops surrounding the Kabul Valley. As it did so, the cabin fell silent and the passengers alert. Women who were wearing lipstick and jeans wriggled into burqas and disappeared from view. Abruptly, the plane made a sharp dive to avoid possible missile fire and hit the runway, military-style, bouncing at full throttle in case needing to abort. It was a breathless, unsettling arrival into the midst of a military encampment. Armoured carriers were guarding the terminal, and soldiers with machineguns faced outwards. The country felt strangely familiar to me. But now there were no more bright colours. There were no skirts of any length in sight; only blue nylon burqas that flitted silently past.

On arrival, I was escorted by our team leader Phyllis Cox—a highly principled American lawyer with peerless experience in leading rule of law projects in many of the world's most difficult places—to USAID. Our funding agency was based inside the American Embassy. This was a huge compound better described as a fortress. The adjoining streets were narrowed by massive concrete blocks to withstand the blast from truck bombs. Behind these blocks were 8-meter walls of sandbags atop of which had been erected slithering coils of glistening razor-wire. The gates were guarded by watchtowers with machine-guns directed at us as we approached. In front of the gates were formidable Delta barriers build to withstand ramming by truck-bombs. A banner was displayed above, without apparent irony: '*Welcome to the USA*'.

Inside, we met the official managing our project. He was a realty attorney from rural Missouri. A military reservist, he wore combat fatigues over his middle-aged tummy and sported a shoulder holster. On his desk was an M16.

'Standing orders for all personnel,' he explained ruefully.

He was also a new arrival and knew nothing about our project. Nor did he seem interested. I'd prepped for this meeting, but it was a formality. We spent the hour in small talk. He lived in a shipping container without windows out the back of the compound and watched lots of DVDs. USAID's (then) budget funded the largest bilateral development program in the world. Even so, it was minuscule compared to that of the State Department which oversaw it. That, in turn, was dwarfed by the military budget which was then estimated to cost USD 300 million each day. After the meeting, on our way to the carpark within the perimeter walls, we passed through a small market. Afghan store holders were obsequiously serving off-duty American moms in jeans and bulging T-shirts, wearing pistols on their hips—just like in Westerns—as they bought brass trinkets for their kids back home. It was surreal, like a scene from *Apocalypse Now*. Aid at the barrel of another invader's gun. I felt tired before even starting.

Our office was set in a lovely garden adorned with damask roses that filled the air with a fragrance of jasmine and exotic spices which momentarily masked the ubiquitous dust. From its upper windows, I could see two buildings standing out across the valley. The first was *Darul Aman* Palace, the 'dwelling place of peace,' which had been built by the king in 1926 as a pretention of European grandeur and modernity. This had been heavily bombarded by the Mujahideen during the 1990s and now lay in ruins, a tortured relic of the failed state. Beside this ruin was the national museum, a far more modest single-story building that was the true symbol of Afghan culture and resilience. After the retreat of Soviet forces, the Taliban had emerged. Originally, they were welcomed as a zealous though small force of religious scholars and eponymous students from Kandahar who sought to eradicate corruption and restore order through a return to traditional Islamic values. In 1996, they had seized Kabul and ransacked the monuments of previous administrations. Most notorious, they destroyed what they saw as the idolatry of the Bamiyan Buddhas. In all the fighting, the museum was severely damaged by shell fire and reduced to another pitiful ruin. But in a less well-known act of foresight and considerable courage the museum's watchman, Najibullah Popal, had buried its treasures, including the fabled Bactrian Hoard, until the Taliban's subsequent expulsion.

On my afternoon off, I was deeply moved to find this tiny museum repaired, its doors re-opened and a collection of its battered artefacts—still undergoing repair—standing in defiant display.

The next day, we were hurrying to another meeting with the Chief Justice, Fazal Hadi Shinwari, a conservative Islamic cleric with a long beard and only the faintest glimmerings of secular law, with whom I grew to enjoy collaborating. The project's 4WD was bucking like a stallion from one pothole to the next along the muddy laneway. We were already late. It was humid, and the air held the sour stench of rubbish and flyblown meat. Eagles circled lazily on the endless thermals above. As the visiting expert, I was again prepping through my notes to refamiliarize our talking points. But the cabin was jolting so sharply it was difficult to hold the papers still, let alone read. I was hassled, hunkering down, when the car lurched to a stop. Now what's stopping us, I muttered. But, at least, I could now read. There was commotion outside. The light on my pages flickered with passing shadows. I kept on reading. Then there was a noise, like a rustle of nesting birds and the chirping of starlings. Insistent. Excited. Distracting. Impatiently, I looked up to find the source of this disturbance. The car was stalled in a crowd. Teeming schoolgirls were erupting from the gates beside us. Bubbling with released energy, they were talking, gesturing, laughing with their friends. Each was immaculately dressed in a pale blue uniform, the crest of the nation proudly displayed on their breast pockets. They kept coming, scores then hundreds, at the end of the school day. The minutes dissolved. The girls of Afghanistan were coming home from school and walking happily towards their futures. I was rendered speechless, transfixed by the beauty of this moment. And since the Taliban resurgence, I still am.

This was a time of resurgent hope. I was working with a team of bright young Afghan graduates who were energised at the opportunity to make a difference. We set about researching the needs of the courts across the country. Under the chaos of forty years of war, first from the Russians then the Americans, the court system of Afghanistan had utterly collapsed. Behind this fog of war, we found a system-wide lack of fundamental judicial competency in legal knowledge, professional skills and judicial outlook, with grave concerns in both the judicial leadership and the public about corruption and the collapse of ethical standards. Foundational deficiencies had de-professionalized the judiciary and eroded public confidence in the courts. Non-state traditional actors such as the jirga, or council of elders, had stepped into the justice gap left by the disintegration of the courts. When we asked the public how they felt about this regression, I found that most people welcomed the traditional jirga to fill its gap. Koranic justice was generally seen to be fairer, more predictable, cheaper, and less vulnerable to the corruption and inefficiency that had grown to characterise the secular court system.

We travelled through the provinces, sometimes escorted by Humvees toting tripod-mounted.30 calibre machineguns, conducting consultations on the needs of the courts and judges—at least to those locations that were still safe with military protection. We reached the Panjshir Valley, beyond the massive airbase at Bagram. Irrigated by the melting mountain snows carried by a fast-flowing river, the Panjshir Valley was an oasis amid the barren surrounds. Entry was along a single winding road between mountain outcrops precipitously close to the torrent's edge. Once this had been the stronghold of Ahmad Shah Masoud—the 'Lion of the Panjshir'—who had resisted the might of the Soviet tanks until he was assassinated by Bin Laden's operatives masquerading as journalists on the day before 9/11. The rusting carcasses of massive Soviet tanks littered the otherwise picturesque valley.

In the Panjshir, the US had built a new court complex for the local community. It was an imperious two-story building with wide steps and ceremonial pillars. Its imposing entrance was heavily chained, and we could only enter through a side door. Our calls announcing arrival echoed down long empty corridors, until finally a figure emerged from a distant cubicle. He was the janitor: No, all the judges were away. The computer in his room was new but unplugged. There was no power; there was usually no power. But he assured us eagerly that the telephone did sometimes work. The complex's many rooms were large and mostly empty. Some were stacked with boxes. Others were filled with the brutalist furniture so favoured in government offices of the region—impossible to move and uncomfortable to sit on—gathering dust. The toilets were unspeakably fouled.

During the many years of war, all disputes had been resolved by the jirga of traditional elders who convened as needed across in the valley. It seemed they were continuing to be resolved there. This magnificent building—one of fifteen across the country—was seen by the community as the latest invader's folly and had never been used.

In the midst of this work, a retired US air force general visited our offices in Kabul to announce an important new initiative to win the hearts and minds of those living in remote communities. This involved the US Air Force being deployed—in between its combat missions to kill the Taliban—to drop solar powered transistors programmed to play American country music. This, he enthusiastically explained, would win 'hearts and minds' by introducing the benefits of the 'democracy dividend'. He invited us to support this initiative. My Afghan colleagues were rendered speechless. Though remaining polite, I could see they were strangling their suppressed mirth. They could see the behemoth with all of its military might was Polyphemus, the blind giant of Homer's Odyssey.

I have worked with some senior USAID personnel over the years, like Wade Channell, who are deeply experienced and capable professionals working with the best available data, who must operate as best they can within the bureaucratic architecture of a sometimes highly ideological and unashamedly hegemonic arm of US foreign policy.

I often debated with Phyllis aspects of what our project sought to do as being foolhardy. She would roll her eyes—whether at the project's design or my unruliness depending. Then she would wearily call in the team's senior local staffer to mediate our conversation.

'So, what do you think, Dr. Arif?'

Dr. Arif had come across from the President's Office and had an assuring grasp of the political economy. He would straighten out one or both of us with scrupulous politeness. Sometimes this meant subverting the design altogether by our burying a ludicrously unworkable activity that had been occasionally concocted by evangelical project designers ensconced in their DC offices.[2] More often, it resulted in our re-interpreting what had never been intended, but always should have been. We would then happily renew our endeavours.

When I talked with local judges about their work, I became aware of the extraordinary disparity in their knowledge and familiarity of the law. Some applied Islamic judgments in strict accordance with the Koran, while others made decisions based on some rendition of state law. Many dispensed justice as they remembered it from before the turmoils or at least as they recalled it from the era of their appointment. When I probed further, I found that word-of-mouth had become a major source of lore, filling the void of legal resources and morphing into the law itself. Despite many idiosyncrasies, what fascinated me was the resilience of these magistrates in outlying courts. I was observing an Afghan version of the game '*Chinese whispers*' where the message mutates from mouth to mouth. Yet these idiosyncrasies were hardly surprising in light of the findings of our research, which were archaeological in their significance. They illuminated an astonishing stratification in the composition of the personnel recruited to the judiciary over the generations of war and, in doing so, exposing the jumbled provenance of its know-how. This in turn exposed the multiplicity of divergent norms which each era of appointment held on the role of the judge, the function of courts and on the core notion of justice itself.

In 2006, we calculated that the national court population was 1415 judges. These judges had been appointed by a host of five disparate administrations, ranging from monarchic, Soviet communist, Mujahideen, Taliban and secular Western. When we examined the qualification of judges, we exposed a seismic cross-section of educational backgrounds. One third of all judges had only attended a mosque, madrassa or secondary school. Almost half of the judges had graduated in sharia studies. Just one-fifth had any degree in Law. Many had never completed any practical induction training known as the 'stage'. As a result, the courts were riven by extraordinary contestation in their delivery of justice: Soviet versus American ideologies; traditional against modernistic outlooks; Islamic orthodoxy vying with secular norms. Given such normative diversity, competing renditions of justice were inevitable. I found myself mystified about how any coherent system of justice could possibly be delivered from such uneven foundations.[3]

While it is my experience and belief that the notion of fairness is universal, even hardwired genetically to humankind, Afghanistan showed me that norms on which laws are built are far from universal. Sharia law reflects more similarities than differences to other secular systems of law, but it also embodies pathologies of patriarchy and misogyny that destine women to be convicted of their own rape and stoned for adultery. I do not, however, consider that these differences endow foreigners with any God-given right to impose their own norms, as history has clearly shown in the many harms inflicted by zealous missionaries. That right can only belong to local actors, though the foreigner may provide leadership and encouragement by showcasing more progressive norms. Norms may evolve, but only ever slowly—as seen in contemporary examples relating to smoking, gay marriage or tax evasion. The foreigner advisor's role, I now believe, is limited to enabling a local contestation of what those norms could become. It may be a long, and slow, journey to fairness.

Many people routinely go without justice in Afghanistan, as elsewhere. But in Afghanistan—which had by then endured a generation of war—there were additional dimensions to these problems. In the Panjshir Valley, I met sharia judges who were totally untrained in even the most basic principles of modern secular law. They could only administer their varying renditions of religious law which were written millennia past and were floundering to deliver justice in a society riven by turbulent transition.

When a country, like Afghanistan, undergoes continual wars and revolutionary change, its values become chaotically jumbled. Each society's rendition of justice is created when institutions such as parliaments make laws which embody that society's norms and administer them through their courts. Afghanistan's rendition of justice had traditionally been embodied in Koranic values. But in the hurly-burly of revolutionary change and intervening wars, it had evolved to include segments of other renditions imported from Russia, America or its neighbours. Broadly speaking, the privileged elite who might also be foreign educated were likely to hold more 'progressive' secular expectations of justice, while those living more traditional lives were much more conservative in both their expectations and ideologies. These divergent expectations of justice were then pitted against each other in the civil war and, in particular, the conflict over women's liberation.

Confronted with these realities, I found myself taking stock of my own expectations about justice, and what I could ethically do to bring improvement. I understood that there was no meta-truth or single 'silver bullet' to create a perfect justice system. Certainly, I had already experienced in Australia that justice was constantly tainted by unfairness, cost and delay. I had also often witnessed Western intolerance to difference, with its frequent disregard, disrespect, even hostility, for Islam, Confucius and other traditions of belief. In doing so, I knew that I must resist the invader's conceit of believing what we knew must be better. In addressing the often-dystopian conditions that I had confronted in development practice generally, and in Afghanistan specifically, my challenge was to make better sense of what was possible in order to bring some order to the chaos and offer practical solutions to immediate problems.

While philosophers may endlessly debate the nature of justice and the role of reform, it was my experience and belief that even a 4-year-old child will immediately recognise unfair treatment from its parents and knows when justice has been denied—that is, I believe that justice is primarily about the pursuit of fairness. This sense of knowing is visceral, a priori and ultimately irrepressible. At my core, I believe that all people should be equal, but where there is inequality, the disadvantaged should be given priority to restore their equality.[4] This principle of fairness transcends both culture and class in its universality. At the same time, I was also learning to understand that each diverse rendering of justice had evolved over millennia to deliver fairness in its own context and culture.

My wish in working in Afghanistan was to make a fairer place by helping the courts to deliver better justice. This was neither evangelical nor a quixotic ideal. I was working to make life a bit better for those who desperately needed help. I was not seeking to impose an intellectual notion of some better form of justice from outside. What this meant for me was to search for feasible ways to help people by adding value to the often sparse and always diverse experience of the judges in the most basic principles and practices of a fair trial. On the dusty uneven ground of war-weary Afghanistan, I found that these centred on the most basic rights of accused people in criminal proceedings to be notified of the charges against them, to have the opportunity to prepare their defence, and to be heard by an independent and impartial adjudicator. So, we set about to focus our work on rebuilding these foundational and indeed universal rights to fair trial.[5]

In reflecting on the divergent norms of Afghan culture, I found myself contemplating the burqa—that ubiquitous blue nylon sack that the Taliban require women to wear for 'modesty' by concealing their faces and bodies. It is relatively easy to despise such restrictions of women's freedom as obnoxious and reprehensible—as indeed, many foreigners do.

But outsiders can often misunderstand.

'Don't you dare be so condescending!'

Laima, a young Afghan American-educated colleague admonished me sternly, behind her smile, for presuming she was a victim of patriarchy. She reminded me of the sexualisation of western culture and assured me she had exercised her own choice to wear a burqa to withdraw from the ever-probing eyes of passing men. Some months later, I was attending a meeting in a large hotel in Karachi, when a busload of well-dressed European tourists arrived. To my astonishment, I was now shocked at the detailing of every curve and crease of their women's bodies exposed, even accentuated, by their clothing.

The more I learned, the more I discovered the perils of my own ignorance. In my head, I knew that every society builds on its own values; that cultures are deeply diverse, and each are different. But now, slowly, I was learning to understand that the significance of the burqa was multi-levelled and far more complex. To ban it, as the French have tried, is extraordinarily controversial, as well as inept. I now strove to be more respectful of such differences, however much they might grate, though this then would roil my wife who finds it contrarian.

All this was during the interregnum of the Taliban ascendancy. Since the Taliban resurgence, and the retreat of the latest invaders, I have not returned to Kabul. They have closed the universities to women again, and almost one third of girls have never even entered primary school. Another wave of human misery has refilled the refugee camps in Pakistan. The presumption of inevitable progress is fraught. There is so much more work to be done.

Looking back now at the beauty of those girls teeming from that school, chattering like starlings, before the Taliban re-erected barriers in the path to their education, I am filled by an intense sense of *monono'aware* (物の哀れ), which is a Japanese Buddhist sentiment that literally means 'the pathos of all things.' Classically, it celebrates the bitter-sweet beauty of the cherry blossom's short life before the spring winds. It describes finding an acceptance of imperfection, impermanence and the inexorable passing of life; and it acknowledges complexity in knowing that both beauty and loss can co-exist.

How do I feel? I remember an encounter near the end of my time in Kabul in 2006. One Sunday afternoon, while scrambling up the hillside to the TV tower overlooking the city, an unexpected gust of wind caught the hem of the burqa being worn by a woman walking ahead of me. To my astonishment, then delight, a defiant flash of harlequin pantyhose was exposed before the hem was briskly closed. Seeing this irrepressible flash of her garment despite the encroachment of Taliban prohibitions was an epiphany giving me hope for the future.

Sometimes the winds are at one's back, at others they are not. This was how it was in Afghanistan. Much of our work was squandered and swept bodily away as in a monsoonal flood. As I now watch the heart-wrenching turmoil that continues, it is difficult, if not impossible, not to despise the pathology of these Taliban edicts however hard I wish to respect their diversity. I wonder about the hopes of those schoolgirls, and the fate of the fragile artefacts in that little museum. But in these moments, I am consoled by the irrepressibility of the human spirit, and must wait for the winds to change, as I know one day they will.

Finding My Path

Choosing Law: University Years

My earliest memories are of the comfort of suckling at my mother's breast, looking up at her face above me. These memories are clear. I am floating weightless in her loving presence. She is the centre of my universe. I have a sense of continuousness which exists before words.

Later, I remember learning to walk on a warm spring day. I am in our orchard in Kent. Daffodils and jonquils are in full bloom beneath the trees. I stand wobbling amid a canopy of petals. Intense bright yellow flowers are all around me. Their fragrance fills the air. My mother is smiling. Later again I play cowboys and Indians with my elder brother Harry in the garden. I have a cap gun whose aim is magical, and a sword with glittering rubies in the handle. Then we get our first bikes. They are gleaming in the sunlight. Mine is blue. I am bursting proud. I remember gliding down the slope in the park, breathless with terror and exhilaration, my eyes watering in the rushing air. Once I tied my younger sister Lydia to a tree in the orchard before forgetting and absconding for lunch. The world is new in the spring of my life. My mother is so young and happy—younger then than my own daughters are now. These are my Arcadian memories of childhood in post-war England of the early 1950s.

That changed when I was sent to boarding school aged eight. Wellington House was what was in those days called a 'prep school', preparing primary level pupils for competitive entry into secondary school. Harry was already there. The fees were expensive, and my mother told me they'd made big sacrifices. My father was a gentle man, an artist, who became a teacher to pay them, for which I remain forever indebted. Money was tight and I remember feeling poor, but not as poor as my friend Peter who lived across the road in a cottage. His dad was a miner. Boarding school was a strange place filled with boys whose parents were still posted around the world in the ember days of the British Empire. I had two 'best friends' against whom all subsequent friendships have somehow been measured. Michael's dad was the police commissioner of Rhodesia, and once he showed us a real Zulu spear and shield. Steven lived in Switzerland. He had an older sister who came on visiting

L. Armytage, *Confronting Injustice*,
https://doi.org/10.1007/978-981-95-3573-6_2

days who was mysteriously glamorous and was whispered about in breathless hushed tones.

The headmaster, known by his initials of HR, was a colonel who had served in the Boer War. He had been wounded and once showed us the scar on his abdomen. He embodied Victorian values of discipline and the virtue of overcoming hardship. Each morning, he made us run through the streets in bare feet. In winter, we ran through snow. Our feet stung until they went numb. Then we had to shower under cold water. I was tormented by homesickness which dulled my curiosity to learn. I found Latin the worst; it was senseless and incomprehensible. This was the era of rote learning, and we recited endless declensions. I could remember only the most basic vocabulary. My parents paid extra for piano lessons and I churned the chords, but never progressed beyond to mastering a tune. One day, I was held back after school because I had failed to memorize the capitals of Europe. Our teachers were called masters, most of whom were generally kind. I had to repeat the exercise while all the other pupils were enjoying their hobbies. The names of unknown cities—Belgrade, Lisbon, Budapest—slithered across the page like tadpoles, then vanished. This went on through the afternoon. It was torture. I was desperate. Finally, I memorised about half before both the master and I gave up. I was slow to read as a child. My sister Lydia, 3 years younger, started before me. I had an astigmatism that made me vomit in movies. After we went to the cinema to see "Around the World in 80 Days", I felt dizzy and emptied my stomach wretchedly from the back window of the car, to the astonishment of passers-by. Later, I was told I had dyslexia. Twice, I was held down and separated from my class rising to the next level.

Another day, at the weekly assembly of the whole school, HR called me out: *Armytage Minor,* (being the younger brother) *will you tell me: are you lazy or inattentive*?

Aged eight, I had no idea. It was an impossible question for me to answer. There was something wrong with me, clearly. I was very stupid and now the whole school knew. I felt tiny and wanted to disappear. But there was nowhere to escape. In the deafening silence, everyone was watching, waiting for my answer. But I didn't have one.

Well then, he resumed, *if you have nothing to say, I will let you think about it, and I will come back to you when you're ready to answer at the end of this assembly.*

Which choice would be less humiliating, I wondered? Round and round this question flitted in my head, like a fly that couldn't be caught. I stood rigid as the headmaster moved on to other miscreants. Which was the bigger defect, I wondered miserably? Finally, I decided it must be worse to be lazy because that revealed a character flaw that I was born with and couldn't be fixed. So, chosing inattention over laziness was my child's best effort to sidestep any moral dimension to my transgression. Long minutes passed. Everyone stirred to go, and I started to hope he had forgotten. Then he repeated the question.

Well, Armytage Minor, what is your answer?

My legs started shaking.

I was inattentive, I replied in a soundless voice. I was to wait several decades before learning that inattention is now recognised to be on the autism spectrum as being a neuro-diverse disability.

Then you shall be punished, he continued. *Go to the Bathroom.*

I wobbled up the stairs alone. His bathroom had black and white marble tiles. It smelt of cologne and leather. Minutes passed. I stood there quivering until I heard the creak of his shoes as HR entered. He held a bunch of birch branches in his hand.

Pull down your pants. Bend over!

From behind me, I heard his shoes creak again as he stepped back, paused, then rushed towards me. There was a hiss of wind through the birch branches. A blinding lightening of agony flared across my senses. Shock, disbelief, scalding pain. A surge of heat, like fire. I gasped. Don't cry! I willed myself. Again, he stepped back. Another pause. Then another strike across the sizzling welts of the first. It was electric, like being bitten. Intense pain flooded out all other thought.

It took a week before the bruises healed and I could sit normally. Later on, he did it again. But I was lucky. Others got it much worse and were permanently damaged. Corporal punishment has since been outlawed internationally as being cruel and inhumane punishment even for adult felons in prison. But however easy it may now be to malign him, I do not believe that HR was a sadist or a pervert. Rather, he was in the rear-guard of the British imperial era. He was hardening the next generation for running an empire, which he didn't yet know had already ended.

Boarding school continued for three years until my parents migrated to Australia at the start of 1964. They told us they wanted to escape the English class system. I remember being filled with relief, excitement and sadness. I never saw either Michael or Steven ever again, and have often wondered where their lives may have led them. This was still in the age of sea travel, and our voyage through the Mediterranean, passing camels along the Suez Canal, and across the Indian Ocean took three weeks watching the churning wake receding behind us. We arrived in Melbourne during a hot southern summer. My father was posted to Wangaratta in the Victorian bush where he taught for a year before moving to the city. Each morning, we were awakened by the raucous lament of the magpies swooping in the wheatfields around our teacher's cottage in nearby Boorhaman. Then I was driven by bus to school across the sparse untidy landscape burnished by the sun, raising plumes of dust from the unsealed road like a triumphant flag behind us. On scorching days, the dust got up our noses and our shirts stuck like gum to the back of the vinyl seats. Even half a lifetime later, a magpie's lament still takes me straight back to those sun-drenched first days in the bush. We had escaped. I shall always be grateful.

Boarding school had inflicted lingering scars, and I had not expected to get into university. But as the years passed, I discovered a mysterious effect. It became an engine that drove me to avoid repeating that humiliation and my terror of failure. I disciplined myself to study hard and did well at school in Australia. I wondered at the revelations of history shaping the present and was enthralled how literature could share ideas that explained people and through its characters myself.

So it was that on my seventeenth birthday, I was offered a scholarship to study my first choice at university. I wanted to be stretched, and the thought of studying humanities felt easy and somehow too comfortable. So, I chose law because it would be more difficult and, by some quirk of logic, thereby more valuable. I was drawn to the notion of law embodying predictable rules of social order, and I found the prospect of learning to work with those tools useful. Law's promise to hold power to account and endow order to society seemed a worthy devotion. Ultimately, though, it was an intuitive choice, a guess. It would take me years of legal practice to distinguish, then disentangle from the law, the allure of the separate promise of justice to promote fairness as the means to improve human wellbeing.

I entered a new world at university. This was the glorious summer of '69, a summer of extraordinary optimism. On 20 July, I remember very clearly watching Neil Armstrong taking his "one small step for man, one giant leap for mankind" on the moon from a TV erected on the campus. We knew that we could only do better than those who had gone before us. Our music told us so. This was the age of Aquarius—Jo Cocker played live at Woodstock; Dylan was blowing in the wind; Mick was jumping jack flash in Kooyong Stadium; Janice got busted flat in Baton Rouge; and Cat Stevens was discovering the wild world. The music of Credence and the Beatles was everywhere.

Yet, it was also a time of confusion and profound bewilderment: the assassination of Martin Luther King was immediately followed by another, of a second Kennedy, then the descent into the quagmire and dissension of the Vietnam War. Australia, as usual, backed the US in volunteering to join this war by conscripting twenty-year-olds. While we were all temporarily exempted as students from the military draft, we joined in the frenetic unity of righteous protests from Berkeley to Melbourne, climaxing in the massive moratoriums that gridlocked those cities' streets. The government fell. Gough Whitlam became Prime Minister, and immediately cancelled the draft, restoring the stunned campuses to their quieter and much duller academic preoccupations.

It was in this cauldron of dynamic change that I settled into enjoying university life. Each morning, I drove to campus, my hair flowing rebelliously over the collar of my shirt, cool as could be in my battered old Morris Major whose floor panels had rusted through, sending glimmers from the road flashing beneath me as I went. I loved the expanse of university, its eclectic mix of people, ideas and activities. Between classes, I discovered the 'small caff' frequented by Arts students who seemed so much more interesting than my classmates in Law.

Here, I explored with friends the revolutionary ideas of Sartre and Camus in that incandescent era before '*Postmodernism*' had yet been given its name. These conversations would spill on to 'the Nott' whose back bar seethed with rebellion over jugs of beer that regularly sloshed over the knees of us all encircling the tables. Some evenings morphed into parties which spread far and wide across town where those ideas fermented unrestrained and later unrecalled. I discovered marijuana and loved the 'hungries' that so intensified the flavours of food and my other senses. It was now that I was first transported by music, awed by the swelling refrain of the Moody Blues' "Question of Balance". Late on many evenings, I drove home in the early hours along emptied streets mesmerised by the rhythmic swish of the tyres beneath me.

In those times, the libraries were still full of books not computers. The Law Library was a solemn place of sepulchral stillness. It was filled with legions of imposing tomes bound in calf leather, sometimes hundreds of years old. Novices, like me, shuffled uncertainly from aisle to aisle searching for our prescribed reading, the most needed books of course being in constant use or hidden in piles awaiting collection. Once I have found the book, however, I found many of the reported cases from which common law was extracted, to be impenetrable in their length, detail and expression. Every judge seemed duty-bound to present their own decision, each based on different precedents from earlier cases. As students, we were required to analyse and distil the 'ratio', or legal rule, from this confusion. My earliest efforts in searching for legal gems found only gritty flint. While other students seemed to bound effortlessly across this arcane terrain, I became lost amid the facts, reasons and law. This was a foreign landscape in which I felt clumsy and ill-suited. My brother Harry now tells me that I was full of fun before studying law, but that I then became solemn. Despite the travail—or perhaps because of it—I felt a compulsion to persevere while some of my companions silently extracted themselves. Deep down, I suppose, I believed that overcoming difficulty would impart value.

I studied hundreds, even thousands, of cases over the next five years. But only two of all those now stand out from those years at law school. The first case of *Rylands v Fletcher* involved a decision by Britain's top court, the House of Lords, in 1868. This established what was then a new arena of English *tort* law to regulate the relationship and rights of private citizens, as distinct from crimes against the state. This case created the rule that one person's use of their land which leads to another's land being damaged as the result of dangerous things escaping, is strictly liable for that damage. This case was seminal in created the notion of civil responsibility for one's neighbour—in this instance, the runoff of negligent or careless work which caused a reservoir to burst and flood a neighbouring mine. The second case was *Donohue v Stevens*, which was another decision of the House of Lords made in 1932. This laid the foundation for the modern law of *negligence* by creating a duty of care for acts that might foreseeably injure others or damage their property. Intriguingly, this case involved the hapless plaintiff or claimant consuming a snail trapped in a bottle of ginger beer. Its ratio, or rule, declared that the maker of any product is under a legal duty to the consumer to take reasonable care so that the product is free from defects which are likely to cause injury to health.

I loved both of these cases for displaying the dynamism and responsiveness of judges in the courts to laying new foundations that redressed injustices where gaps existed in the law. They showcased judges upholding the sacred promise to serve as the guardians of the constitution by improving the law to deliver justice. It was this promise that had intuitively drawn me to the law in confronting injustice and dealing with what Thomas Hobbes had classically described as the 'brutishness of man in nature'.

Years later, I had the opportunity and privilege to work closely with many senior judges, those very people who are charged to serve as the guardians of law's promise to deliver justice. One was Murray Gleeson who was then Chief Justice of NSW, and later of the High Court of Australia. One day, I gave him a brief document to read. He swivelled his chair, placed the sheet of paper on his knees and proceeded to silently read. He sat motionless for some moments as his eyes swept each line rhythmically, reminding me of a vacuum cleaner extracting tiny threads of lint from a carpet. Only when he had finished did he move and give his response. In those moments, he epitomised the juristic qualities so celebrated in law school. I was galvanised by his attention to and command of precise detail, however minuscule. This command is the hallmark of many judges and the barristers who appear before them. It embodies the canon of 'stare decisis' which brings uniformity and predictability to court decisions by strictly following the ratios or rules set in earlier cases to ensure equality of treatment.

In my early years in law school, I looked up at the senior students five distant years above me with a mixture of awe and vertigo. They seemed so complacently confident. How could I end up like them, chuckling together with their hands contentedly in their jacket pockets, as they stood on the cusp of professional life? Years later, I briefed Julian, one of those students, who was by then a senior barrister, or *silk*, experienced in litigating cases to the High Court. Momentarily, I recalled his student self, strolling so assuredly along a straight path, while mine felt so uncertain and yet to be mapped.

In my second year, I arrived late to the first lecture of Indonesian language and literature which I had elected to study. The theatre was already full. I looked for a seat at the back, but none were available. There was only one spare in the front row. Trying to make myself as small as possible, I tiptoed through the row to find myself sitting beside a Japanese girl with gleaming ebony hair whose beauty caused me to gasp involuntarily and took my breath away. When she glanced at me settling, I felt giddy and blushed. I hardly dared look at her. From the corner of my eye, I noticed her exquisite handwriting, and tried to conceal my own scrawl behind my arm. When the class ended, I fumbled clumsily with my papers, as I searched for something to say. Anything. I was tongue-tied. Whatever sprang to my mind seemed trite. Yet she also seemed to linger. I can't now remember who suggested coffee, but in the moments it took us to walk over to the small caff, I found some words and we were grinning at each other. Suddenly, everything was intensely exciting. Her name was Miyako. She was astonishingly lovely, with deep brown eyes the colour of freshly-ground roasted coffee beans under cushioned lids and a curiously beautiful mouth that behaved so gracefully as she spoke. I was lightheaded she was sitting so close that I could smell her hair.

From that day, we shared two marvellous years together before she returned to Japan after completing her studies. We met again after a year, when we became engaged. We exchanged literally hundreds of letters, now seemingly in slow motion taking a week to arrive and another to return, before finally going our separate ways after another year apart, wrenching my heart.

Twenty-five years later, I had an itinerary from hell flying between Phnom Penh in Cambodia to Port au Prince in Haiti. It took a total duration of 52 hours, crossing the grain of all major flight routes with four different airlines. First, I had an 8-hour layover in Bangkok, then another 9-hours transiting in Japan, then finally an overnight in Miami—all before hopping across the Caribbean to Haiti. I was already bleary-eyed from fatigue as we descended towards Narita—notorious for being one of the world's dullest airports, situated 90 minutes out of Tokyo. Rebelling at the prospect of further boredom marooned in another airport corridor for the day, I took an excursion into the city, on a whim, having about 3 hours to explore.

But, where to go? I needed to pick a destination for the train. Tokyo is a massive place—the world's largest city with a population of 32 million, even then. I had heard about the Ginza, but its glitzy nightlife reputation didn't appeal at 6 am on a wet morning. So, where to go …

Then I remembered dimly that Miyako had started a job in a college downtown teaching English to civil servants when she returned to Japan those many years before. Well, perhaps I could go there and look around at the places where her new life had taken her. It might be interesting, more interesting than the airport at least. I still remembered the name of the school from all the letters I had written. So, I rang the telephone operator for directions. In those days, very few Japanese spoke any English. But I was lucky; this operator did. She found the address, gave me its telephone number and told me the nearest station. I boarded a train which needed to change at Shinjuku. Shinjuku is the world's largest station serving as the hub for 12 major train networks through whose gates 3.5m passengers pass each day in 6000 trains on 52 platforms, disgourging commuters through 200 exits. It was a truly intimidating space, and it was now rush hour. The main concourse was a tsunami of converging commuters weaving deftly through each other in all directions. I couldn't find any directions in English, and felt like a blinded man. But somehow, I found the right platform and arrived at Yotsuya, a smaller station which had only 6 exits. Disorientated, I clambered the stairs of one and contemplated the wet grey cityscape that surrounded me. So, what do I do now? Across the intersection, I saw a brightly lit stall selling lottery tickets. For want of anywhere better to go, I borrowed their phone and called the school's number. I felt like a pilgrim searching for an old temple that he expected to be closed.

'Could I speak to Miyako, please?'

Having, by then, never having held the same job for more than 5 years, I had not the slightest doubt about the answer. But then the receptionist said, 'Hold the line, please.'

The ground fell away from beneath my feet, and I suddenly had difficulty breathing.

'What?', my voice sounded muffled, like I was under water. I had to swallow.

'She's in class at the moment. Can you leave a message?'

Dazed by the unexpected, I mechanically gave my name, and said I was standing at the lottery stall near the station. I don't know how long I stood there, immobile. Maybe twenty minutes. And then there she was, smiling, exactly the same.

Miraculously, we met again totally unplanned in that vast city where I was a complete foreigner. We shared 40 minutes in a coffee shop. The years vanished and so did any sense of strangeness. We had by then both married; I with Lisa and now had two lovely daughters. Our conversation resumed with excited curiosity. As the minutes melted before returning to the airport, I confronted a choice that would later disrupt the course of both our lives, and those of our families. I asked for her telephone number, and then called her from Haiti. After two years of profound and often painful transition, we married.

Miyako has stayed at my side ever since, sharing my life with its many adventures, enabling me to experience and learn from all that came in the chapters that follow. Later, she told me that she'd picked me out that morning walking late into class without a worry in the world.

But what took you so long? she asked.

Evidently, I was still a very slow learner.

Before graduating, I dreamt of sailing into the vast Pacific to do good works whatever that meant. That dream would take days to forget, but decades to realise. First, I needed some tools to make myself useful.

Clerkship: Acquiring Tools

I entered the legal profession at a time of profound upheaval in early 1974. Gough Whitlam had just won the Prime Ministership on a reformist ticket and passed a swath of new laws. They were revolutionary in their impact. The *Trade Practices Act* introduced a radical regulatory regime for business accountability and consumer rights; the *Family Law Act* abolished fault and introduced irretrievable breakdown as the sole grounds for divorce and, in a single stroke, purged the pathology of private detectives spying in the marital bedroom. Other initiatives abolished conscription for the Vietnam War, revitalised the arts, and liberalised tertiary education. It was an invigorating time of national rebirth, until the chaos of inexperience created scandal, constitutional crisis, the dismissal of the Prime Minister and ultimately defeat of the government. All of this was a windfall of new work for lawyers.

On my first day, I felt my stomach tighten as I boarded the rush hour train for the city. My employer was one of the coveted 'top 3' commercial law firms handling major commercial transactions, which occupied the upper floors of Melbourne's most prestigious office tower. This status was assiduously cultivated in a vertiginous hierarchy. At the pinnacle, godlike in their glass-walled offices with views overlooking the city's central business district were the partners, who were bonded by their memberships to 'the Club' - being the most prestigious Melbourne Club - and their bristling mutual dislike. Far below them were the aspirant associates, winnowed mid-career lawyers lean and hungry for the prospect of their ascension to the pinnacle. Much further down the corridors were the junior lawyers scurrying about to win the attention and approval of their superiors. The secretaries came next. They were both the first glimmerings of humanity yet fierce gatekeepers to the partners. Then came the law clerks, destined by modest qualifications and poor connections to toil through their lives in windowless cubicles beneath the stairs. Here, I was introduced to Mr. Barrington who, to my dismay, exposed the pain of his forlorn career as a conveyancing clerk by ruefully boasting he had just 1258 days left until retirement.

L. Armytage, *Confronting Injustice*,
https://doi.org/10.1007/978-981-95-3573-6_3

Finally, lowest of all, came the article clerks, who were universally despised by everyone but the pitying secretaries. I was one such. We huddled in partitioned workspaces in the middle of an open-plan section, comprising two chairs with a benchtop, a file tray and shelf for books from the library. We shared a telephone, but no computers in those days. How small I felt; my pickings were truly meagre pecking about the office for titbits of work no one else wanted from the desks of all those above me.

The firm's hierarchy also extended outward from the city receding into the haze of the dormitory suburbs through the nature of the work undertaken. At the centre reigned the plush office towers of corporate, commercial, financial, equity and tax specialists servicing the business elites. And at its farthest edges were the dwindling shopfront offices of those who practised in family, property and litigation matters for ordinary people.

I had dressed in my first suit of mid-weight dark grey wool, despite the heat of summer, 'sensibly' purchased by my mother in a nondescript style that was assured never to be affected by fashion. Over the coming months, I would learn the arcane art of dressing as a lawyer within these hierarchies. Suits were both our armour and uniform. They were most often navy and sometimes grey, only occasionally and courageously brown, but never green. These orthodoxies constrained any expression of personality to the selection of ties, socks, shoes and watches. Absurd sums could be misspent on a silk tie in disciplined patterns and restrained colours. Mid-career lawyers sporting carnival socks were a sure sign of mid-life crisis and an increasingly desperate hunt for a marriage partner. Brown leather shoes were a big mistake with a navy suit that suggested provincial origins. Sports watches were best left at home, but too often weren't. Pocket handkerchiefs were the flourish of the over-assured wanker with political aspirations. Finally, the white crest of a *Montblanc* 'writing instrument' discreetly signalled discernment from the shirt breast pocket. Other office workers went about the streets more comfortably in open collared shirts—but nobody bothered much with them unless, of course, they were clients.

Each morning at 10 am, the aging Mrs. Wilson would earn her widow's mite by wheeling the trolley of stewed tea or 'instant' coffee, serving us in descending order of hierarchy. For a few minutes, we were permitted to raise our heads over our desks to chatter like sparrows. Sometimes, too often, we would avert our eyes as Geoff, the firm's youngest partner glamorously endowed with a mop of boyish blond hair, would favour our lowly domain. He liked to explore the boundaries of his privilege by loitering at the stationery cupboard near the young secretaries in the typing pool, who would giggle excitedly like trapped chicks behind the protective glare of their matron.

Entry to the legal profession requires practical training as well as academic qualifications. At that time, the usual way was as an articled clerk in a law firm. The merits of 'articles' were that they were supposed to fuse real-world experience with on-the-job mentoring. In reality, the quality of mentoring depended on the principal. I was one of twelve articled clerks with whom I sometimes shared a hurried spaghetti at bustling Campari in order to gaze at close range on the lunching giants of our new profession. We were a mixed bunch whom I had never met during law school. In later years, Doug scaled all the rungs of the hierarchy to make partner. Stephen became a barrister and later followed his father to become a judge of the Supreme Court. Others included Mark who became Attorney-General, Peter who became Defence Minister and Rowan whom I met years later as an international judge at the Khmer Rouge Tribunal of Cambodia. But not all paths were so illustrious. I witnessed the stifled anguish of Kate, a prodigiously talented lawyer 3 years my senior, who had made it so far despite overcoming the herculean challenges of being blind, on being told she would never make partner because of her gender.

I was assigned to a partner specialising in major international transactions requiring extensive overseas travel. Bill's office was minimalist, with two telephones but only ever a single file on his stark black lacquered desk. His only overt display of personality was an outsized astronaut watch with illuminated red dials glimmering within the raised bezel of a scoured stainless-steel case and matching bracelet, that he had been awarded by one of his American corporate clients. From the outset, Bill was usually absent, but when present was distracted by my presence and frustrated by my inexperience. When away, his mail would come to my desk. One day a request for advice arrived from a major Arab oil interest via Skadden Arps, as it was then known, its NY 'global powerhouse' attorneys.[6] It was urgent and required immediate response. In those days there was still no email, zoom or even fax. The advice hinged on interpreting the application of a new tax provision that the Whitlam government had just enacted. At its crux, the critical issue was binary: either their proposed investment would be exposed to liability for withholding tax, or it would not. The New York attorneys were also canvassing competing investment prospects in other jurisdictions.

With this unexpected assignment, the pressure on my novice shoulders was abruptly burdensome. I searched along the corridors, but everyone above me was busy and no one was available to provide any guidance. I was alone. I scurried to the library and read through the legislation, then the commentaries. The more I poured over the provisions, the more the applications of liability slithered like goldfish around the page, just as the capitals of Europe had done more than a decade earlier. The more I pondered, the more slippery they seemed. Liability could go either way. Finally, I reasoned 'Yes, there would be exposure to liability.' One week after my principal returned, he wrote a letter apologising and countermanding my entire advice. With the abruptness of a slap, a carbon copy appeared on the file. When nervously I asked, he explained so tersely, I couldn't understand but dared not inquire further. For the remainder of my articles, he gave scant acknowledgement to my presence, except to nod on my departure. My reference was a bare two paragraphs that confirmed my employment but was so scant in endorsing the pursuit of my 'chosen' career—that is, some other career—that it could never been used. I felt betrayed and abandoned by the firm that had formally undertaken to mentor me. But I was now in the grown-up world and had to sink or swim. I would roam the corridors scrounging for scraps of work on which to keep busy. Sometimes, I found a will to draft, a tiresome client that no one else wanted to take to court, or documents to file at the Titles Offices. It became a melancholy ordeal.

Yet despite my abandonment, I did learn some useful things. Occasional work involved drafting an 'advice' to a client. There was a peculiar formality and structure to this correspondence. The letter was characteristically impersonal, as though neither the author nor the recipient had any human relationship. The 'client' would 'instruct' (usually) his lawyers to answer a question which was framed in the first paragraph. The second paragraph would recite the relevant 'facts.' The third paragraph would outline the relevant law. The final paragraph—or section—would then supply the 'advice' in terms of the legal implications and recommend the action to be taken. These letters were invariably completed 'sincerely,' but *not* 'faithfully' and never 'with best wishes,' and they were only signed by a partner. Next, came the challenge of expression. In the early days, I was firmly rebuked for using the verb 'feel' rather than 'think', 'argue' or 'conclude'. However stylised, I nonetheless enjoyed mastering this method. A well-crafted advice is clear, short and incisive—a rare joy to read.

On other days, I would escape from the office when tasked to 'brief counsel' in court. This involved assisting the barrister with whatever (usually) he might need me to do: scrambling around for missing documents, rescheduling the attendance of witnesses and the like. Those days formed some of the most interesting of my articles. In my role of 'instructing solicitor', I would sit at the bar table facing the barrister and the courtroom beyond with my back to the judge.

It was during the travails of my articles that I met some truly impressive lawyers. It was in these courtrooms that I first met Robert Richter, who even as a young barrister was regarded as the sharpest blade in the criminal bar. He wielded a scalpel of devastating mental precision in an arena where the liberty of the innocent swung in the balance. Under an unruly mane of flaming red hair, he inspired me in the principles of criminal justice and the presumption of innocence—even, many years later, for Cardinal George Pell whom he successfully defended in the High Court in his appeal against conviction for condoning clerical paedophilia. Despite this presumptive victory, however, Pell was shamed in the public eye and fled back to the Vatican to die in opprobrium.

Another was Appellate Justice Frank Vincent who had cut his teeth in Central Australia defending Indigenous people on legal aid against the systemic oppression of the 'white fella' justice system. He went on to mentor me among generations of young barristers in his footsteps as the exemplary champion of criminal justice. He carried the weighty load of hearing only the gravest trials involving multiple murders, gang rapes and other atrocities. On only the rarest occasions—and never while sitting on the bench—would he allow a shy smile from the backstreets of working-class Brunswick to soften his ascetic visage, etched as an outsider who had ascended the bastions of privilege through the acuity of his intellect and the tireless resolution of his conviction. He'd seen it all; the good, the bad and the bizarre. He recounted in his memoir how in one homicide, the accused had stabbed his fiancée repeatedly to death over the design of their wedding invitation.

As I embarked on my professional life, I found a need for these people who became my role-models, sources of inspiration and subjects of aspiration. They lit a flickering candleflame to guide me through the new spaces ahead of me. From time to time, there would be others with the stature of giants like Justices Michael Kirby, Shafi'ur Rahman and Samdani and Nobel Laureate Amartya Sen who will each appear on later pages. As I learned to navigate this world, and now look back, I understand they were heroes who inspired me. Their presence was much-needed, precious and reassuring. I respected them for showing the boundlessness of what we can each achieve, and gifting me their examples with which to set my own direction. We need these people in our lives, who go ahead and light our paths wherever they may lead, as I hope I may now in my turn for others.

As most of our cases were substantial, they were conducted in the Supreme Court. This gave me ample opportunity to observe the rituals of the trial process and study the grandeur of the court chamber. The two-story building was a grim icon of colonial power which occupied an entire city block on William Street, forming the heart of the legal precinct. It was crowned with a monumental dome. Within the echoing stone corridors of the ground floor were the court chambers, nestling around the judges' library with its leather-bound tomes on laden shelves under the vaulted dome ceiling. Above were the judges' chambers. Each of the fifteen massive courtrooms displayed the majesty of colonial power in the raised judge's bench, with a fence separating the barristers' table from the public pews. Heavy unforgiving ebony benches lined the gallery beneath the gilded crystal chandeliers, and pastel-coloured ceiling. How much power and grandeur were crafted to loom in these mighty courtrooms. The court clerk loudly hammered the gavel, and the barristers silently rose to bow to the bewigged 'Honourable' judge as he (invariably) entered the court in his black gown and sat on the raised bench to portentously start each day's proceedings.

Those days in court were long and often slow, causing my eyes to glaze over as routine evidence was presented. That grandeur was however once shattered to my astonishment, and then rapidly suppressed delight, during a tedious afternoon when the slumbering judge's chair rolled off the bench causing the recumbent occupant to disappear, however momentarily, from sight. This misadventure went resolutely unacknowledged by all in the chamber.

One of our clients, Scotty, was the director of a mining company in WA. The company had a number of troubling irregularities when it went bust in the last mining boom, and he was being prosecuted by the regulator. Bill had accepted Scotty as a client but held him in barely concealed contempt. Whenever Scotty called, Bill ordered his secretary to transfer the call to me to take messages. It was also my job to 'instruct' his barristers in all of his court hearings. There were many of these, for each of which he would commute across the continent on the dreaded 'midnight special' to arrive crumpled for the next ordeal.

"Where's Bill?" he would ask tetchily.

"He apologises for being really busy on other urgent matters, today." I would wearily repeat.

As the hearings progressed, I had little to do other than to study the conduct of the barristers. The firm usually briefed senior counsel, known as 'silks' denoted by the black rose embroidered on the back of their gowns. In major cases, these silks would be supported by a 'junior,' who were themselves mid-career. The style and manner of each barrister was unique, and I enjoyed observing their techniques. The best conveyed an artistry to navigate the infinite complexities of the law with what seemed effortless simplicity. I soon learned that what seemed less was predictably more. Unlike courtroom scenes on television, the best avoided histrionics, embellishments and repetitions, to steadily construct a structure of clear argument whose strength could be measured in its clarity and apparent simplicity. One barrister would gently clink the arms of his spectacles as he knitted them together in his hands while patiently sculpting his witnesses' evidence. Another gently chided difficult witnesses under cross-examination to admit they were being 'liberal' with the truth. The best barrister could transform the multifaceted complexity of the law into an illuminated path leading irresistibly to a single destination. I could find myself transfixed by the elegance and persuasion of their arguments.

Over those months of hearings, Scotty and I got to know each other quite well. He was a wily Celt who treated me kindly and was stoically philosophical about being charged at full partner's fee rate. While there was little doubt that he had been 'careless' with some of his financial responsibilities, the firm shielded him with two hefty barristers from prison-time. But his costs of litigation were astronomical, in the order of hundreds of thousands of dollars today, with equally hefty fines. This was the deal I now found myself made a part of.

Observing the passage of these trials until their completion allowed me to contemplate the quality of justice to which I was now an apprentice. In jury trials, in particular, I would weigh the evidence and then compare their verdicts. I was fascinated by how often a jury, selected from the community of ordinary people without any legal expertise or prior experience, could award verdicts of damages in claims that fell within predictable patterns of similar cases. The uniformity of their assessments displayed an intuition, even a visceral sense of rightness, which was mysterious, if not mystical, and gave me some reassurance in the existence of a shared humanity in courtrooms across the land.

But I also found myself reflecting on the role and ability of counsel to influence the outcome of those cases. Skilled counsel could evidently affect the result for their clients. Indeed, their skill is precisely what impels the wealthy to pay the often-astronomical fees that they can charge. I was learning that the judge could—even should—be led by the more able lawyer. The judges in our 'adversarial' system are like the umpire in a sporting event, responsible for administering the rules between contesting sides, then delivering their judgment. The notion of the parties jousting their competing claims to attain justice is fundamental to our system, but the fairness of its outcome heavily presumes the equality of the trial process. So, it rankled me that justice could become a commodity to be bought by those best able to afford it, like those as fortunate as Scotty. In the other 'inquisitorial' system of many European countries, the judges are more like the detective who investigates what has happened and then applies the law. Each system pursues fairness but in different ways. Either way, if the law unfailingly applies itself spontaneously to the facts, then there would of course be no need for lawyers. But this rarely happens, and hence the need for lawyers.

My own first foray into court was altogether humbling. I was tasked to present a 'plea' for the mitigation of a sentence for a traffic offence that threatened the cancellation of my client's driving licence. Since my client was a tradie, a plumber, who depended on his ute, being a utility vehicle or small tradesman's truck, for all his work, the stakes were high. These were still the days of 'police magistrates' who, despite the presumption of innocence, routinely accepted the evidence of police unless incontrovertibly refuted. My job was to limit the damage by convincing the magistrate that it would be unreasonably harsh to cancel my client's licence. I arrived early to find my client nervous, glum and uncomfortably dressed in an ill-fitting jacket and garish tie. He asked me questions I'd already answered seeking reassurance about the extent of my scant experience.

The courthouse was filling with lounging policemen seeming unnaturally friendly chatting with their mates. Once my case was called, everything went smoothly until it came to my recital of the reasons for mitigation. I had prepared the defence carefully the evening before and practised it in the mirror before leaving home to the point of learning it by heart. But now, facing the magistrate and watched by so many police and other lawyers, my script fogged in my hands, and my voice became muffled. Then it faltered. I paused, then stalled.

Moments passed.

The court clerk looked up, then slowly started to frown. But thankfully, the magistrate seemed preoccupied.

The prosecutor coughed.

Where were my words?

I felt the looming stillness of the crowded room behind me. They must all be staring, but I dared not look round. My heart was now thumping. I thought I might faint. Then, my legs started shaking so hard the material of my trousers was flapping against my knees. Could everyone see? I looked down at my notes, but the words were blurring and jumbled, just like back at school. More moments passed.

Finally, I clawed at a string of words to cling to and stutter them out. I had jumped some lines, but there was no going back. Hurriedly, I pushed onwards to urge the magistrate to exercise his discretion for leniency.

How long had my ordeal been—was it half a lifetime, or just a second or two amplified by adrenaline? I will never know. When I'd finished, the sounds and movements of the courtroom returned, as though nothing had happened. Perhaps no one had even noticed, I hoped. The clerk ordered my client to stand. The magistrate then convicted him and announced his sentence, which doubtless he'd been drafting during my address. My client was fined, but he kept his licence. The next case was called. I have no idea whether my plea had made any difference whatsoever. But in those glorious after-moments we shared our relief; briefly, I was his conquering hero.

Prior to completion of my articles, I was summoned to the office of the managing partner who notified me that my contract would not be extended. This was a cheerless ritual. But to our mutual surprise, I felt a huge smile of relief spring irrepressibly across my face. By now, I had discovered that I was not a corporate lawyer; and nor did I ever wish to become one. The aspiration for justice was only rarely, if ever, evident in the daily practice of that firm which instead was flourishing in using the courts as an economic tool to consolidate wealth. Discovering who I was not was a crucial first step in discovering who I wanted to become.

At my admission ceremony in the Supreme Court, I wore a radically red tie and an earring in mute dissent. Then I descended hurriedly from the firm's tower to explore the world, and never looked back.

Partner: Mastering Craft

I spent two years travelling the world, backpacking across Australia's vast red flatlands to Darwin, then on to Bali and overland ultimately to Europe. I travelled solo, discovering many intriguing, wonderful places—Afghanistan, Pakistan and Nepal—that I would return to in later years. In Greece, I was hospitalised with a severe hepatitis fever so debilitating that it took me three weeks to recognise the Acropolis through the window across the bay. For days, I just lay there on a drip, utterly wasted. I felt like my battery pack had been removed. Slowly, after several weeks, I started to rebuild my strength humming along to Gloria Gaynor's hit of that time, *'I will Survive'*.[7] First, I could only shuffle down the corridor clutching the rail, next very slowly up some stairs. Then I tottered outside to discover the hospital's vegetable garden, where I sat thawing under the shy spring sunlight. One day, I heard a commotion from the chapel nearby which was celebrating the orthodox Easter mass. I was greeted at the door and felt warmly welcomed. It was a beautiful service, and the space was filled with a quiet serenity. After some minutes sitting in the congregation, I noticed that the priest was missing an ear. Oddly, then, the verger had only a part of his hand. Slowly, very slowly, I turned to find myself amid others, disfigured but smiling, all around me. I was in the leprosarium. Luckily, it is very rare to catch leprosy from casual physical contact.

When, after 18 months, I finally returned home to Melbourne, I joined a small family-run general practice in the suburb of Moorabbin at the periphery of the profession, where my new view of legal practice was altogether different. My principal, Rolly, was a gruff elderly man who'd climbed up the long back stairs of clerkship after being demobilised from WWII to finally become the local solicitor with a shopfront practice. He patiently shared his vast experience and taught me to provide valuable service to ordinary people by working hard with the law. Rolly's clients were local business owners, their families and friends and sometimes passers-by laden with shopping or weary from work. They were not the massive corporations with their complex machinations and glossy executives jostling to evade their tax liabilities. They brought a mix of human problems that needed fixing: car crashes

L. Armytage, *Confronting Injustice*,
https://doi.org/10.1007/978-981-95-3573-6_4

involving serious injuries and property damage, workplace injuries and chronic disease, family break-ups, domestic conveyancing, business advice and wills. This was the full mix of general practice, and I was stretched to become useful across their expanse of travails. I grew a beard to disguise my sparse experience in advising clients my parents' age on their family breakups. I witnessed the tragedies, hardships, caring and dignity of people in the cloistered privacy of these consultations. Some days, I was nailed to my desk all day; others I'd attend the local courts or occasionally journey back into the city on bigger cases. I enjoyed being a part of the community, getting to know local businesses and chatting with my clients in the street. For many of these people, life was a struggle that was confounded by these problems. I learned quickly to give it my best shot. I drew up papers to transfer the milk bar across the street three times over just two years in the mid '70 s, witnessing the heartbreak of each newcomer as their dreams turned to nightmares and their retirement savings were exhausted by ever-rising costs and the unrelenting erosion of the OPEC 'oil shock'. By then, I'd started to learn what I was doing. And in doing so, I'd grown into a caring lawyer providing useful services that were valuable to real people.

I then moved back to the city joining a mid-sized firm specialising in civil litigation. Here I discovered I enjoyed the intensity and focus of building and contesting cases in court, and soon I became experienced in a range of increasingly substantial disputes. I found my strengths in building, then negotiating and resolving these cases by avoiding the delays and unpredictability of court hearings. It was not long before I developed a substantial practice in major litigation; and it soon became clear first to my partners, then myself, that I had a flair for handling high volumes of serious cases that contributed substantially to the profitability of the firm.

Soon I was handling major claims, severe injury cases: paraplegia, quadriplegia, brain damage, fourth degree burn trauma that fused human tissue, grisly industrial diseases like asbestosis, and fatalities. I recall one in which my client, Cate, a young woman who was enjoying a summer drive in an open-top sportscar when it lost control and caught fire trapping her in the passenger seat which melted the skin, nerves and muscles of her spine. Another, Lucia, was wearing her seatbelt while flying to a business meeting when the plane hit turbulence causing the attendant to spill scalding coffee into her lap inflicting unspeakable burns. Following a massive settlement, the airline's insurers insisted that henceforth all hot refreshments be poured in the aisle. Another case involved a toddler, Zoran, who fell from a slide in the playground of a movie drive-inn causing brain damage. After that settlement, the insurers withdrew all insurance cover, resulting in the demolishing of drive-inn playgrounds.

It was a blessing to finalise these cases early and generously. I learned to negotiate these cases, and many others liked them, to settlements with the maximum of available budget at the earliest possible opportunity. But it was never enough. Deep down inside, even now so many years later, these memories make me cry. Perhaps I was too soft. But, at last, I was discovering why I had entered the law. I was no longer acting as a technician helping the wealthy to become richer; now I was starting to find my way as best I could to bringing justice where most needed by mitigating catastrophic misfortune.

But not every case had a happy ending. Andy fell from an open train doorway on his way home from school. He survived the fall. But a passing train instantly severed both his legs. Years later, I needed to inspect his now healed injuries. He came to our office with his father. At my request, he removed his trousers to unstrap the prostheses. I rose from my desk and reached the door. I just managed to close it. Then I fainted like a felled tree in the reception area outside.

I was startled to wake up looking at my secretary's shoes in front of me.

Are you alright? she asked, which seemed even then to be a ridiculous question.

Of course, I muttered senselessly as I gathered my wits.

Then I opened my office door. Ashen faced, and sweating profusely, I tried to behave as though nothing had happened. Inanely, I apologised vaguely for the unexpected interruption. They exchanged bewildered glances and pretended not to notice.

Andy's claim against the railways hinged on whether we could prove the carriage-door was defective. Their defence was that he had been skylarking, dangling from the hand-straps hanging from the ceiling when the train turned a corner. All his school friends were mysteriously unobservant, which did not bode well. Ultimately, we were unable to gather any evidence to establish his claim, and it languished.

Managing a caseload of 500 Supreme Court writs at every stage of completion is a juggling act that requires considerable attention and a good operating system. When everything is going smoothly, it is like a tightly spinning top, in suspended equilibrium, with periodic injections of activity to sustain momentum. These included conducting client interviews, organising investigations and obtaining expert assessments, providing preliminary advice on liability, attending procedural hearings, exchanging and answering questions (called *interrogatories*) and obtaining documents from the other side (called *discovery*) in pre-trail (or *interlocutory*) procedures that filled many months with activity and only then, when prepared, briefing barristers (or *counsel*) for advice before each claim could join the long queue of others awaiting trial.

Mislaying or overlooking a file at any critical time amid all this work was my nightmare. This could easily happen with a busy list of many cases each moving at its own pace. Occasionally, it did. Once I was appearing in court on a case, when I was startled to see Jan, my assistant, signalling frantically from the sidelines. Somehow, we had overlooked the hearing of another case on the same morning. Fortunately, it was in a neighbouring courtroom. After a furtive but torrid discussion, she was able to reschedule it. On other occasions, I was stirred by compassion—as much as personal relief—at the spectacle of a hapless colleague scrambling deranged across the busy traffic of William Street clutching bulging files that had evidently been overlooked.

I found the best way to manage the colossal juggling act of a large practice was the simplest. Each of my files had a space on the cover for the date when it would next be reviewed. This was usually monthly, unless it was urgent, when it stayed on the top of the desk. I entered the next date for every file in my diary. Periodically additional events, like calls or letters from the other side would prompt additional actions. Every day, Jan would retrieve these files for review before whatever court hearings and appointments had already been scheduled. Most cases progressed steadily, however sluggishly, over a year or two. But difficult cases that needed special investigation or evidence tended to snag and sometimes languish for months on end until finding the time to attend to them. I was able to finalise or 'settle' most cases, perhaps 70%, once the court date had been fixed, in 'the shadow of the courthouse door', when the client's attention—and that of her/his lawyer also—were galvanised to all the risks and costs of proceeding. Many cases, perhaps 20%, got as far as giving evidence for a day or two in order to gauge the credibility of key witnesses. Only a fraction, perhaps 5–10%, went the full distance to be completed with the judge delivering a judgment. This was usually because of the sobering impact of the massive legal costs mounting on both sides, which the losing party was always at risk of being ordered to pay. Some clients insisted 'on principle' to having their day in court—at least, that is, until they fully apprehended the costs of those principles which could, on occasion, even exceed $50k in today's terms each day. If the hearing continued for any more than a day or two, it rapidly created another nightmare of delaying all my other cases, which was an additional incentive, at least for the lawyers, to settle the matter as expeditiously as possible.

When this system worked, which was most—though never all—of the time, it was a dream. My cases progressed to completion, their bills were rendered, and the fees accumulated in the partners' monthly reports—as though by magic.

As a practising lawyer, my time was quite literally money. The legal profession operated, at that time at least, a process of recording time worked in 6-minute units, that is, in ten units in each hour. Every unit had a dollar value: the highest being for partners, the lowest for clerks. This process existed—and possibly still does—for billing purposes and required all 'fee-earners' to record how they spent their time working on each file. Ostensibly it was used for costing files. But in practice it was also used as a management tool to keep lawyers working productively. Generally, lawyers were required to charge around three-quarters of their time to clients, the rest being allocated to administration, marketing and training. Unsurprisingly, this system encouraged fee-earners to record a 2-minute 'yes/no' phone call as a legitimate chargeable unit—trebling its actual cost. This regime instilled grinding efficiency, but it was the bane of practice for both lawyers and clients alike.

It was during this period that a friend, Ronwyn, asked if I could give a full-day class the next day on civil litigation in the lawyers' practical training program. Their instructor, who was a barrister, had become jammed in court with a case taking longer than expected. I had never thought about doing this, but when I did it sounded interesting. So, I agreed to try on their assurance that the students had already been given a practice manual, which I nervously read that evening. The next day, I found that I really enjoyed the experience, which seemed to come almost effortlessly. I saw the students' eyes light up as I gave practical examples, hands-on experience and anecdotes to enliven the materials. I found teaching refreshed my own understanding of my work and punctuated the routine of practice. So, I became a regular instructor and later, as my own experience grew, designed a new course on negotiation skills for lawyers.

By now, I had found a niche specialising in civil litigation. Over the next couple of years, I found myself rising through the ranks in a sometimes-giddying exhilaration of promotions. An avalanche of new cases led to expanding the firm's practice. It employed two new lawyers, then another two, until I was heading a dynamic team of five energised young lawyers who, between us, became the firm's biggest fee-earners. At twenty-nine, I was unexpectedly invited to join the firm as an equity partner and then co-managing partner responsible for all litigation.

Suddenly, I realised, I had 'arrived' as a lawyer. This was strange for a kid who'd been held down twice at school, then dumped in his articles. Immediately came status, staff and benefits. I felt like a princeling. This was a time of wearing Zegna suits with tailored waists, crimson silk ties and expense accounts for clients in very fancy restaurants that I couldn't afford to bring Lisa, my then wife, with whom I shared eighteen contented years. Graham, the firm's trusty accountant educated me on those benefits.

Buy a bigger house, he told me.

But, I protested, we already had what we needed. We had recently borrowed our first 30-year mortgage and proudly bought a weatherboard cottage in Caulfield. It seems ridiculous, now, for just $34,500. I drove a recent model Golf VW. Neither was flash, but both were fine.

At Graham's further urging, I test drove a Porsche. It was astonishing, like riding a prancing horse. But to my surprise, it was fool's gold. Now that I could afford to purchase one on lease, it lost its enticement of being unattainable. I realised that I had no interest or need to outpace revving teenagers from the traffic lights. That was not who I wanted to be.

'Use it or lose it,' he warned.

'Then spend it on wine', he told me. I bought a bottle of Penfold's Grange costing $47 on special, which even then—before speculators had discovered it—was expensive. It was nice, but still never *that* nice. Now this wine costs twenty-times at $1000 each bottle.

The workload was heavy. But I had learned to work really hard experiencing a quiet joy in the elegance of efficiency. No time was wasted, and few minutes went uncharged. I was working to the max. Every minute of each working day counted—except for weekends which I firewalled for my young family. The 6-minute costing system locked my focus. At lunch, I walked through the city streets for a 30-minute break, clearing my head before returning to the office. Some days, I would lie under my desk to straighten my back on the floor and descend into a deep refreshing nap. It was during one such nap that Jan found me and nearly had a stroke fearing I'd suffered a heart attack.

Each year, I finished at lunchtime on the breakup for Christmas. I would roam then through the department stores in a daze, gathering fancy treats for the family. I would buy on a whimsy: cakes, marmalade, Scottish shortbread. These sprees became a happy ritual. I felt stoned, in the nicest possible way, disconnected and floating in slow motion. I would return home laden with goodies for Christmas with the family. And then, I would hibernate for 4–5 days sleeping continuously to emerge only for meals and grunt monosyllabic greetings before disappearing again. In all the years since, I have certainly worked smarter, but never have I worked harder.

After some months, when the buzz of partnership had receded, it sometimes felt like I was sitting at the base of an enormous sand cliff; the faster I finalised cases, the more rapidly new cases fell over my head. It felt like I was being smothered by my own hand. Soon my file load exceeded those of my partners. When I looked around more closely, I found they were earning higher profit shares than me, but many seemed to be working less and were certainly rendering fewer fees. Slowly, it started to feel that as a new partner I was subsidizing them rather than each of us supporting each other evenly. Having never before looked beyond the goal of making partner, I was now startled to question that achievement.

Then I looked beyond my partners at the profession around me. I had ascended to a plateau which, however high, was now a flat place. I sensed a slackening of my climb. I looked across at John, my senior partner, who was nationally respected in the field and undoubtedly more skilled than me, but only incrementally so. After the excitement of achieving partnership had passed, it dawned on me that it would take me decades to attain his height. My ascent would now become slower. At dinner parties, I also started to notice that my sphere of interest was narrowing to my specialty and I had become blinkered. I suspected I was becoming boring, paradoxically knowing much more about much less. But surely, that was back to front, I pondered. I was also troubled by the expectations of lifestyle that were accumulating around me. I sensed that the quest for a bigger house, faster car, more flashy holidays was infinitely seductive, but unquenchable and never-ending. Already, I could see the beginning of massive mortgages and school fees inexorably locking me ever more tightly into my law firm because only my position in it as a partner could afford them.

At the same time, I was starting to find the rewards were strangely disappointing. This was unexpected because, for the first time in my life, I was earning beyond what most could ever aspire to. It wasn't disappointing because there wasn't enough, but rather because it might never be. I was discovering that money itself wasn't actually satisfying. Yes, of course a sufficiency was necessary to survive and enjoy life. But it didn't really matter how big my house was, or how fast my car. I already knew it didn't really matter. They were proxies for something that I'd expected to be satisfying, which actually wasn't there. I was slowly encountering an emptiness in the promise of practising law.

I was starting to feel confused, conflicted and increasingly listless. I had 'made it' to the place I'd dreamt of, where most others couldn't reach. Everything should have been fine. But I guessed I'd never before looked very closely at what lay beyond the accomplishment of partnership. I was now confronting some choices that I hadn't had to consider before.

Beyond the aura of success, I remained troubled by the problems of unfairness, cost and delay that hobbled the courts from delivering justice and confounded most ordinary people from being able to use them to solve their problems.

The risk of these dangers is recognized in the European doctrine of the "*equality of arms*" which is a legal principle derived from the right to a fair trial, as enshrined in Article 6 of the European Convention on Human Rights, though not explicitly in Australian law. This principle ensures that both parties in a legal proceeding have a fair and equal opportunity to present their case, without any undue advantage being given to one side over the other. It is a fundamental element of procedural fairness. It requires that each party has the opportunity to be represented by legal counsel. If one party cannot afford legal representation, measures should be taken to ensure that they receive adequate legal aid or assistance. But in Australian legal practice, as sadly is too commonly the case, this foundational doctrine is usually honoured in its breach.

Indeed, the impediment of cost was so acute that even I, as professionally privileged as I now was, could not afford to retain my own services without confronting the imminent risk of having to sell my home. Taken singly or together, these impediments were barriers to any notion of accessible justice that often rendered the courts unfit for purpose. But, as a partner, I was now benefitting from the very system that disabled the courts from delivering justice as they should.

Aged just thirty, I now sensed my options were diminishing. Despite being a litigation specialist, I felt fraudulent being unable to afford the time needed to acquire the forensic skills of trial experience by regularly appearing in court. With so many matters queuing in my filing cabinets, I could really only appear in court for a few hours, a day or two at most, from time to time. I was becoming locked into a situation of having to brief others as counsel, which became a vicious cycle preventing me from ever conducting my own trials. It dawned on me that this was no longer a path building the skills and experience to develop further as a lawyer. I talked with my partners about resolving this dilemma. But there wasn't much the firm could—or would—do. I was now too valuable where I was, doing what I was already doing. Soon, I might need to send my daughters to schools with massive fees that only my partnership position could afford. The more I looked, the more I found myself becoming imprisoned within the walls of my smart office, shackled by fears of the unknown beyond it.

This discomfort grew until one afternoon, exasperated by losing a lengthy slab of dictation due to a malfunctioning voice-recorder, I found myself poised to hurl a chair through the window onto the street below. The force of that impulse was shocking and quite frightening. Could I control it? Could I even explain it? This was *not* alright. Something was wrong, and I needed it to stop.

Practising law is a worthy devotion. I had learned to carry a massive caseload to provide useful services that were valued by my clients. Best of all, I found a quiet joy in bringing justice to the needy by mitigating catastrophic misfortune through major litigation. But I now acknowledged that I would never flourish amid the minutia of legal technicalities like some of my colleagues: Julian who became the human rights silk challenging government in the High Court, Stephen who would one day become a Supreme Court judge, or Mark the Attorney-General. And I also now knew the money, however much, would never be enough.

Despite acquiring the lavish trappings of partnership with all the toys of a princeling, I had heard a murmuring question. '*But is this all there is?*' In some turmoil, I retired from the firm to the astonishment of my partners, half a lifetime earlier than expected, to continue searching for what I could not yet name.

Crossroad and Catharsis

The '90s were a time of profound turbulence for judges and courts around the world, as much as for me.

In Australia, this turbulence exploded through the double barrels of gender and race: first in a series of rape trials presided over by judges who were seen as being out of touch by the communities they were supposed to serve. They had expressed beliefs and opinions about women 'inviting' rape by the provocative way they dressed, or being presumed to have consented to sex by their presence only. Most rapes are never reported; some researchers estimating fewer than 10%. Of these about 10% result in convictions; and of those, the average penalty is about 30 months, with remissions. Shockingly, that may be less than for stealing a car. Why would anyone in their right mind even dream of approaching a court system to protect them when it fails to deliver anything more than the prospect of excruciating public humiliation under cross-examination, and an infinitesimal prospect of justice.

The second blast exploded when the over-representation of Indigenous people in the criminal justice system hit the headlines. In 1991, the Royal Commission into Aboriginal Deaths in Custody found that Indigenous people were 17.8 times more likely to be in prison than non-Indigenous people. It revealed an enduring race and class war that deeply shook the nation's pride and confidence in itself. The genocidal horrors of the frontier wars could no longer be treated by middle class Australia as an historical anomaly[16].

These twin blasts brought the skies crashing down on the Australian judiciary. Public outrage fanned by the media was immediate and intense. Newspapers openly questioned the credibility, and challenged the authority, of the judiciary to the mystification of the judges who huddled in their chambers, shielding themselves with their independence. Their response was then seen as remote, unaccountable and non-transparent. It was a very difficult time. Abruptly, the judges were seen as being the problem: patriarchal, reactionary and out of touch with the communities they were supposed to serve. Facing the imminent threat of government intervention, the

L. Armytage, *Confronting Injustice*,
https://doi.org/10.1007/978-981-95-3573-6_5

judicial leadership finally acted by introducing a program of judicial education, among other measures.

Until then, there had never been any formalised education for judges in Australia, or most other places in the common law world. Judges, particularly senior judges, stood so close to god that they were presumed to be born gifted with their talents, and hence it was heretical for any other mortal to teach them. This was plainly a conceit for anyone outside the judiciary, but it took a massive external controversy to displace it. So it was that I packed my young family in the car and moved to Sydney. It was my new job to fix the problem as a director of the Judicial Commission of NSW, responsible to educate the judges and magistrates of Australia's most populous state. My entry into this new field was generously facilitated by John Hudzik, Emeritus Professor of political philosophy at Michigan State University who was visiting Sydney and introduced me to his colleagues working with the courts in the United States.

Having left legal practice, I had been drawn to build on my earlier teaching experience which I had enjoyed. Doubtless because of my own learning difficulties as a child, I had become interested in the mystery of learning which had led me through a succession of jobs educating first lawyers and then other professionals after leaving my law firm. This transition was not however without bumps. My station in the world had plummeted and I was no longer a princeling. Gone was my team of assistants and secretaries. Now I did my own typing, at first slowly and very clumsily. People also treated me differently. There were some strange looks, a holding back from former colleagues, even pity in some expressions. Some thought I was deranged. By resigning my partnership, I had rejected an orthodoxy that money trumped everything. In doing so, I had somehow betrayed my partners and peers, and the values they shared. My earnings were certainly lower, hence presumedly my value. It was a sometimes-jarring transition. But I already knew there was no turning back when, after just 3 months, a friend offered me to interview for another partnership position with a larger law firm famed for its class action litigation. I could not in good conscience even accept their plane ticket for an excursion back to Melbourne for their interview.

As a child, I was a late reader, suffering from an astigmatism and dyslexia. So, it was a belated wonder when the pages finally yielded their secrets, and I discovered the epic adventures of a red bus that magically appeared from behind the letters on the page and parked there forever in my memory. Doubtless because of these learning difficulties, I became fascinated by the profound mystery about how human beings learn and, from there, how I could facilitate that learning in me and later in others.

This mystery is exquisitely framed in Schon's paradox:

> The paradox of learning a really new competence is this: a student cannot at first understand what he needs to learn, can learn it only by educating himself, and can educate himself only by beginning to do what he does not yet understand.[8]

This mystery spurred me to research my master's thesis which was later published as the book: '*Educating Judges*'.[9] By then, I was now working at the Judicial

Commission. I had amassed plenty of practical experience in training lawyers and other professionals but felt a new need to master my craft in the more challenging and sometimes contested environment of working with judges. While a series of public controversies had driven the upper judiciary to accede however reluctantly to continuing education, this had been given, in reality, on the basis of the needs of others, such as lowly magistrates, rather than for those as close to the gods as themselves.

When I started researching the field, most of my searches came up empty to my bewilderment and consternation. In part, this reflected the infancy of information technology before Google. But equally it reflected the nascency of judicial education. I persevered devoting all my spare evenings to this research as well as many quiet afternoons in the office, jesting that my job was now the most generous government scholarship available to any student.

Given the public criticism of the judiciary's gender and racial biases in the mid-90 s, the timing was opportune to professionalise their training. I had so much to learn—not just about education, but also how to research, write and argue academically. After 3 months, I submitted a draft of the first chapter of my thesis to Terry, my supervisor. It took another 3 months for me to understand that his feedback of my draft as being 'encyclopaedic' was *not* in fact a compliment. I had stumbled on the first step of gathering endless data with which to fill the expanse of my ignorance, but I had yet to discern the difference between gathering data, however relevant, and building an argument. Daunted, I stared blankly at this cliff-face blocking my path. It took many weeks to realise that first I needed to pose an idea, then gather data from which I could sift evidence, that I could then organise logically to support a conclusion that would either establish or refute that idea. Only once mastered did these arcane techniques of academic argument seem effortless.

I began researching education and what was then known about cognitive psychology, behaviourism and humanism in my exploration to educate judges, and I enjoyed testing the efficacy of their theories against my actual experience.

Around this time, Malcolm Knowles framed the then novel proposition that adults learn differently to children. He argued that adult learning is problem-focused, autonomous and self-directed.[10] This was a timely elaboration in explaining our judges' aversion to any suggestion of disempowerment, or condescension, by outsiders seeking to 'teach' them anything. Patricia Cross then clarified that since adults are problem-oriented learners, the more sharply they defined any problem, the less satisfactory traditional classes would be.[11] There were many others like David Kolb and Ned Hermann illuminating the canvas of our understanding how humans learn.[12] Collectively, their insights and reasoning opened up the altogether new space of facilitated learning.

These insights spurred me to focus on the learner, rather than on the content to be taught, which introduced the transformative shift from passive to active learning. I now began to see my role as facilitating the self-directed learning of others. Not only did I need to guide the (sometimes reluctant) learner towards what they needed to learn by demonstrating its relevance and utility, but I also needed to ignite their interest and incubate their ongoing inquiry. I stood in their shoes to steer that process. Updating judges about new laws was relatively straight forward. But John Hudzik cautioned me from his own experience that judges didn't already know it all, however much they felt they might, as ever more complex civil and criminal litigation proliferated. My challenge was to guide the learner along the path of what they didn't yet know they didn't know but still needed to find out in new and unfamiliar domains, such as DNA, AI, minority rights or Indigenous disadvantage.

I now found myself reflecting on the never-ending process of learning. I recalled my endless struggles as a child to learn to read, tell the time, then to ride a bicycle. Each of these steps was massive. Yet first, there was another even more ambitious step—learning how to learn. Once mastered, this is taken for granted. Yet the mystery of Schon's paradox persists. We still understand so little about how we actually learn. It remains a form of magic that happens every day; and I now had the privilege of facilitating this magic.

I was particularly excited by Donald Schon's focus on the notion of professional artistry which I found much more intriguing than the mundane but prevalent preoccupation with attaining basic competence. He used artistry to describe how experts actually handled unique challenges in daily practice. He argued that this required the application of intelligence or 'a kind of knowing' built through experience that embodied the art of identifying a problem, the art of implementation and the art of improvisation in the messy swamp of daily practice. The professional must first construct problems from ambiguous situations before they can be solved. Thus, he saw 'problem setting,' or problem diagnosis, as more important than 'problem solving' in being the key to professional excellence. I tested each of these theories against the practice of my own experience, and found it revelatory that I already understood this notion innately but had not yet been able to articulate it.

I found active learning—where adults learn through doing—tilted the education process towards problem-solving exercises and debates and away from conventional lectures and seminars. For example, I would raise judges' self-awareness of their biases by organising debates where they had to confront, reflect on and justify their differences among their own peers. Much to their surprise, they usually found such activities to be fun.

I soon reached the conclusion that while learning can be pushed along, it is likely to be better when curiosity is animated to motivate and direct that learning. This is a continually evolving process, from child to young adult, and then from adult to seasoned professional. I argued that judges appointed on merit from the upper bar were characteristically intensely autonomous and highly successful professionals who are distinctive as a cohort of adult learners. Learning can often embody radical relearning in a cyclic process of ever-deepening understanding. No one is static. Moreover, norms may shift over a lifetime. As a father, I have found myself keeping up by watching my daughters Rosita and Danika, who are now both mothers with their own children. They update me regularly on the latest technology and gently but firmly re-educate me on changing attitudes and social values, when they might find me sometimes expressing delinquent attitudes that were accepted in bygone decades but no longer, for example possibly now regarding the pronouns of transitioning.

I had a mysterious experience, while completing this thesis. I am not generally given to mystical experiences, but at various times during the more harrowing parts of the research, I became aware of a benign presence standing at my shoulder offering me encouragement. It assured me that I was doing something worthwhile and was on the right track. It took a number of such encounters with this sensation to surmise that it was the spirit of my maternal grandfather, Geoffrey Grant Morris, whom I had never met. One hundred years before, he had been a Classics don at Corpus Christi, Cambridge.[13] His scholar's gold medal, dated 1908, had silently gleamed beneath a fine layer of dust on my shelf since it had been handed down to me. Now it seemed that I had received his ancestral blessing, however unexpectedly. When the thesis was done, I was in turn awarded the university medal and, in the following year, it was published as the first monograph in this nascent field.

I found the opportunity to research and develop this altogether new program of education for judges to be immensely exciting. From the outset it required considerable thinking about its purpose, scope and content. I wanted to help the judges earn public respect, but not just technocratically. Ignorance of law was not the core problem. The judiciary was appointed from the upper ranks of the bar and generally competent in knowing the law. The judges were however seen as being out of touch, failing to reflect—and indeed to lead—community values, and being beyond the reach of accountability. In effect, they were failing much more seriously in their social responsibility as leaders. I wanted to design a program that provided a bridge to address this underlying problem.

In doing so, I was fascinated to see inside the inner sanctum of the courts. In the upper ranks there are some truly extraordinary people with astonishing vision, acuity and talents. Michael Kirby presided over the Court of Appeal, and later the High Court, to change the nation in the profoundly important matters of human and Indigenous rights. He was a generous mentor to me and a secular saint for many others. Another was Justice Jim Wood who headed the criminal division of the Supreme Court who, as a former surfer, gave that grim court a much-needed humanising face. Later he led a Royal Commission to clean out corruption in the police force, which he miraculously completed blemish free. Others were quirkier, like Roddy Meagher, a brilliant eccentric, whose shambolic chambers were adorned with original Degas, Monet and Picasso paintings hanging drunkenly askew behind piles of files threatening to spew their papers at any moment across the floor.

Most judges—if pressed—begrudgingly agreed that professional education was a good idea—but mainly for their peers and subordinates, rather than themselves.[14] But like any profession, it was of course a mixed bunch of novices with skills to acquire and those getting tired who could benefit from refreshers. So it was that I was challenged to steward the attitudes and values of a privileged and sometimes recalcitrant cohort of high achieving professionals. Much of my challenge lay in persuading habitually self-directed achievers that this program could provide them with something of value. Besides making their jobs easier by providing timely updates on new law, it involved stretching their horizons in important new directions. In particular, this was a time to guide the judiciary to listen to and understand the unheard voices of women—most of whom felt re-victimised when they resorted to the courts for justice—and Indigenous people—many of whom had spent most of their adult lives incarcerated in prisons on their orders. Hearing these voices from outside their privileged corridors was often revelatory and even transformative.

To accomplish this, I departed from conventional lecturing to introduce much smaller informal workshops where outsiders could share their expertise with judges and magistrates in a safe space for them all. Some were highly skilled experts in ballistics, DNA evidence, forensic pathology, complex off-balance sheet accounting or juvenile psychology. Others had no formal qualifications at all beyond the authenticity of their personal experience and insights of the courts.

Kevin was an unconventional presenter. He came from Brungle, a tiny township in the foothills of the Snowy Mountains on the traditional lands of the Wiradjuri people. Hal Wootten QC, a member of the Royal Commission, had suggested I talk with him. Kevin, who was aged 34, had already served 19 of those years in prison—most of his life—for numerous offences including the very serious crime of armed robbery. He had helped the Commission as an advisor on Indigenous matters.

'He's a quiet fellow, but perspicacious,' Hal confided.

When I met Kevin, he wiped his hands on the back of his pants before shaking hands. He had intense eyes and a gentle manner. After a few minutes of chat, he gave a constrained chuckle like an awkward smoker shielding his cigarette in his palm. I instantly liked him. So did the judges.

Kevin gave workshops on what it was really like to be an Aboriginal man in prison. They were based around a video titled "*Who Killed Malcolm Smith?*"[15] This narrated the history of the first suicide in custody investigated by the Royal Commission. Kevin had shared a cell with Malcolm for several years before he had killed himself. Somehow Kevin had survived his own turmoil in prison. He had little formal schooling but was a moving educator. Before starting, he was shy and needed reassurance. Once he got going, however, he affected the magistrates with his quiet authenticity and direct insight.

I had designed this training program to provide judges and magistrates with a broader understanding of Indigenous people's circumstances and raise their awareness of the problems still confronting Indigenous Australians in the justice system. It was a radical method in dismantling the power and authority of judicial officers by lowering them to the same level as, even indeed at the feet of, Indigenous people during these sessions. It exposed the judges and magistrates responsible for sentencing offenders to the world and perspectives of Indigenous people, many of whom had spent most of their lives behind bars.

When speaking to the judges and magistrates, some of whom had actually convicted him of earlier offences and sentenced him to jail, Kevin was gently spoken, patient and without rancour. He narrated his lifetime of continual arrests and imprisonment without bitterness, anger or blame. The room fell totally still while he spoke. A seasoned magistrate silently wept. Another, clearly dazed, told me later: "I never realized that it was like that." Kevin had that effect on many people.

During these sessions, Kevin was joined by Bobbi Sykes. Bobbi had won a scholarship to Harvard without having completed secondary school. She was the first black Australian to be awarded a PhD. She established a foundation that awards scholarships for distinguished Indigenous women to also study there, many of whom now hold professorships and other eminent positions. Bobbi was also a founding member of the 'tent embassy' in Canberra and a prominent activist for Indigenous rights. Despite her reputation in the media as a firebrand, I recall her thoughtfulness and forbearance when answering the many questions about those whose lives were far outside the privileged circle of the judges' experience.

The last time I saw Kevin was outside my office on George Street some months later. When he called, his voice was strained and hardly recognizable. He was haggard and tense. He'd had a row with his wife about needing to leave the city and return to his home in the Snowy country. He had walked barefoot all night through Redfern to clear his head. He told me of his mounting frustration; how all the encouragement and excitement arising from his experience of working with the Royal Commission and the judiciary had failed to deliver any promised solutions. He was unemployed again and broke. He was staying off the grog however, and assured me he had resisted the temptation to do another armed robbery.

'It would be so easy. But I'm never going back there (to prison). I wouldn't come out again.'

He asked me for a loan for his travel money to get back home.

'It's not easy asking,' he said. His eyes were squeezed up, as though staring into the sun.

It was an awkward moment for us both. I hesitated, just a moment, before going to the bank, neither of us wanting his promise to repay it with his next dole cheque.

Three weeks later, Bobbi rang to tell me Kevin was dead. I thought I had misheard. Then it hit me. I had that sinking feeling of being in a lift in free-fall. I was gutted. I should have been more generous; then he would definitely have got home.

My shame continues to this day.

The program I developed aimed to build the competence of judges in many ways. Another presenter, Rich, was a visiting expert in assessing witness credibility, truth, an art close to the heart of judging. His research had tested the abilities of various occupations to assess truth including the CIA, the US secret service, police, and tax and customs officials. In these tests, Rich had measured the participants' ability to correctly assess whether 'suspects' were lying. Overall, most were correct about half the time. Two occupations were outstanding: customs officials and the secret service. He had found that customs officers identified smugglers through their non-discrepant body language: nervous ticks, over-friendliness and evasive eye contact. He also found the secret service had developed an intuition or 'sixth sense', which they didn't fully understand but knew worked. When they scanned a crowded place for a possible assassin, they were actually searching for unexpected behaviour. For example, when the US President entered a room, they searched for the one person who was not smiling in that direction, but instead who was looking down or had a grim expression.

I invited Rich to measure our judges' ability to assess witness credibility. Surprising to me, but as he predicted, their scores conformed to those of the average population at around 50%—that is, their 'skill' was soberingly hit-or-miss. He argued this was also the norm for judges in the United States. Curiously, our magistrates scored discernibly better than the judges at around 66/33; that is, they were more often right than wrong. Rich's findings suggested that the magistrates, perhaps due to dealing with a much higher volume of cases, had more opportunity to hone their assessment skills than judges—and, consequently, had acquired a specific skill—however intuitive—in assessing credibility. While it remained unclear to us both whether we could formally develop these skills beyond imparting some self-criticality of their probable absence, that alone was at least an initial step in the right direction.

It was during this time that I had a series of four metaphorical experiences.

The first of these was driven by my formative fear of failure from prep school. I learned to study hard to avoid the repeat of such humiliation. After graduating, I had worked with Rolly for two years in his suburban practice while I had studied for my Masters in the evenings. This required honours-level performance, that is a mark of 75% or higher. In the first year, I came first in one subject and well in the others. I was cruising comfortably. At the start of the second year, I arrived early to class. To pass the time, I rolled a cigarette. The lecture theatre filled, and the professor began. He made introductory remarks, then he paused, looking slowly around, to let his eyes rest momentarily on me before swivelling to a 'No Smoking' sign on the wall. My mind was dwelling on his introduction, and I failed to notice. I passed the first essay, then the second, but failing to qualify at honours level. I passed the next subject, but likewise not well enough to qualify. I took a supplementary course, for an additional semester, which again I passed but not well enough. I then met with the Dean to seek his indulgence. But he refused it. Abruptly, I had failed, again. I was filled with shame and self-loathing for months, even years. It was a bitter lesson. I had become careless. When finally, I tried a second time, fifteen years later, I won first class honours, the university medal for outstanding research, and published my first book. So the bipolar nature of my learning has remained a confounding mystery to me to this day.

The second of these experiences was equally cathartic. It came before I had overcome my fears of the unknown to master the courage to step away from the security of my law partnership. It was during the summer preceding my resignation from the firm. I was climbing a mountain in Lamington National Park, on the Queensland border. It had a ridge which from the valley flat looked innocuous. But as the ridge ascended towards the escarpment, it became narrower and more precipitous on both sides. Finally, after scrambling upwards for about ninety minutes, I reached the saddle. Here the path narrowed into a razorback for some twenty-five metres in length. I had to cross along this razorback to reach the grasslands beyond. It just a rock or two in width. The surface was uneven and weather-worn, little more than an outcrop of stones embedded in crumbling clay. On both sides were steep descents that concealed their depths below the canopy of trees. The scrub on the walls was sparse, offering no handholds or protection. If I lost a footing, there would be no arresting my fall many meters below. Looking across, my sphincter tightened involuntarily. I stalled to contemplate my options. There was no turning back. Actually, I knew already that this was why I had made the climb; I had to get across. Slowly, I inched my way forward. The dried clay was cracking and unstable. Pieces fell away beneath my feet. I shuffled searching for footings. It seemed impossible to go on. Frozen, I stopped halfway. I could feel the prickle of fear climb up the inside of my legs which were now trembling. Then it gripped my back and shoulders in a claw as my muscles involuntarily spasmed.

I could feel the void drawing me from both sides.

Don't look down, I ordered.

I started to turn back. But the ridge was too narrow. My feet were shaking, and the footings were crumbling.

Try going backwards, I thought.

But that was worse. I couldn't see where to place my feet.

My breaths were now coming short and fast.

I could feel the panic prickling my scalp. I could fall—really fall—and there was no help within reach. I'd heard that three people had already died from falling off this saddle some years before. I could be the next. If I stayed rigid, I'd soon get tired and lose my balance.

I knew then I could only go forward—and must.

I had to master the terror, or it would all be over.

So, I did. With an inner voice that I didn't know I had, I told myself to look ahead, step forward and cross. Just get it done, *now*! I did. The void was still all around me, but I defied its call. I shifted my weight, leaned forward and clambered slowly but surely along the ridge. I felt the danger dissolving like a morning mist as I went. Relief surged and filled me.

Reaching the grasslands, I lay back giddy with exhilaration to savour the clouds above me, then the view. After some minutes, I made my way back across the razor-back and clambered down the ridge. I was as weightless as the eagles floating above me. The following week, I resigned from my legal partnership, and launched my journey into an unknown future from which I have never looked back.

The third experience was discovering my love for running. By this time, I had started to run regularly to keep fit with the lawyers' sedentary lifestyle. It was convenient because there was no need for elaborate equipment or rigid time commitments. I found that I most enjoyed the early mornings and settled into a rhythm of 12 km runs that I could complete comfortably in an hour before work, bounding along silent streets through the predawn gloom, then celebrating the sunrise as the steam rose from me into the chilly air, while the world still slept. This became a special space in which my spirit could roam reflecting on the past and contemplating the future. I felt a joy in running well, my body and mind in harmony.

Soon, the road opened before me. I became drawn to the prospect of running longer distances, then the marathon. At first, this felt hopelessly beyond me. My body was just not able to do it. Yet it was contesting this impossibility that drew me on. I mapped out a training plan and started to slowly stretch the distances. If I could run 10 km, I told myself, then I could learn to run 15 km. When I reached 15 km, surely, I could manage 20 km. That was almost halfway. As weeks grew into months, my range incrementally grew. Soon I was running 20 km. Then I set my sights on the unimaginably long 30 km distance. Keeping a steady pace, never racing, monitoring my feet, my heartbeat, my heat, I astonished myself by completing the distance. I even felt good the next day. It was then that I knew there was no alternative: I must step up to the marathon.

I remember that day, standing with hundreds of others behind the starting line, at Frankston, twitchy with apprehension. It was a fresh spring morning and my bladder had contracted. I had to pee several times before the starter's gun. When finally, it sounded, I surged confidently past scores of older runners over the first 10 km and then the second around Port Phillip Bay. But by 30 km, I was struggling to continue by just reaching the next telegraph pole. Then the next. It was agonising; my lungs heaved, and my legs were leaden. My nipples rubbed raw by the singlet stung from the sweat. Finally, I ground to a halt, crouching for rest, gasping breath. After just five minutes, I wished I hadn't. It was so much harder on my trembling feet to start again. At 35 km, those older runners glided unstoppably past me. At 42 km, I shuffled over the finish line at the Melbourne Art Centre in a numbed daze, then euphoria. I had made it!

Completing this marathon was a major lesson and became one of the commanding metaphors of my life. I had done what I believed, and knew, I could not do. In doing so, I learned that I could do whatever I wanted, provided that I was serious about it. Over the following years, I completed many other marathons—in New York, with its boisterous street parties in the Bronx, Queens, Harlem and Central Park; in Cambodia through the ancient temples of Angkor Wat early in the morning before the sun relit its furnace; and around Australia. In one, I crossed over the line 'in overdraft' having depleted my muscles dry of their glucose, literally exhausting all of my kinetic energy. I had to be carried across the parklands to recover, restoring glucose by quaffing a tub of iced coke and then ice-cream—the best I've ever tasted. In another, I cooled in a piping hot bath as it transferred all its heat to my frozen body, like thawing a slab of mutton on a butcher's hook. But no marathon was ever better than that first run around the bay when I discovered that I could go beyond my limits—to live beyond my expectations, irrespective of all the difficulties and improbabilities. This experience became a commanding allegory for my life with which I would later grow in many unexpected ways.

By the middle of my five-year contract with the Judicial Commission, I found that it was no longer demanding to work within the constraints of its edifice. By then, I had introduced an entirely new professional development program for all the judges and introduced an extended range of new services. With the onset of routine, the excitement of innovation had diminished. The pace became lethargic. The work was no longer challenging, and the skill that I had most sharpened in legal practice—timely decision-making—seemed not to be valued; indeed, it seemed strangely anathema in government. It took several years for me to understand that public service was about managing stasis rather than steering change. My CEO was paid handsomely to maintain equilibrium which essentially meant managing—and maintaining—the routine. This was systemic rather than an accident, but it was an anomaly to me. I was now finding myself working at less than half power which was not only enervating but was corroding my self-esteem. To redress this, I would need to return to the more turbulent world in the private sector that demanded timely decisions and value for money.

It was at this time that I had a fourth experience: I became captivated by the prospect of hang-gliding. I found myself drawn inexorably towards the intoxication of soaring silent and weightless through the air, ascending effortlessly on thermals to float in the heavens above. So, I travelled down to Stanwell Park where there was a launching site about 90-minutes' drive south from our home in Sydney. The park overlooks the Southern Pacific Ocean, offering an elevated escarpment that captures offshore updraughts well-suited for hang-gliding. I felt ready to confront my terrors of falling from the skies like Icarus. Three times I travelled down to this park; and three times the weather and winds were inclement. Each time I remained grounded and returned disconsolately home. It was only many years later, after I had resigned from the Judicial Commission and was flying around the globe busy in my consulting practice that I understood this frustrated impulse. Actually, I had thrown myself off the metaphorical cliff in my working life and, in doing so, no longer had any need for this recreation.

I see now that catharsis has presaged many significant stages in my life: prep school, graduate studies, shedding my law partnership, and then plunging into self-employment. My experiences at Wellington House had evidently become a part of me. While trivial on any scale of the world's horrors, HR's reprimand had scarred that carefree child with a fear to avoid any repetition of such humiliation ever again. This fear made me weak. But unknown at the time, it could also make me strong. It became the engine that would drive me with considerable power into unexpected spaces. For this, however unpleasant, I am grateful.

Fear of failure is a potent force. Over the years, I have learned to understand, respect and listen to my fears in the long nights when they were most intense. These fears have been like my night manager, attending to unfinished business that was overlooked during the hurly-burly of the day. They have warned me of the dangers that I confronted on resigning from legal practice and then again from government. The prospects of failure were clear and present dangers that threatened to jeopardise my responsibilities to support my wife Lisa and our two daughters. The magic of those fears was their power to stimulate. Lying wide-eyed awake in the night, I heard their admonitions to do whatever it takes. And in doing so, I learned that personal crisis is often the prelude to catharsis and metamorphosis, like a fish leaping upstream or the transformation from caterpillar to butterfly. Life presents opportunities to confront our fears of the unknown and, I have discovered, the tools to soar in the skies when we trust ourselves to do so.

Like most children of that era, I had been taught in school through repeated affirmation to believe in god. But as a teenager I could no longer maintain any belief in the gods of religious scriptures. Instead, I found a spiritual practice called Subud in my early twenties. Here, I learned to find a quiet still space in which I have developed a deeper understanding of myself and my relationship with the universe. In this space, I am continually filled with a sense of the numinous in the many wonders and mysteries of life, and cannot now imagine my life without it.[17]

So, once again, I stepped through my fears ready at last to make my start.

Confronting Injustice

Unequal Australia

I had read the statistics many times, but that never lessened the shock. Most times when I entered a prison in Western Australia or the Territory, I found myself to be the only white man in sight, other than the guards at the gate. It was like entering a filmset of America's deep south. But this was modern day Australia.

In 1991, the *Royal Commission into Aboriginal Deaths in Custody* found that "the Aboriginal population is grossly over-represented in custody. Too many Aboriginal people are in custody too often." Overall, Indigenous people were 17.8 times more likely to be imprisoned than non-Indigenous people. But in Western Australia, Indigenous adults were 22.7 times more likely to be imprisoned than non-Aborigines and juveniles were a staggering 48.3 times. It found "glaring deficiencies" in the care which had been provided to many of those who died in custody, who were often given unduly harsh, inhumane and degrading treatment.[18]

My work with Indigenous people had started in the early '90 s. What had begun as a technical task at the Judicial Commission caused a disturbance inside me which smouldered and then ignited into outrage that forged my vocation in justice reform. My job then had been to implement the recommendations of the Royal Commission with the judges and magistrates of New South Wales. The Royal Commission had starkly illuminated the complexity of the problems confronting Indigenous Australians and racial relations in Australia. It had recommended that government improve the overall welfare and wellbeing of Indigenous Australians, including health, education and social security, policing and prison procedures. In particular, it cast a guardianship role on the judiciary and recommended that judicial officers undergo special training in contemporary Indigenous custom to sensitise them in overseeing the quality of law enforcement. It was this recommendation that had prompted my work with Kevin, Bobbi and later Noel.

After leaving the Judicial Commission, I had launched my own consulting practice advising government, the courts, universities and major law firms on delivering better services. This practice was going well. My clients included major government agencies like the Law Reform Commission, Taxation Office and Trade

L. Armytage, *Confronting Injustice*,
https://doi.org/10.1007/978-981-95-3573-6_6

Practices Commission, as well as the Federal Court, the Administrative Appeals Tribunal and the prestigious law firm Mallesons among others.

In 1996, Rob Clifton-Steele, a businessman of shrewd insight, considerable ingenuity and deep compassion, and I started to work together for the Aboriginal & Torres Strait Islander Commission to improve the effectiveness of the Aboriginal Legal Service (ALS) around Australia. Despite both feeling hugely underqualified for this work, we won the tender and spent the next three years advising Indigenous communities across the continent on how better to address their legal needs.

We entered an altogether different Australia to the one with which I was familiar. We travelled across the vast expanses of Queensland, the Territory, South and Western Australia. In the remote Kimberley of far north western Australia, I was awed by the greetings of hands stencilled on rocks countless millennia ago—mute evidence of our shared humanity connecting profoundly different lives. Then south to Kalgoorlie with its colossal 'open cut' mines, and outlandish bars where topless girls with eyes glazed with boredom served jugs of beer to equally bored miners in a sad ritual devoid of either beauty or desire. From there, east to Cairns on the Barrier Reef and Australia's endless beaches vanishing into Pacific haze; then down to the wretched forgotten townships of Brewarrina and Walgett in outback NSW, and south to Hobart mired in its glowering history of genocidal denial.

Some nights I lay exhausted in a swag beneath the infinite canopy of stars shimmering through the tree branches until the comforting patter of rain enveloped me. The Territory was still very much *blackfella* (Indigenous) country through which *whitefellas* (non-Indigenous) happened occasionally to pass. Western Australia and Queensland remained fraught contested spaces with massive over-policing where the '*black wars*' (Indigenous extermination) continue to be fought. I encountered Indigenous communities cleaved between traditional and urban living with fundamentally different needs that rarely overlapped. I needed to stay tightly focused on what I could do in order to avoid being paralysed by the seemingly overwhelming injustices and entrenched despair of indigenous people. Each time I flew home, I was jarred by the chasm in wellbeing that a 3-hour flight back from Alice Springs to the evening glitter of Sydney's harbourside streets would expose.

We had many life-changing revelations that immersed us in both the wonders and despair of Indigenous life. From Alice, the legal service provided outreach to remote communities like Papunya, Yuendumu, Yulara and Utopia scattered across the Macdonald Ranges. Each of these communities comprised a scattering of run-down houses, a store with heavily barred windows, abandoned rusted car hulks, and sparse shade over the hot red dust. Yet it was in these apparently forsaken places that a vibrant sense of 'country' existed, and truly splendid art was being painted. Travelling to these remote settlements in the Central Desert, I now discovered the vitality of Indigenous art, which was often the largest, even only, source of livelihood.[19] Many artists—Emily Kame Kngwarreye, Gloria Petyarre, Kathleen Petyarre—were already internationally acclaimed. The magic of their art shimmers in the paradox of its mysticism, expressed in forms and colours that were otherworldly. Most of these artists are female, and I soon experienced that it is usually the voices of women, the matriarchs and 'aunties' who hold these communities together, and gave me the deepest insights on their needs. These women are the guardians of tradition and culture. Their art was painted on the red dirt of the desert floor: in one that I have collected, the paw print of a dog is rendered as it walked by; in another, there are smudges from the wind or falling leaves.

There were visionary leaders, moving orators and inspirational storytellers. I had first met Noel Pearson some years earlier while he was still a law student. I was organising the first conference of the judges of the Supreme Court, and had gambled on inviting him to present a lecture on the recommendation of his professor, the legendary Garth Nettheim. When I greeted him at the lift, he glared at me suspiciously before slowly smiling. He was an astonishing orator. Even as the youngest person present, just a student, his presence captivated the full chamber of the Supreme Court in rapt attention. This was the portent of his later speech at the funeral of Prime Minister Gough Whitlam whom he eulogised with the warmth of deepest respect as 'that old man'. Much later again, he would speak with considerable intellectual power to advocate the case for Indigenous recognition in The Voice to Parliament referendum on the ABC's most prestigious *Boyer Lectures* of 2022.[20]

It was also during this time, that I was learning from the truth-telling of Bruce Pascoe[21] and Stan Grant[22] who disabused me of my earlier education at Wangaratta High School. On arriving in Australia in 1964, I had been shocked to be taught that 'Aborigines' were a dying race who had no culture. Now I was learning the profound revelation of the lingering cult of silence in Australian history about the Indigenous injustices woven throughout its fabric. Then after watching Rachel Perkins' '*Australian Wars*,' I was further shaken to realise another ancestor George, in my father's line, who had built the first watermill near Hobart in 1830, was doubtless complicit, if not a protagonist, in the '*black wars*'—a genocide which tainted that colony, and later the squatters in my ancestry who stole the lands that had made them prosperous in the 'western district' of Victoria as well as respectable in gifting their homestead Como House in modern-day Toorak to the National Trust.[23] This was not my guilt; but it is my shame, horror and sorrow that I now acknowledge.

Since the early 1990s, I had been captivated by the grace of Bangarra Dance, each time it visited Sydney. While I was mesmerised by the vibrancy of its dance, as well as Indigenous art, and re-educated by recent scholarship, I was confounded by the hardship and disadvantage of the people living in these communities. This disadvantage spanned every aspect of human wellbeing as measured in life expectancy, infant mortality, physical and mental health, nutrition, housing, education, employment, income, standard of living, suicide and self-harm. Alcohol, petrol and other stimulants were sedatives to dull the ache of their despair and the layers of generational and epigenetic trauma, even for children under the age of ten. Travelling just one kilometre from the boisterous busloads of tourists marvelling at the majesty of Uluru, I entered the Indigenous community of Mutitjulu—a shanty settlement at the very heart of Australia, consisting of Soweto-style tumbledown shelters, mouldering rubbish and mangy dogs roaming in the dust. The men sat listless while the women, often visibly disfigured by the scarring of domestic violence, went about their work, and the children wobbled past clutching plastic bags of petrol to their noses. The wretchedness was palpable.

We made many visits to communities to see how people felt about the service. Early on, I met Maree whose arm was freshly bandaged when we spoke.

'How did you get this, I asked?

'Nev hit me when he got home from the pub. Said his dinner was cold.

'Have you been to the legal service, I asked?

'Yeah, but they sent me away.

'What! Why?

'They already act for Nev and told me they couldn't talk to me.'

When I made inquiries, the director explained their guidelines prioritised cases involving prison-time. This was their '*Black on Black*' policy. The legal service couldn't act for both Nev and Maree, because that would create a conflict of interest. So, they had to refer Maree to the legal aid office. But this left Maree—the victim—abandoned and unsupported by a defender whom she trusted. It happened so many times, often after a big night several times the next day.

While in Alice, I visited the prison, which they called the little Big House (the Big House was the adult prison in Darwin). I asked the warden to let me interview Indigenous inmates about how they felt about the legal service.

'Watch out. You'll get an earful 'round here,' he warned with a wry grin.

As I did. Then they took me to Solitary where I met Jason. I think he'd just got bored, so he said he wanted to see me. Probably anyone. He was a big lad, tough, but nice looking.

'Watch'ya in for, I asked?

'Joy ridin, he replied.

'But *why* are you in here, in Solitary?

'I'm 14, he said with a shrug, so they keep me separate.

Juvenile remandees—at least at that time—were detained in solitary confinement in the maximum-security wing of the Alice Spring adult prison for periods of up to 14 and 21 days. This was explicitly contrary to law. But there was no juvenile facility in Central Australia. Unexpectedly, Jason took some pride in it. It came to serve as his rite of passage, his act of initiation as a modern indigenous man.

These injustices were starkly visible in the criminal justice system every day. Like A&E wards in hospitals, the courts showcased the symptoms of dysfunction and social breakdown which remain the unresolved legacies of colonial history. The Aboriginal Legal Service was positioned at the end of this breakdown, struggling like a first-aid dressing station in the trenches of WWI to staunch the continuing injuries from that history. Its efforts, however valiant, could do little more than bandage the wounded and nothing to prevent or lessen the continuing carnage.

In our travels across the continent, we found some oases where ALS outposts were well positioned to deliver efficient and generally effective legal services. These services almost invariably focused on the criminal defence of Indigenous people, usually young males. I was awed by the stoic resilience of these people and, equally, the dedication of their ALS defenders. Day after day in a dizzying merry-go-round of appearances before the courts across the land, their lawyers fought for justice against overwhelming odds. They were champions of the Australian criminal bar working under the harshest conditions to defend the rights of Indigenous people. In the most remote communities, a single lawyer supported by an indigenous field worker confronted massive caseloads defending as many as 40 clients in a single sitting day in the outback boxed-in by scheduling of the chartered plane that permitted minutes, and sometimes only seconds, to take instructions and give advice, often without an interpreter.

We heard many stories where either the defendant was too shy or didn't understand the "guilty" plea or his possible defences and so ended up being convicted. One time, Rob was sitting outside a court in a remote settlement in the Gulf region talking to an old fella who said:

'You know that young bloke inside, charged with a sex crime. Didn't do it - he wasn't here!'

The defendant hadn't understood what was going on and was about to be convicted by the fly-in magistrate until Rob went inside and intervened. That magistrate was legendary in getting pissed with the cops at night and singing till the early hours. Yet in that community, disadvantaged as it was, male and female 'ceremony' still remained strong.

The ALS is the incubator of many of Australia's finest criminal lawyers, including Justice Frank Vincent of the Victoria Supreme Court. It is under these torrid conditions that he and many others forged their forensic skills. But these ordeals often caused burn-out that mired the service to constantly haemorrhaging its most experienced lawyers who were then replaced by well-intentioned novices in a perpetual churn of under-resourcing.

The challenges confronting the ALS are enormous and often overwhelming. They are expected to balance limitless needs with chronically scarce personnel. Severe underfunding causes too many people to be imprisoned too often for too long despite the best endeavours of their defenders. Without fundamental changes in the status quo, there is no realistic prospect of breaking the cycle of exposure to over-policing which entraps hapless juveniles in the notorious '*trifecta*' of petty criminal offences (offensive language, assaulting police, resisting arrest) that relentlessly fills police lock-ups night after night.

We heard many stories in the Territory about men who were taken out of their community to Darwin because of some violence-related charge, then bailed with no backup resources until the next hearing. They were sent a letter or told to come back for the next hearing which they obviously didn't receive or understand because they were away from home living in 'the long grass' surrounding the township. When a warrant was then issued because of their non-attendance, they were further charged with obstruction or other charges and ended up being mandatorily imprisoned. Meanwhile, back in the community, their wives would usually want them back, but was left unsupported. We heard the same story countless times.

Years later, I was myself exposed to the menace of this '*trifecta*' which was usually reserved by the police for targeting Indigenous men. I was visiting a wine district in rural Victoria. It was around 5 pm on a very hot Friday afternoon. The summer sun was finally descending, and I'd decided to explore the township. The streets were deserted, so I ambled to the water tower, then around to the old nunnery that had closed and converted into a guesthouse. As I moved past houses, sprinklers were relieving the baking flowerbeds. After making a circuit to the closest vineyard, I found my way back to the main street. A patrol car cruised slowly by. A pedestrian waved. A local, I thought, and continued my return to the motel. My reverie was startled by a male voice behind me:

'Can I have a word with you.' It was not a question.

I turned to see the police wagon had returned and was now idling behind my shoulder. Surprised, I looked in.

'With me?' I asked.

'Yes, what are you doing?' countered the voice from the shadows of the driver's seat.

'Um, I'm taking a walk,' I replied.

'Why?'

'I'm having a look around the town.'

'Are you alright?'

'Er, yes, thank you, I'm fine. Is there any problem?' I asked, feeling him eying me.

'Have you been on Gunn St?' he retorted.

'I don't know, I've been for a walk to the water tower.'

'We've had complaints about you', he then accused.

'Oh, really?' I straight balled, 'what complaints?'

'There's been a man up there fitting your description waving his arms about.'

'Oh, that's odd, I didn't see him.'

'Are you sure you're alright?' he repeated.

'Yes, thank you, officer, I'm still alright,' I said, now looking him straight in the eye.

He was an overweight police sergeant with a leer on his face. He was having some fun.

'What is this about, I asked?'

'What's your name?' he blocked.

'My name? It's Livingston,' I replied.

'Where are you from Livingston?'

'I'm from Sydney.'

'Whereabouts in Sydney?'

I told him.

'Nice is it, up there?'

'Yes, it is.'

'So, what are you doing here, Livingston?'

'Well, Officer, this is a wine region and I'm a visitor.'

'Oh, so have you been enjoying the wineries, have you Livingston? '.

'We have visited one, yes,' I replied now carefully emphasising the number.

'Are you sure you're alright, Livingston?'

'Yes, thank you, Officer, I am still alright,' I said now looking back at him hard.

This went for about ten minutes. There was no reasonable cause to stop and question me. I had been within my rights to refuse to supply my name, but had volunteered to do so to avoid obstruction, while his silent colleague ran my name through his database. I never felt at serious risk. But, at the same time, he was making it altogether clear that if he had any inclination to pull me in, I would be stuck in the lock-up overnight and then the full weekend, before my solicitor's office opened on Monday morning. His smirk was to communicate that I was entirely in his hands. I played it straight, assured with the confidence of being a lawyer (however out of date) who could summon help if I needed. It went on just long enough to show me how arbitrary the exercise of police power can be and how wide its ambit to demolish my holiday weekend by replacing it with considerable inconvenience. And long enough, now, for me to personally experience just how easily I could have been pulled-in, had I been black and tired of being picked on by unrelenting 'over policing'.

After innumerable consultations, Rob and I offered our best advice to our client, the Aboriginal & Torres Strait Islander Commission. We also presented our recommendations to each legal service.

At its best, the ALS provides criminal defence services which are without doubt essential. But ultimately, it is a service which is overwhelmed by the sheer volume of needs and chronically operating beyond the limits of its capacity. The ALS stoically fights each case battle, but it is clearly losing the criminal justice war. The profound problems and needs that the legal service confronts overwhelm its capacity and destines its best efforts to be a band-aid rather than a cure. Moreover, there is a fundamental imbalance between the power and resources available to the government, police and prosecuting authorities and those to the Indigenous community. This imbalance continues to deny most Indigenous people adequate defence and any meaningful access to justice. Accepting that most of the causes of Indigenous disadvantage and crime lie beyond the realm of the courts, it is impossible to expect the ALS alone to fix those causes of crime. This pins the ALS to a treadmill of perpetual injustice. It clearly provides vital services but, as presently structured, these services are evidently futile, and essentially symbolic. To become strategically more effective, they needed to reposition.

We advised the Commission to restructure the role of the ALS to redress this mismatch between needs and resources. By reallocating its resources, the service could become considerably more effective in conducting targeted test case, public-interest and class action litigation that offered the prospect of benefitting the wider community, particularly in protecting women and children. We urged each ALS to prioritise the under-servicing of (usually female) victims of intimate partner violence. These victims were routinely unrepresented due to the perverse consequence of the '*Black on Black*' policy. This policy avoided any conflicts-of-interest by prioritising the representation of alleged (usually male) offenders who would otherwise face imprisonment, to the disadvantage of the female victims.

Once done, our advice entered the swirling political cauldron of competing agendas and interests. Many of the legal services adopted all or part of our recommendations. Separate Indigenous women's services have been introduced and expanded; class action and public interest litigation is increasing; and the 'Black on Black' rule has been moderated.

Since then, there are now many powerful drivers of changes. Truth-telling has entered our mainstream conversation. This started in a conversation between Eddie

Mabo and historian Henry Reynolds in Townsville which instigated the movement for Indigenous land rights and germinated in the High Court decision of *Mabo v Queensland* (2) on June 3, 1992 and led to the Native Title Act.[24] There have now been 594 successful land claims under this legislation. In 1997, the report of the National Inquiry into the Separation of Aboriginal and Torres Strait Islander Children from Their Families, known as the *Bringing Them Home* Report, was published with the opening words, "Grief and loss are the predominant themes of this report."[25]

In 2005, Tom Calma's *Closing the Ga*p report galvanised governments across Australia to attain equality for Indigenous people in health and wellbeing, education, employment, justice, safety, housing, land and waters rights.[26] While these targets have not yet been reached, there is some ongoing progress, but it is slow.

There are many working to improve the situation, like my friend and colleague Natalie, a shrewd and caring lawyer who is reworking government policy in NSW in an endeavour to circumvent Indigenous juveniles becoming trapped into the churn of reoffending.

Since the Royal Commission, the rate of over-representation fell from ×17.8 to ×10.1 in the wake of remediation efforts, before now settling back to ×15.2.[27] This is a measurable reduction of 15%, however marginal But it is so slow.

At the time of first drafting this book in 2023, I believed that Australia stood at the cusp of a reckoning with its unresolved colonial history with the national referendum on a 'Voice to Parliament'. This referendum aimed to amend the Constitution to formally recognize Aboriginal and Torres Strait Islander peoples as the First Peoples of Australia. As Noel Pearson had painstakingly explained, the 'Voice' was essentially symbolic; it was intended to be advisory on matters affecting Indigenous communities, without any legislative powers. Yet it provided an opportunity of hope for us each to make a difference. That referendum was however abruptly rejected, and hope has again faded. I am still trying to understand. Why was Australia so mean-spirited? Eliminating injustice is not a zero-sum game unless, that is, there are those who profit from such injustice. I had believed that we could unite in our wish to improve the lot of Indigenous Australians. I had felt Kevin's despair, heard Noel's frustration and seen the rapidly suppressed flash of Stan's anger. But I have now discovered most Australians did not understand or share this wish. They chose instead to retain the familiarity of this inequality, which I find despicable. These are my people, but who are they? I am shamed as a member of this heartless community.

While the over-representation of Indigenous people in Australia's prisons remains at calamitous levels that taint our nation, we had played a small part in making some improvements. Now, at last, I had discovered why I had chosen the law. We can each make a difference, however small. But there is still so much more to do.

Palestine & Israel: Conflicting Histories

On the road to Jerusalem, I passed a young woman hitching a ride. She was smartly dressed as though heading to a meeting. She was carrying an Uzi machine gun slung from the shoulder over her blouse. Later, I saw kids, hardly older than teenagers, socialising with friends at a bar. Under their table was a jumble of automatic weapons. But what I found even more startling was that I'd stopped noticing all the weapons after two days there.

My arrival in Tel Aviv was a shock. Even in 1997, a time of relative peace between the *Intifadas*—the Palestinian 'uprisings'—it was like entering a war zone. There were guns everywhere. The airport was full of hard-faced men whose eyes were constantly scanning the crowds. Outside, others were watching the cars. There was an alertness in the air. They were soldiers braced for combat.

That evening, I went down to the seafront where couples of all ages promenaded in the cool of the evening. I sat on the parapet above the sand to contemplate the view. Beside me a middle-aged man and his friend were playing cards, chuckling quietly together. The butt of a Glock was hitched under his belt. The light settled quietly on the evening as if nothing was amiss.

I arrived naïve but excited, expecting my challenges to be in the technical nature of the work. This visit to Palestine was my first overseas assignment as a consultant. The World Bank had offered to pay my airfare and expenses but no fee. As a novice, I was eager for overseas experience, so I had accepted. But instead, over the course of this and following visits, I was confronted by the dead hand of history which submerged my head into systemic, unrelenting and seemingly intractable injustice. Gasping for breath, it was all I could do to witness and learn from what I experienced. What an induction this would prove to be.

Over the next three years, I made several visits to help the Palestinian Authority establish an Institute of Law to train its judges in the West Bank. These were in the early days of judicial training, and I started work by producing a bench-guide on everyday practice for the new judges. As the training began, I soon became aware that they faced the immovable threat of their jurisdiction being trumped by the

L. Armytage, *Confronting Injustice*,
https://doi.org/10.1007/978-981-95-3573-6_7

Israeli military courts intervening at any time on security grounds. Their work was constantly overshadowed by the ever fermenting and unpredictable political situation, during the period between the *Intifadas*, which could shut down the West Bank and its courts by imposing 'closures' inhibiting all movements without notice at any time.

Every morning, I commuted with a colleague from my hotel in the then Arab quarter of Jerusalem across the West Bank to the Palestinian University at Bir Zeit, north of Ramallah. At that time, the barrier wall had not yet been built. We travelled across sparse rocky landscapes diminishing into endless haze. Emaciated goats grazed in wiry olive groves. As we bounced over the rocky terrain of unsealed roads, I couldn't help contemplating the irony of how hard this arid land has been fought over through the centuries.

Israel is so small. Even Tasmania is three times bigger. This was my very first impression, even before the shock of seeing weapons everywhere, as my plane crossed the Mediterranean beaches and flew over the rooftops of Tel Aviv to land at Ben Gurion. It felt as though I could throw a stone clean across this tiny country—in some places, just a 30-minute drive from side to side. Yet its geopolitical significance is so large and complex. Lebanon, Jordan, Syria and Egypt press in around it.

No wonder there was such tension in the air. Nowhere else had I seen such rage on the roads—not as I might have expected between Israeli and Palestinian, but exploding between Israelis fighting with their fists and curses over minor issues such as a parking space, seemingly just a microsecond from drawing their weapons. Everywhere there was the tension of existential fear, an epigenetic legacy of the Nazi Holocaust.

At twilight, after working at Bir Zeit, I bundled myself hip to hip with nine other passengers into a Palestinian taxi, the signature yellow 7-seat battered Mercedes limo, for my journey back across the corrugations to Jerusalem. Every trip, we would be stopped at Israeli checkpoints. A young conscript, shirt untucked, a rifle with M203 grenade launcher dangling from his shoulder, would sullenly inspect the passengers. His bored eyes would linger on the male students sitting around me. At the jerk of his head, they would wearily disentangle themselves and depart for interrogation. The soldier's ritual was performed with barely concealed boredom. Sometimes one or more of the passengers would be taken aside, then the taxi silently resumed the trip without them. Mysteriously, I was always invisible. Was it my hair, my eyes, my clothes? I could never discover the cause of my invisibility. Later, I might see the same Israeli youth in a café in Jerusalem, transmogrified to an innocuous teenager checking out the girls with his pals.

Jerusalem is a minuscule walled city. It has an enchanting maze of laneways to shrines that are holy to Jews, Christians and Muslims alike. It is divided into four quarters: Jewish, Arab, Christian and Armenian. Each visit, I lived in the Arab quarter. Within this swirling multicultural society, the golden Dome of the Rock is venerated by Jews as the Temple Mount built by King Solomon, son of King David, and also by Muslims as Al Aqsa Mosque to mark Mohammad's ascension to God. Nearby is the fabled Via Dolorosa, the path taken by Christ as he carried the cross to his crucifixion at Calvary.

The old city is a rabbit warren of shops offering antiquities including Roman coins and pots of sometimes dubious provenance. After work, I loved making my way through the tangle of laneways surrounded by the cacophony of blaring music and the tantalizing aroma of exotic food. I sipped the scalding sweet mint tea, refreshing and bitingly tart in the way that prickled the skin under my eyes. Here I discovered the finest medjool dates—the plump, finely textured caramel of the desert—grown in the contested Jordan Valley of the West Bank. It was while exploring this maze of laneways that my pockets were picked. Early one morning, a horde of kids bounded boisterously towards me. They offered trinkets to distract me as they swarmed around. At the same moment, a silken hand deftly lifted the wallet from my pocket, and they bounded noisily away. When I reported the theft to a Palestinian policeman, he shrugged. But when I mentioned I was a foreign visitor working for President Arafat's Authority, he hurriedly disappeared. In just 5 minutes, he returned with my wallet, missing the cash but with all its cards intact. I was impressed: those kids were remarkably skilled.

History and religion pervade what is called the holy land. When I retraced Joseph's epic donkey ride to Bethlehem, it took just twenty minutes in a rattling taxi with the smell of dust and exhaust overpowering the scent of the sycamores that lined the roadway. The fabled grotto was a disappointment, culminating in a garishly illuminated plastic shine. How often had it been reconstructed, even relocated, over the centuries, I wondered? But the café across the square was much more captivating. Its walls were lined with sepia images of TE Lawrence on a camel, General Allenby in a car and Australians troopers wearing slouch hats on horseback. Beneath, among the fading paraphernalia, were the spidery inscriptions of the fourth Australian Light Horsemen celebrating their charge to Beersheba in payback for Gallipoli. One Ottoman defender described them 'not (as) soldiers at all; they are madmen'. So, the ANZAC myth began. I gazed at the jaunty smiles of those farming lads from Geraldton and Wodonga. Would they have smiled had they known what lurked ahead in the bloodlands of Passchendaele near Ypres and later the despair of the Depression? Not knowing what their futures held was a quiet mercy.

My dealings with the Palestinian Authority were uniformly frustrating; they were characterised by centralised decision-making, endemic inefficiency and arcane tribalism which was opaque to the outsider. Doubtless, this was due in part to the factionalism that still cleaves the West Bank and Gaza between Fatah and Hamas. The West Bank (of the Sea of Galilee) lies beside Jordan and is run by secular Al Fatah; while Gaza, squeezed against Egypt, is run by more Islamist Hamas. At that time, Israel physically separated the two with military and economic blockades, and occupied them both, as well as occupied East Jerusalem. Between the *Intifadas*, I had difficulty experiencing Palestine as a unified entity on the ground, let alone as a functioning state. It seemed impossible to unify the Palestinian judiciary where the jurisprudence of the West Bank was traditionally Jordanian and that of Gaza Egyptian, each with altogether different traditions and procedures. These differences are however not just legal or political, but fundamentally historical, ideological and cultural. Palestine seemed no more a cohesive state than Afghanistan, both being fragments of disparate histories, colonial traditions and military occupations.

For these reasons, the Palestinian Authority has long been a political misnomer which has only occasionally spoken in a single voice—traditionally that of Yasser Arafat's PLO—against the tyrannies of Israel.

Despite these challenges, we helped to establish the judges' school which was headed by Professor Camille Mansour, a Palestinian scholar who was educated in France, and Dr. Ghassan Faramond who had taught in the USA. I gave them tools to take forward the training, but all the successes rested with their team using them, working with the Sharia Courts across both polities as they did to overcome their differences.

In doing so, we made numerous visits to Gaza. The 'Strip' is a truly dismal territory on the south-eastern corner of the Mediterranean, 40 km long and 10 km wide, which is the size of the tiny island of Malta. But with four times the population of two million, it is one of the most densely populated places on Earth. Most of this population are refugees or descendants of refugees from the *Nakba* (the 'Catastrophe'), the forced displacement of Palestinians during the establishment of Israel in 1948. Refugee camps make up many of the townships of dilapidated dwellings lining squalid laneways of rubbish and open sewerage. It is with grim irony that some scholars have likened Gaza to a ghetto encircled by razor wire.[28] Entry can only be made at the Erez and Rafah crossings which are guarded by Israeli soldiers who control entry and egress with studied lethargy and unrestrained contempt. These guards are a stark military presence. But, Ghassan taught me, much more powerful was Israel's control of the economy. What tourists and pilgrims never saw during this period was the throttling power of the 'closures.' These closures routinely blocked all movements of workers and produce, choking the Palestinians' livelihoods and starving the population. Now it's occupied territory, and the inexorable spread of 'settlements' across the West Bank severs Palestinian communities, displacing and exiling them from their traditional lands. They then become another wave of refugees to further inundate the Gaza slums. Over the years, the incursion of these settlements has been unrelenting in tightening the pressure on the Palestinians until, finally, it has exploded in the *Intifada*s of 1987 and 2000 and, most recently, the Hamas outbreak and atrocities of 7 October 2023.

On one visit, we met the Attorney-General of the Palestinian Authority. While he kept us waiting in a lengthy display his authority, friends visited and departed. Eventually, we were frisked by two large unshaven gentlemen in poorly cut suits and ushered into his offices. Busy chatting with his friends in Arabic, the Attorney waved me to a chair and gestured for tea. I inspected the room. A portrait of Arafat in his signature black and white keffiyeh adorned—if that is an appropriate verb—the wall. Heavy curtains struggled to hold back the scorching heat and blinding sunlight outside. Elaborate plaques of achievement lined the bookshelves. His attendants sat impassively near the door, their two Kalashnikov automatic rifles leaned against his desk. When the conversation with his friends ended, I prepared to exchange business cards, a formal ritual in which only the most senior officials participated. The Attorney reached into his right-hand drawer. While he was rummaging for his card, I was astounded to see him shift aside a small pistol. He then extracted a crumpled card from under some rolls of US dollars, freshly minted $50 s and $20 s that glinted malevolently from the gloom. As Ghassan adeptly steered the way through our agenda, I found myself distracted by two questions: why was there so much cash in his drawer, and was it incoming or outgoing? I could never decide which was more disturbing. Some months later, I read that he had become entangled in a factional fracas, managing to escape with his life, somewhat ignominiously, through the toilet window.

Some evenings, back in Jerusalem, I would sit on the roof top overlooking the Old City to sip a beer and contemplate the unfathomable history that surrounded me. History frames the world we live in, embedding many injustices that contaminate the present. This history has continued to twist violently—even as I write, then re-write, this chapter—for the Palestinians who have endured 75 years of displacement and occupation.

Given all this history and the heft of its geo-political significance, it seemed stupefying to me that neither Israel nor Palestine had actually existed as states before 1948. Jerusalem has been a cradle of humanity's quest for God and a fulcrum for continual conflict since the Roman Occupation and Christ's crucifixion more than two thousand years ago. In the seventh century, it was captured by the Muslim Caliphate, and in the centuries that followed, became the lure for countless vainglorious Christian crusades to reclaim it. Jerusalem remained a part of the Ottoman Empire however until the First World War, when Beersheba fell to the antipodean horsemen in 1917, and Turkey was defeated. It was in this lead-up to the demise of the Ottoman Empire that Britain promised the 'Palestine mandate' to the Jewish people as their homeland in the Balfour Declaration.

After the Second World War, Zionists agitated guerrilla warfare to undermine any continuation of the British mandate. Zionism is a nationalistic belief and movement that calls for the return of the Jewish people to their homeland and the resumption of Jewish sovereignty in the Land of Israel. This belief is distinct from Judaism, which is the religion of the Jewish people, encompassing their beliefs about god, man's purpose and their religious responsibilities. The world expressed its contrition for the *Sho'ah*, the Hebrew word used by the Jewish people to describe the Holocaust, one of the darkest chapters in human history, by supporting the creation of Israel and the partition of Jewish and Arab states. For any visitor to Yad Vashem in Jerusalem, there is no denying the horror of the mute mountain of children's abandoned shoes, nor the black and white evidence of the collapse of modern civilisation in the hollowed eyes of Auschwitz survivors as they stared at the camera. To its collective shame, the world had been acquiescent—if not complicit—in those obscenities. Doubtless driven in part by this guilt, Britain ceded independence to the state of Israel which was established in 1948. INSERT F/n here and in Backmatter: UNGA Resolution 181, 1947[29].

But resolving the competing claims to the 'holy lands' has remained immensely contentious. Zionists forcibly expelled every Palestinian from their homes and lands in Jerusalem in the *Nakba*, justifying their entitlement for evicting 700,000 Palestinians in a Dantean calculus against the Holocaust extermination of six million Jews. Numerous massacres and atrocities followed spurring the Palestinian *fedayeen*, the resistance or simmering civil war, which ultimately escalated into four

Arab-Israeli wars. The third of these, known as the 6-Day War in 1967 was a triumphant victory for Israel. The Arab armies of Egypt, Syria and Jordan suffered humiliating losses of territory, equipment and casualties. Israel captured the Golan heights, the Sinai Peninsula and the Gaza strip. They also drove the Jordanians out of the old city of Jerusalem including the Temple Mount, as well as the West Bank. But it was not all over yet. In 1973, the Egyptians and Syrians simultaneously attacked Israel's southern and northern borders to reclaim their losses in the fourth war, known as the Yom Kippur war.

Even forty years later, when I visited the Golan Heights with Gary, my program manager, I was shaken by the carnage. Gary was living in Tel Aviv with his diplomat wife. He had formerly served in the Australian tank corps and could explain the ferocity of the battle with insights that I could never have gleaned. Heavily outnumbered, the commander of the Israeli garrison, Avigdor Kahalani then aged just 29, marshalled his duty battalion of 36 centurion tanks to charge the invading army frontally. Wounded and blown from three of his tanks, he held off the invasion until reinforcements could arrive four days later. The Syrians retreated leaving more than 700 destroyed tanks many of whose rusting hulks remain to this day on the plains, now called the 'valley of tears' (עֵמֶק הַבָּכָא, *Emek Ha-Bacha*), to remind Israelis of their existential threat. Many had their turrets blown off. Others were pierced by shells which had detonated with such intense heat that molten 'magma' (around 1000 °C) had fused holes through 10 inch (25 cm) steel armour to incinerate their occupants.

Seeking resolution of the Palestinian claim to territory has been extraordinarily vexing and the graveyard of America's best diplomatic endeavours. In 1974, the UN voted to endorse a 'Two-State Solution.' This required Israel to implement the 1967 borders which partitioned the West Bank and Gaza from Israel into separate states. In 1978, US President Jimmy Carter brokered the Camp David Accords leading to the first peace treaty between Israel and Egypt. The treaty was signed by Israeli Prime Minister Menachem Begin and Egyptian President Anwar Sadat. Conflict however continued, ultimately leading to the 'Oslo Peace Process' which US President Clinton facilitated between Yitzhak Rabin and Yasser Arafat in Washington DC in 1993. But Yitzhak Rabin was then assassinated in 1995 for what was seen by rightist hardliners as his capitulation to forfeit the occupied territories to the Palestinians. Since then, all serious peace negotiations on a 'Two-State Solution' have stalled.

Israel's conflicts with its external neighbours were further exacerbated by conflicts inside its borders. The Palestinians launched the first *Intifada* between 1987–1993, and the second *Intifada* between 2000–2005, between which my visits occurred. The second *Intifada* was sparked by Ariel Sharon's visit to the Al-Aqsa Mosque and the demise of the Oslo Peace Process. These conflicts killed some 1500 Israelis and fourfold Palestinians. During the second *Intifada*, Israel constructed the West Bank barrier wall in 2002 ostensibly to prevent Palestinian terrorism, despite it being outlawed by the International Court of Justice. This consolidated Israel's settlement plans into Palestinian territories that had previously been recognised in the Oslo Peace Process.

From its birth in revolutionary struggle for freedom from the British mandate, Zionism fermented through this period into a fundamentalist, supremacist ideology that advocated for the dispossession and expulsion of all Palestinian people from their traditional lands. This ideology legitimised settler occupation of Palestinian land, creating ghettoes in Gaza and the West Bank which are contained and enforced using military force. These settlements are protected under Israeli law but illegal under international law and in breach of the international humanitarian law obligations of occupying powers. In effect, Israel became an apartheid state which has politically and economically disenfranchised the Palestinians, enacting parallel laws that apply only to Palestinians in occupied East Jerusalem and the West Bank. Each year, settler colonisation has bitten inexorably further into their land. The passive violence of dispossession and often overt and excessive violence of occupation have continued unrelentingly with unprecedented amounts of Palestinian land taken.

The 'One-State Solution' is unacceptable to Israel because, in simplistic terms, it would render Jews into the minority. On one calculation, less than half of the total population of Israel including the West Bank and Gaza is Jewish. The majority are from diverse ethnic, religious, cultural and national backgrounds. Most are Palestinian Arabs, who in turn are mainly Sunni. The remainder are Christian and Druze. These demographics are however themselves contested. According to the Israeli Bureau of Statistics, Jews make up 74% of the Israeli population, at seven million people, that the Arab population of Israel is 21%, or almost two million people. The Palestinian Central Bureau of Statistics put the population of the West Bank and Gaza at almost 5.5 million people. When added to the two million Palestinians living in Israel, the total is nearly 7.5 million—more than Israel's Jewish population. The Palestinian population is also significantly younger and therefore growing faster.

But not only is the One-State solution fundamentally unacceptable to Zionists; it is also unacceptable to hard-line Palestinians, notably the military wing of Hamas, which spearheads a Sunni extremist movement which until 2017 was formally committed to the destruction of Israel and remains in armed resistance against the Zionist project. Indeed, while Zionist extremists who now occupy critical portfolios—such as defence—within the Israeli Government and members of Hamas' military wing remain in the ascendancy, at least in Gaza, compromise and accommodation seem impossible.

It is no surprise then that internal peace has remained precarious, and is presently shattered, when much of Palestine remains under military occupation in breach of international humanitarian law. While Zionism canvases a spectrum of beliefs, in recent years it has acquired an uncompromisingly expansionist ideology in the upper reaches of the Netanyahu government that has been unflinching in expropriating traditionally held Palestinian lands. Successive Netanyahu governments have continued to build settlements across the West Bank provoking sporadic Hamas rocket attacks on Jerusalem. These are characteristically followed by massive retaliations in ever-increasing efforts of deterrence. During the writing of this book, Hamas broke through the Gaza fences on 7 October 2023 to terrorise Jewish settlements killing 1269 mainly civilian victims and committing appalling atrocities, including taking 240 civilian hostages. The right of Israel to defend itself is indisputable, and the Israelis are understandably very serious about their security. But this has in turn sparked another Israeli invasion of Gaza, inflicting some 50-fold retaliatory casualties of biblical dimensions, bombarding schools and hospitals to ruins reminiscent of the firebombing of Dresden. From what we can see on the news, it seems inescapable to conclude that Israel is using siege and famine as weapons of war against a civilian population. The indiscriminate levelling of homes has reduced Gaza to a moonscape of ruins. It is the monstrously disproportionate extent of Israel's retaliation that renders it obscene and unlawful under the accepted norms of the law of war in the minds of most lawyers and jurists. At the time of final editing, the Israeli government openly signals its plans to exterminate and expel the Palestinians from Gaza in what amounts to a second *Nakba*.[30] Watching the horror of the Palestinian genocide becoming normalised on daily television makes us all complicit.[31] Even writing these words here, today, is fraught. This wretched history of unresolved injustice and escalating conflict eclipses all prospects for any genuine and sustainable peace in the near term.

Having come to the Middle East with no particular grasp of the complexity and the tragedy of this history, I was ambushed by the polarizing nature of these competing interests. As an outsider, I needed to understand the endemic sense of existential threat arising from being surrounded by five hostile countries, that is then conflated with epigenetic trauma from the Holocaust that continues to be suffered by many Jewish people. Yet I also found myself inexorably drawn to the Palestinians' cause by the overwhelming injustices and brazen impunity that I repeatedly witnessed.

Under the continuing protection of the United States which, in more recent years, has surrendered any pretence of its former stance to neutrally broker a just peace, Israel in 2024 now wields its power over Palestinians and controls their land, employment and opportunity without restraint. The administration of justice lies in the hands of the powerholder. While Israeli courts rule on the law which is imposed under the force of the gun, there will never be any justice for the Palestinians. I have struggled with this conundrum: surely, the Israelis can understand—so much better than anyone else—the toxicity of persecution, injustice and genocide. Yet the zero-sum vision of Zionist politics continues to squeeze the Palestinians into the desperation of having nothing further to lose. This must be obvious to all, except these Zionists themselves. Even during the lull between the *Intifadas*, I found it impossible to avoid the bitter irony of the legacies of persecution, as I witnessed the spectacle of the victims becoming the oppressors, resowing what their own oppressors had heaped onto them. What the Jews suffered at the hands of the Nazis, the government of Israel is now meting out to the Palestinians. To be Jewish can mean many things. This term may refer to a person's ethnicity, religion, shared culture and history or a sense of peoplehood. These dimensions may overlap without always coinciding. But in the present conflict, it is crucial to differentiate—and never to confuse—a person being Jewish from the political and military actions of the government of Israel which is presently lead by Benjamin Netanyahu. Continuous persecution ignited the *Intifadas* which were inevitably followed by escalating dispossession which in turn ultimately exploded in the latest outbreak of 7 October

2023. Until there is some mutual respect and equality of treatment, there seems no prospect of justice or any lasting settlement. As history is already critically weighing the injustices of Israel's maltreatment of the Palestinians and finding it direly wanting, the impunity and unenforceability of the International Criminal Court and the International Court of Justice is visible eroding the normative authority of international law.

At the end of my first visit, I was subjected in an unexpectedly ritual. At Ben Gurion Airport there were long queues for each step of ticketing, luggage stowing and immigration before entering the departure lounge. I entered this shuffle and let my thoughts roam across the impressions of my visit: the old city, my new friends, all the history, culture, food, and the opportunities and challenges that awaited my next visit. After some time, my reverie was broken by an attractive young woman standing quite closely beside me who, for some reason, I'd not noticed before. She was saying something to me. We started to chat.

'Yes, sure, I had enjoyed my visit.'

'Yes, it was my first time. I'd really liked the old city. Wasn't it amazing, so much history!'

'Where else did I visit? I stayed in the Arab quarter where I enjoyed the music and food.'

'Were you alone?'

'No, I was with some colleagues.' She seemed intrigued.

'Oh, so what was I doing there?

'Well, I've been working in Ramallah.'

Now she was looking at me so directly, it was making me a little uneasy. She smiled slightly with the mouth but not her eyes, then seemed to lose interest.

That's a bit odd, I thought.

The queue shuffled forward.

After ten minutes, I arrived at the immigration counter. The uniformed official asked me directly what I had been doing at Bir Zeit. He then asked me where else had I been. When was I in Gaza? Why did I meet the PA? My answers didn't satisfy him. Step aside, he ordered, unsmiling. I felt a shiver settle around my shoulders.

Three plain-clothed officers wearing latex gloves emptied my bags, item by item. Every file was fanned open, shaken, pages examined. They shook my case to test its bottom. Luckily, the contents were all so dull, they finally decided I really must be working for the World Bank. With a wordless nod, they left me to repack the shambles of my strewn luggage, and moved on to the next suspect. Fortunately, I'd come early and had plenty of time. Another member of our project, an eminent judge, was not so fortunate. Something he'd said had evidently displeased them. After undergoing the same experience as me, he was subjected to the indignity of a full cavity search. Then they dismantled his computer. Very slowly. He missed the plane.

On my next visit, I warned Miyako to be prepared for the ritual of a covert interrogation by a young man. Sure enough, I watched the security service assign young women to the male passengers and young men to the females. After the initial chat, they retired to compare the answers with the formal interviews. If they found any discrepancies, the hapless passengers were taken aside and disappeared from sight.

Sometimes I have felt that what I was really doing in Palestine, as elsewhere, was trying to clean up the detritus of Empire. The Middle East is particularly complex, a seemingly intractable mess created in the wake of its extraction from the Ottoman, French and British Empires—which I likened to Ireland during 'The Troubles'.

This was my first overseas job. We laid foundations for the judges' school at Bir Zeit, and the courts in the West Bank and Gaza have now started working together to deliver justice despite their many differences. I was learning so much about how to make a difference, however slowly. I was learning so much more about the long arm of history, and the problems that its shadow casts over us as we navigate the present. I was also starting to understand the intractable complexity of competing interests both within and between each side, and to contemplate the challenges those create to confront the future. Pursuing justice is an infinite journey fraught with such challenges and is all the more precious because of them. My belief and hope then, as now, was that the exhaustion of all other options will ultimately revive a more just balancing of the competing interests. For the present, that remains elusive and seems far beyond reach until, that is, I remember Ireland which is now at peace however tenuous.

Pakistan: Chaos and Charm

On 11 September 2001, I was in Quetta, Baluchistan, just south of the Afghan border. So was Bin Laden, according to the CIA, though our paths never crossed. I had been working with the courts and staying in the lovely Serena Hotel built in traditional mudbrick by the Aga Khan. Baluchistan is a seriously exotic place in the Hindu Kush populated by veiled, dark-skinned women with the astonishing green eyes of Alexander's armies and Pashtun warriors wearing the black turbans of Taliban affiliation.

That morning, I had boarded an early flight to Islamabad which would get me back at my desk in time for coffee. The passengers were an assortment of locals and a motley gaggle of post-doc adventure-seekers. I had a window seat beside a Balochi girl, aged about 16, who averted her face. The plane climbed steeply after take-off through sparse mountain peaks into cloud. After ten minutes, the clouds darkened, and we plunged into a massive storm. The seatbelt sign flickered, and the cabin crew scurried up the aisle to their seats. Soon the plane was bucking wildly as lightning strobed through the cabin, then groaning against the crashes of thunder. It got darker. The plane was being thrown around. The wings were trembling and flexing like a bird. The incessant protests of the fuselage became alarming. Then it tilted steeply downwards as the pilots searched to escape from the turbulence. Through the thick cloud I got a glimpse of the ground immediately below. Then it was gone. Suddenly I was frightened. We kept careering downwards. White-knuckled, I gripped the seat rests more tightly, however impotently, as I looked at the ashen faces of my fellow passengers, all staring sightlessly ahead. The young girl beside me then seized and gripped my hand fiercely. Wordless, she drove her nails deep into the back of my hand.

When we finally landed, I was still shaken but much relieved, and hurrying to put the flight behind me. The girl collected her case and walked hastily away without any acknowledgment of the recent intimacy of our shared experience. The terminal was strangely still. Crowds were milling at the flight displays, staring intently. As I hurried past, anxious to get going, I glanced at the screen.

L. Armytage, *Confronting Injustice*,
https://doi.org/10.1007/978-981-95-3573-6_8

That's odd, I thought, there's a tall building billowing clouds of dense black smoke. Somehow, I sensed it was not a movie. The world was pivoting.

Days later, President Bush declared the 'war on terror' to cleave the world with his new crusades against Islam, rushing out to invade first Afghanistan then breathlessly next Iraq.

Some months earlier, I had been invited by Hamid Sharif, a perceptive Pakistani lawyer at the Asian Development Bank with the best professional network of colleagues I've ever seen, to lead a substantial law and justice reform program in Pakistan. Miyako and I had arrived in the national capital, Islamabad, which is a diplomatic city defined by its monumental buildings atop grandiose steps and ceremonial flags. Its wide empty streets with nary a human being in sight is strangely similar to Canberra or DC. It is a matchbox city of stately ambassadorial residences in tidy suburbs for diplomats and senior bureaucrats jokingly described as being situated just 15 km from (the real) Pakistan in bustling Rawalpindi. We enjoyed our first week in the front wing of the Marriott hotel which nestled below the deceptively tranquil Margalla Hills. Then we moved into the smallest residence we could find. It had a wide marble staircase, crystal chandeliers, and five bedrooms of palatial proportions, each with its own distinctively coloured jacuzzi ensuite. There was even a servant's room behind the house. After 9/11, we were issued a guard with a shotgun who spent most evenings snoring loudly beneath our bedroom window.

I returned often to the Marriott for work functions, and sometimes dinners with Miyako. Occasionally we used the pool and gym. But this all ended some months later when the Taliban detonated a truck bomb outside. The explosion left a crater 60 metres wide and 10 meters deep demolishing the entire front wing and killing 54 occupants; how flukishly lucky we had been.

The Islamic Republic of Pakistan is an extraordinary mix of maddening chaos and beguiling charm, deep opacity and unfathomable complexity. This chaos was showcased in the first week of our arrival during a flight to Karachi to meet with the provincial judiciary. As our plane taxied for take-off, the smell of smoke seeped into the cabin. Then an emergency claxon sounded the fire alarm. The cabin crew scurried up the aisles in a state of abject confusion like startled chickens. Meantime, the plane continued to taxi towards the runway without hesitation. The passengers around me seemed oddly unperturbed. Then to my horror, the turbines powered up and ignoring the alarms, the plane started its run and lifted into the sky. Surely, it would circle and immediately turn back. But no, on it went. Later, the captain announced that a fire in the toilet had been put out. Only I, the novice, had been disturbed, for this incident was apparently normal. As we descended, he made another announced:

"*Insha'Allah,* (if it is God's will) we will land shortly." Having been relying on the pilot's skill and experience until those words, I hardly felt reassured. But as the months passed, I found myself becoming as blasé as everyone around me. This was, after all, Pakistan.

After leaving the airport, the chaos resumed as our taxi became entangled in the cacophony of fast cars, slow trucks and families clinging to camel-drawn carts in a miasma of dust and diesel exhaust.

Much of what seems inexplicable in Pakistan is best explained, and better understood, by reference to the geopolitics of the colonial period. History and politics are rarely remote in Pakistan. History shapes the canvas across which the present is drawn to explain the 'unfinished business' in contemporary events through which we walk. History, most recently of the British Raj in pre-partition greater India between 1858–1947, laid the stage for many of the misadventures of modern South Asia. Britain's exhausted and ungainly extraction from South Asia precipitated the Partition of India, separating what is now predominantly Hindu India from Muslim West Pakistan and East Pakistan. The exodus of Muslims from India was bloody, then leading to the Indo-Pakistani War of 1971 and the *Gonohotta* (the Bengali genocide) that ensued, culminating in the 'liberation' and ultimate formation of Bangladesh.

Pakistani politics has been turbulent and brutal, characterised by the execution, assassination and banishment of many of its leaders. Since independence, it has suffered four coups (by Ghulam Muhammad in 1953, Ayub Khan in 1958, Zia ul Haq in 1977 and Musharraf in 1999), spent many of its formative years under military rule, hanged its democratic leader Zulfikar Bhutto, and assassinated his daughter, former prime minister Benazir Bhutto. Its future as a democracy constantly seems precarious, at least to me. Indeed, many locals explained to my bemusement that democracy was 'poorly suited' to the shenanigans of Pakistani politicians. Moreover, the state operated more efficiently under military leadership, at least initially. Most recently, former Prime Minister Imran Khan, whom my very canny Pakistani friend, Judge Dr. Rai M Khan (no relative) regards as one of Pakistan's finest politicians, had just been sentenced to 14 years of imprisonment, and confronts an apparently endless queue of further prosecutions.

Dr. Rai and I worked together at the Punjab Judicial Academy where we were building the faculty of judge trainers. Here I found our teaching roles were often reversed with the best exchanges arising unexpected over coffee or lunch in the canteen. I remember his explaining the many and varied nuances of '*Insha'Allah*'.

Insha'Allah (إن شاء الله) is a magnificent Arabic word which literally means 'if God wills.' It is used in many Muslim cultures to express the belief that nothing happens unless God wills it. It is also exceptionally versatile. It can express piety, acknowledging God's sovereignty over all matters. Important as this sentiment undoubtedly is, it can have many other meanings. It can be variously used to express intention, as in "I will visit you tomorrow, *Insha'Allah*, (provided nothing untoward intervenes). Or, hope, acknowledging uncertainty, recognizing that it is not possible to completely control the future. It can portray a humble approach to life's unpredictability. It can be used in casual conversation to express agreement: *Insha'Allah*, I will return your call later today—meaning, I will if I can. It can be used in legal documents to indicate that an action or event is conditional upon circumstances beyond human control, reaffirming a reliance on divine will. Interestingly, it can be used ironically, with humour or scepticism. For example, if a student who never studies says they'll get an A on an exam, their friend might reply, "Sure, you'll get an A, *Insha'Allah*," to indicate doubt. It can also connote improbability. For instance, "I'll win the lottery tomorrow, *Insha'Allah*," when the chances are extremely low. *Insha'Allah* is a most useful word, unique in its range of subtle meanings, that I rapidly learned to treasure and use often.

In the earlier example of the pilot, its usage was to connote his intention to land the aircraft shortly unless, perhaps, the plane's guidance system has been damaged, in which case it would more likely be a prayer. With the toilet having already been on fire, it could indeed have been either, or simply resignation after a lengthy career with that airline.

The complexity of Pakistan's hostility with India is opaque to foreign eyes. The centrality of these hostilities is ceremoniously displayed in the ritual changing of the guards at the Wagah border midway between the Punjabi capital of Lahore in Pakistan and the Sikh city of Amritsar on the Grand Trunk Route in India. Here, each evening, adoring crowds of supporters sit in orderly rows on either side of the border dressed in their finest shalwar kameez and saris to witness the flag-lowering ceremony. To the trill of bugles, soldiers selected for their extraordinary height and manicured moustaches parade in ceremonial uniforms and brightly plumed headgear. They march stamping and kicking their glistening boots shoulder high as they glare belligerently at their opposing number to the cheering delight of their supporters. This histrionic theatre is a national tonic for all but, Rai explained, it is also a symbolic display of a complex but collaborative balancing act between these sparring nuclear powers.

The Pakistani army has always been important in managing this delicate equilibrium, both ceremonially and actually. Established to protect Pakistan from foreign intrusion, it has grown hugely important not just militarily but also politically, economically and socially. Ever since Pakistan's formative years, the army has stood as the de facto ruler behind the throne. On four occasions, it has seized and sat on that throne. It is Pakistan's largest property and business owner, consuming a remarkable 3.8% of GDP—more than that spend of defence by the USA (3.4%) and double that of Australia (1.9%). It is also the largest single employer not just of the poor but also of the elite families whose sons' careers are routinely apportioned between the army, government and business.

During our time living in Pakistan, we were evacuated twice: first after 9/11 with the invasion of Afghanistan by the US and its allies, then again in the next year with the potential nuclear stand-off with India over the Kashmiri 'Line of Control' (LoC). During the displacement of those experiences, I found myself reflecting on the apparent perpetual instability that characterises the region. I asked Rai why this stalemate was allowed to persist despite the dramatically escalating risks of nuclear war between the two neighbours. His answer was both complex yet simple: I was asking the wrong question. Contrary to all external appearances, the LoC was in fact entirely stable and robust because both countries had invested heavily in achieving that delicate but mutually desired balance of affairs. The real question, he suggested, was to ask: Is Kashmir a problem or a solution? The British extraction from colonial India in 1947 had destabilised the balance of competing interests across the region. Managing the ensuing disruption was a massive undertaking. Both Pakistan and India had struggled to agglomerate highly diverse domestic populations with profound ethnic and religious divisions. While two-thirds of the Kashmiri population share ethnic or religious roots with Pakistan, Kashmir has been occupied by India since Partition, resulting in the threat of an uprising constantly simmering, for example in the flare-up of 2003. The UN had intervened in 1948, ordering a plebiscite but this had never been held. Hamid then further clarified these events to me: Nehru who was the founding prime minister of India, was a Kashmiri and didn't want to let it go. So, he engineered Kashmir's accession to India, and then did everything he could to undermine the plebiscite. Meantime, it became most convenient for the Pakistan Army to justify its massive and ever-increasing budget by living off this arguably non-existent threat.

Behind the public posturing of both Pakistan and India, Kashmir remains strategically significant because of its geopolitical location as a buffer zone for Pakistan, India and China. At this crucial juncture, this tiny mountain kingdom with its relatively minuscule population of just 12 million provides both its much larger neighbours of Pakistan and India with a shared threat that unifies their respective domestic divisions against a mutually convenient external enemy. Hence, for many observers, the supposedly elusive problem of Kashmir would never have been resolved through the obvious device of a plebiscite precisely because the elites on neither side really wanted it to be. Kashmir is a delicately balanced but deadly serious regional pantomime for their respective domestic stakeholders. The ostensibly warring parties are actually agreed on its perpetuation. Behind the opacity, I was learning that there was in fact order.

Over the years, I had often felt that much of my work arose from the need to clean-up the mess of the colonial period and the rubble of Empire. Across South Asia, it is history that again explains much of the intrigue that has played out on Pakistan's western border with Afghanistan. The colonially imposed Durand Line arbitrarily divided ethnic Pashtun people between Afghanistan and Pakistan. This imposition explains why Pakistan's secretive security service, the ISI, often appeared to undermine the Musharraf's public position as an ally in the US's 'war on terror' in Afghanistan, by supporting the Pashtun Taliban.

It is this history that makes Pakistan so interesting. Pakistan is complex, unpredictable and often incomprehensible to the foreign eye. Characterised by chaos and intrigue which is often instigated by the ISI, it is important however to understand that this chaos is however rarely an accident; rather, it is a covert operating space within which the elites manoeuvre.

Some months after our arrival, Musharraf chose to side with the US by offering staging facilities for US forces in their invasion of Afghanistan. In return, I was reliably informed by Hamid that someone 'very senior' in the State Department had instructed the Asian Development Bank at the highest level to reward his support. To our astonishment, the funding for our program was then magically increased from USD 75 million to USD 350 million overnight. The largesse that tumbled over us was a political expedient which was totally unplanned. It seemed ludicrous; my job was abruptly transformed into piloting what had become the world's largest-ever law and justice reform program which, had I known at the outset, I would have found too intimidating to accept.

As it was, we scampered about trying to put this windfall to best use. The major justice problem that we confronted was endemic backlog and delay in the disposal of court cases. The oldest case that I found in the mouldering court stacks was 64-years old. It was still being slogged out between the great grandchildren of the original litigants. Most cases were between 5–10 years old, though it was not uncommon to find many 20-year-old cases on the laden shelves. In essence, the courts were overwhelmed with literally millions of aged cases submerged beneath a constant deluge of new ones. This logjam had complex causes. Certainly, these included understaffing of the courts and dilapidated case management systems. But our research revealed a distinctively Pakistani flourish. Whenever a party found themselves in a legally indefensible situation, their lawyers would rush into court in order to initiate proceedings with the intention of seizing control of the litigation process. But their purpose was not to expedite the outcome. To the contrary, their tactic was to mire the case in pre-trial proceedings in the hope of finally exhausting their opponents. Lawyers also quip that the courts are just in that the judges accept bribes from both parties. The result was an eruption of vexatious litigations that clogged the entire system.

To redress this problem, we introduced a pilot scheme to eradicate chronic backlog and streamline new cases. First, we purged all cases older than 10 years which were moulding forgotten in the stacks. Literally hundreds of thousands of dead cases were painlessly shredded and eliminated from the system, unless a party stepped forward to reenergise proceedings. Next, we introduced limits on the number of adjournments, having ascertained that there was on average an astonishing 156 adjournments in most civil cases. This practice arose from judges, overwhelmed by the number of cases in their lists, acceding to most adjournment applications to dispose of their daily caseload, exacerbating the problem by wasting their time churning the cases without any productivity gains. It was dysfunctional, systemic chaos. Then we introduced time limits for each stage in the passage of cases from start to finish. Finally, we trained judges and court staff on these steps, and created a reporting system where the judges could compare their performance to stimulate competition.

We also introduced a range of other measures including law reform, building infrastructure for new courthouses, and supplying much needed equipment like computers, and of course training. I enjoyed a lot of my own time training judges to become the trainers of other judges both at the Federal Judicial Academy and later in Lahore at the Punjab Judicial Academy.

This work would have achieved little without the quiet leadership of Shafi'ur Rahman, a highly respected retired Justice of the Supreme Court. Shafi'sb (respectful postnominal, indicating senior counsel) could open even the most closely guarded doors of provincial chief justices suspicious of foreign intervention. He had started his career in East Pakistan, surviving the war of independence with all of its dislocation, and had the comforting chuckle of one who had weathered many misadventures. We often shared lengthy drives along the Grand Trunk Route of Rudyard Kipling fame to Peshawar, capital of the then North-West Frontier province. On these journeys he was my mentor, educating me on many things. On one, he shared his turmoil in choosing to re-swear his oath as a judge after the coup of General Zia ul Haq in 1997. He explained he needed to remain a judge because the judiciary had been weakened and there were so few judges of principle remaining. This turmoil never left him, though it was rarely shown, giving him a gravitas that all could feel. I was privileged to work with him, listening to his cadences in Urdu to win over his audience's trust before passing the microphone on to me.

Pakistan is also a land of extraordinary charms. These charms are tightly held and among the world's best kept tourist secrets. In addition to the welcome and hospitality of its people, many of these we found far above the scorching heat of the southern plains. The high country to the north is sculpted by three of the world's most formidable mountain ranges: the mighty Himalayas, Hindu Kush and Karakorams which intersect at the Indus River above Gilgit, forming an historically impenetrable buffer zone between India and China.

Miyako and I took many trips up country, some with Doug Porter, another Australian who was now running our program at the ADB and is the best-read development thinker I know, and his wife Rae. Doug, once an academic, is a voracious reader with a breadth of experience far exceeding my own who, during my doctoral research a decade later often had me scurrying for the dictionary to ponder the ideas he sprinkled, like teleology and ontology, to explain the development issues around us. One such trip was to Murree, a pleasant 90-minute drive from Islamabad. This was the first of many adventures that we have shared extending into friendship to the present day. During the colonial era, the British built hill stations across India from Darjeeling to Murree to shelter from the heat. Overlooking Kashmir to the east, Murree nestles in the foothills and forests of the Hindu Kush range above Islamabad. Though now dilapidated, elegant buildings with vaulted ceilings still dot the slopes, like dowagers resting in the afternoon sun. Also dating from the colonial era is an incongruous brewery that still makes beer for those infidels who drink alcohol. When I applied for a liquor permit to purchase this beer, I encountered the dour humour of the bureaucracy that required applicants to certify that they were an alcoholic undergoing medical treatment. I meekly complied.

We then explored the Swat Valley. The road from Islamabad heads west along the Grand Trunk Road towards Kabul before turning north, climbing into the cool air and scented orchards of the Swat Valley. It then cuts across the Malakand Pass where Pashtun tribesmen fought two fierce battles with the Imperial British Army in the 1890s. Ensign Winston Churchill was garrisoned here during the siege of 1897, in what the British Empire then called the North-West Frontier Province (NWFP). His faded signature is still displayed in the fortress guarding the Pass. Swat, also known as the 'Switzerland of the East' because of its spectacular views of snow-capped mountains, was until recently a Taliban stronghold. It was here in 2012 where Malala Yousafzai, then aged 15, was shot in the head at close range by the Taliban for speaking out for girls' education. Remarkably, she survived, was awarded the Nobel Prize for Peace and later completed her education at Oxford University.

Our longest and most dramatic adventure took us high into the Karakoram Mountains. This mighty range rises beyond Murree. From there, it takes three days of resolute driving to reach the Chinese border at the Khunjerab Pass through some of the most formidable and unworldly country I have ever seen. Chitral is a remote former princely capital in the Khyber Pakhtunkhwa (formerly NWFP). Its views of the surrounding mountains are other worldly. It is also a resting place for the nomadic Afghan Kuchi people who graze their flocks of goats and sheep across this sparse mountainous region. Nestling close to the Afghan border is also the home of the Kalash, an Indo-Aryan Indigenous minority who claim to have descended from the army of Alexander the Great who invaded in 324 BC. Following a polytheistic sect of ancient Hinduism, their unique culture has long enthralled anthropologists. We visited their remote villages that straddle the border and were greeted by womenfolk in distinctively colourful clothing doing their washing in a stream, boisterously unrestrained by the constraints of Islamic modesty.

We then travelled onwards along the Karakoram Highway which wound its way painstakingly through spectacular valleys to Gilgit on an exhausting journey along a tendril of the ancient Silk Route. This highway had been built over twenty years by the Pakistani army to supply its outposts on the contested border with India and China. It was hewn from the rock wall, bored through tunnels and under waterfalls, often beside dizzying drops of up to 800 meters to the Indus River swirling distantly below on its own way from Tibet to the Arabian Sea. By the time the highway finally opened, more than one thousand army engineers had perished in explosions, avalanches and rockfalls. Labelled the eighth wonder of the world on its completion, the highway—which described its elevation rather than its breadth—was often wide enough for just one single lane of traffic teetering above the ravine. There are many switchbacks so sharp the corners are blind, and horns must be used repeatedly on approach. The road was often unsealed, deeply potholed, with jagged rocks that slashed at tyres. It didn't pay to speed. Occasionally, we would glimpse the mangled carcass of a rusting truck or bus on the slopes below. There were frequent avalanches, and sometimes severe earthquakes, that regularly swept away entire sections of this highway. Every winter, the route is closed for months by snow. Every spring, the engineers must clear the way again. It was at times a sphincter-tightening journey.

From here, the Highway continues to climb above the tree line and enters a barren moonscape that defies scale. There is only rock and dust beneath the clouds that skitter between the rising peaks. Only the colourful splash of a truck labouring wearily across the horizon gives any scale to measure the distance. These ancient 5-ton Bedford trucks display garish art unique to the region. Hand-painted in flamboyant colours, every inch of the truck is covered in portraits of gods and film stars, floral or geometric patterns and fanciful motifs, often with messages or mottos for a product or cause. Each truck features a distinctive wooden prow fixed crown-like above the cabin, decorative wooden panels and elaborate bumpers with chains or coloured garters dangling from them. They are always massively laden with bails of wool, building materials or agricultural implements perilously spilling over their sides.

The views on this journey are quite astounding. The road passes the mountaineers' turn-off to K2, which at 8611 metres is the second highest mountain in the world. Then the peak of the Nanga Parbat rises silently to 8126 metres beyond the horizon. At various points, flocks of sheep blocked our way. These hardy alpine sheep, with bloated misshapen rectums that stored precious fat for the winter, grazed the desert moonscape. Periodically, the road descends to the valley floor where aging rope bridges loll often drunkenly over the roiling Indus offering villagers the only terrifying means of crossing its churning waters, before resuming its endless climb.

Then the valley opens to the evermore remote Kingdom of Hunza perched beneath Altit Fortress on a tributary of the Indus. Here the road offered us the panorama of seven peaks, each over 7000 m in height. Finally, we passed the mysterious conical formation of the *Passu Cathedral* with its fast-retreating glacier before reaching the Khunjerab Pass that crosses into China. It was an otherworldly journey completed in spellbound silence but for the grinding gears of our jeep, the torment of the winds through surrounding outcrops, and occasional lament of golden eagles surfing the thermals overhead.

It is this context of the brutality of Pakistan's history and the monstrous precarity of its mountain landscapes that framed Khwaja Muhammad Samdani as a hero of the rule of law. Justice Samdani was a diminutive, quietly spoken man who became the mouse who roared and thence a giant of the judiciary.

When General Zia ul Haq seized power in the army's third coup on 5 July 1977, he imprisoned Prime Minister Bhutto. Sitting in the Punjab High Court, Justice Samdani granted Bhutto's application for bail. Zia punished Samdani by removing him from the bench and transferring him to the administrative role of secretary for justice. Zia then ordered all judges to retake their oaths of allegiance to his government. Most of the judges did so. The chief justice urged Samdani to join them, but he refused. Instead, he resigned his judge's commission and returned to his family home, having just 350 rupees (about US$2.5) in his bank account. In 1988, Zia was killed in a mysterious plane crash, with many suspecting he was assassinated by the CIA. His name has remained reviled in history.

Justice Samdani understood that the constitution is important as the 'law of all laws' of the land. Even more importantly, the constitution enshrines the aspirations, ideals and values of the nation, while the laws embody the norms, standards and rules of its society. Among these values are democratic government and judicial independence. Democracy ensures the citizens' right to participate in their own governance by voting, and independence protects the judges who in turn protect the constitution and apply its values by delivering justice fairly. Pakistan's many tyrants have seized power by flouting the constitution and disregarding both democracy and justice. Justice Samdani was a fearless judge who spoke truth to power. He challenged the coup-leader Zia not only in his courtroom but also to his face. But he paid dearly for these ideals.

"I read the text of the oath, which was an oath of allegiance to the martial law regime as against the constitution" he explained to me. "Judges have neither gun nor sword in our hands. But instead, we have the pen with which to write verdicts that *insha'allah* are more powerful than the sword."[32]

In his memoir, Samdani recounted an encounter he had with Zia who had a grudge against law abiding civil servants in the administration. He quoted Zia as saying, 'I would like to strip the secretaries (in Pakistan being the middle-aged male ministry heads, rather than female members of the typing pool) naked and hang them upside down.' This 'unparliamentary language' was too much for Samdani to swallow. He retorted that he would like to see a couple of Zia's generals hung by their ankles with their pants off. This left the gathering stunned. He was summonsed to Zia's office, where he was ordered to apologise. Samdani refused until Zia did first. There was an impasse. Three months later, he was quietly returned to his judicial duties.[33] At his death, Justice Samdani was eulogized by the president of the bar: "He leaves behind a legacy of honesty, dignity and an absolute adherence to principles. He did not merely possess a strong moral compass, he served as its very definition."[34] There is now a Justice KMA Samdani Memorial Lecture on the Independence of the Judiciary. Last year, this lecture was presented by the Chief Justice of Pakistan.

Then, it all happened again. One quiet morning in 1999, I was visiting Pakistan for the first time to present a paper at an international judges' conference. I was sitting at breakfast in my hotel in Rawalpindi when I read in the newspaper that General Musharraf had sacked the entire judiciary. As commander of the army, Musharraf had earlier ousted the government in a fourth bloodless coup the previous year. He was now insisting that all judges re-swear a new oath of allegiance to his regime at noon or face immediate unemployment and possible imprisonment. It was like living through those decelerating moments after the flash of a bomb exploding, but before its report could be heard. I saw the flash, like a strobe freezing everything in a microsecond in the silence before the blast of detonation. Around me, everyone was oblivious, chattering over their breakfasts as normal. But, in that instant, I knew that judicial independence and the justice it guaranteed had again been flattened under another soldier's boot. Within a day, this dismissal was front page news around the world. But by then, all the judges had already been obliged to confront the anguish of making their decision. Most—though not all—once again decided to pledge their fealty to the dictator, abandoning the constitution and all its values that they had sworn to protect. Later, the Supreme Court, irretrievably compromised by its own oath-taking to Musharraf, bent over backwards to validate this coup by invoking some nonsense about the doctrine of necessity.

Some years later, the same court dismissed Musharraf for high treason and sentenced him to death. But by then, he had fled the country to die in ignominy in Dubai. Such is the continuing chaos of democracy and justice in Pakistan.

The values of democracy, justice and the rule of law are precious because they protect the citizen from tyranny. But the evidence of history shows that they are also fragile. Zia and Musharraf may once have had noble intentions and believed that the end justified the means. But that evidence shows that the lure of power is corrosive and irresistibly strong.

No one may be exempted from Samdani's testing, though few of us will share his fortitude. *Insha'Allah*, we can each make a difference. So it is that history continues to build its path behind each of our steps, however small they might sometimes seem to be.

We invited Justice Samdani to address the judges conducting the delay reduction project who he inspired. Remarkably, in less than one year, this project reduced decades-old backlog by 30% and increased disposals by 250%. These were transformative results in delay reduction. Independent research later attributed a 2–3% increase in Pakistan's GDP to this success in securing much-needed investment.[35]

I have reflected on this remarkable success and can reach only one credible conclusion: while we were the so-called experts, we were *not* the key ingredient; it was the judges themselves. We had acted as agents of change by bringing knowhow and training. But more importantly, we had injected reinvigoration and revived their enthusiasm. These mid-career pilot court judges were overworked, under-incentivised and exhausted by twenty years of frustrated efforts. Our presence had disrupted the statis of routine and given them some time-out to reflect and exchange experiences. Justice Samdani inspired them. Collectively this enabled them to reclaim their ideals as judges eager to make a difference. I was now learning that my role, at its best, was to reenergise their best efforts. When I am able to work well in this role, it can be quite magical.

Some years after I had completed training the judicial trainers, Dr. Rai confided in me that the Supreme Court had just tasked him and his colleagues at the Judicial Academy to undertake a strategic planning process for the courts, and then to revise its curriculum to support and implement its changes. This was a huge job that they were embarking on themselves.

I was at first disappointed not be invited. But then I was delighted to find that I was no longer needed. Evidently, our earlier training was now working.

Papua New Guinea: Colliding with the Present

When I visited Mt. Hagen as a student in 1969, married women were dressed in pandanus skirts and walked about the market bare-breasted. Some of the men had brightly painted faces and wore adornments of shells, pig tusks and feathers across their torsos. The township had been 'discovered' by Europeans just 35 years earlier. I had entered another world and time; and have remained smitten ever since.

I had arrived in Port Moresby a few days before. It was equatorial, colonial and mind-blowingly exotic. Expatriate administrators and 'kiaps'—patrol officers—lived in quaint wooden bungalows sheltered by fragrant frangipanis and painted picket fences, overlooking the panoramic expanse of Ela Beach. From Moresby, I was jolted in a small plane through dense clouds over jagged volcanic peaks and lush forests to reach Mt. Hagen. The highlands enjoy massive rains, humidity and fertility, ideal for cultivating copra and coffee. The few expatriates that I encountered were plantation managers and administrators. At the sports ground, a British police sergeant was drilling the riot squad in clearing the local pub. They were equipped with axe handles, helmets and shields. Later, I hitched a truck ride down the unsealed 'highlands highway', shuddering in first gear past waterfalls and rock-strewn ravines. Reaching Lae after nightfall, bone-shaken and exhausted, I roamed deserted streets and spent a sleepless night in stifling humidity riven by the endless gurgling of an emphysemic expat occupying the next cubicle.

When I returned in 2003, more than thirty years later, there were truly astonishing changes. PNG was now an independent state. It had a parliament and supreme court beside a golf course. When the Whitlam Government granted independence on the 16 September 1975 in the face of the gusting new seasonal winds of decolonisation—exactly fifty years before this time of writing—there were just eight university graduates to take over the reins of government. While possibly apocryphal, the colonial era was abruptly over, leaving many locals with grand and noble hopes of independence, but also a deeply conflicted sense of nostalgia and resentment for the 'Big Brother' who had exploited then dumped them.

L. Armytage, *Confronting Injustice*,
https://doi.org/10.1007/978-981-95-3573-6_9

PNG has massive resources. Vast gold and copper deposits had been discovered and mined. These mines were guarded by 'mobile squads' of para-military police bearing M16s privately funded by foreign companies. The rain forests were being logged and massive reserves of liquified natural gas promised boundless riches. Incrementally over the intervening twenty years, planes endlessly arrived to disgorge miners, surveyors, entrepreneurs and assorted fortune seekers to be housed in condominiums sprouting above Ela Beach offering breathtaking ocean views. There was even a yacht club in the harbour where they could moor their boats. Moresby was now a frontier town proud of being among the world's most expensive cities. The cost of hotels rivalled those in Manhattan. Pubs offered a host of new entertainments for the throng of expat miners including mudwrestling competitions with strapping local gals deft at upending them to the hilarity of their mates.

The mining boom had created many riches. The roads were now sealed, at least in Moresby, and the freshly laid pavements were stained crimson with splashes of betelnut spit. Most townships had a clinic and school. Some kids were going on to university. But much of these riches was expatriated while Australia turned a blind eye to the mansions of PNG's politicians that lined the Cairns esplanade. Only the tailings of that unquantifiable wealth remained to find their way into public services.

Some of the colonial bungalows were still standing, now slumping bow-roofed and unpainted in the shadows of the apartment towers sheltering behind coils of glistening razor wire and the security paraphernalia that characterised the postcolonial cityscape. Once unspoiled, Ela Beach was now a wilderness overflowing with refuse, avoided by all due to the prevalence of violent crime. The residences of the Australian Mission had been relocated behind 10-foot razor-wired walls, informally called *'Fort shit-scared.'* The food in the supermarket was imported and more expensive than in Australia. The fortunate drove ever bigger, faster four-wheel drives while the gap between the 'haves' and the 'have nots' was widening at an alarming rate. The country's collision with modernisation and the so-called 'resources curse' was traumatic. Tribal and family authority structures were rapidly crumbling for those displaced in the squatter settlements around Moresby. It was heart-wrenching to witness those hopes of progress gone awry.

It was into this torrid environment that the Australian Government had sent me and many other development practitioners 'to make a difference'. PNG is the oldest and largest recipient of Australia's foreign aid. Australia is committed to the long haul of improving PNG's law-and-order situation. By 2005, its support had increased to \$110 million for the law and justice sector alone. This had sounded to me like a lot at the time, until I learned that it was comparable to the operating cost of the regional hospital in Canberra. PNG was spending its own budget mainly on salaries, and there was nothing much left for improvements. So, what Australia offered in assistance was all that was available to bring any improvement and change to law and justice. My role was to lead a small team to advise the Australian Government and monitor the progress of its endeavours.

Despite the lavish budget, the challenges we faced were enormous. The size of the need to bring peace, law and justice to the citizens of PNG, riven as it was by its collision between tradition and modernity, the rush for resource wealth, the fragility and limited capacity of the state, and the limited resources available were profoundly mismatched and over-ambitious on any measure. They still are. While difficult to generalise given PNG's internal diversity, customary authority structures had disintegrated in Port Moresby with the influx of workers from other regions seeking jobs in Moresby and many other parts of the country. Tribal warfare erupted in parts of the Highlands and violent crime were endemic in urban centres. The plunder of resources seemed out of control, and many in Australia lamented PNG's descent into anarchy, citing simmering tribal wars and the 'Sandline' Mutiny that had threatened civil war between police and the defence force.[36]

I was guided by Sinclair Dinnen, a quietly spoken Scot at ANU with unruly hair who is the most knowledgeable scholar of PNG that I've ever met. Many of the law-and-order problems were already evident before independence and should not be attributed to it. He saw the notion of PNG as a 'failed' or 'failing' state as particularly unhelpful because it implied that at one time it was a 'strong' or 'successful' state that had subsequently 'failed'. That had never been the case. He argues that PNG is better understood as a nascent state still in the process of being formed. State-making in a country like PNG is profoundly challenged by the absence of a shared sense of political community or nationhood. With so many different groups with local (rather than national) identities and allegiances, he taught me to understand PNG as a classic case of what another scholar had called an 'imagined community'.[37]

Given the recency of independence, and the impenetrable nature of the mountainous geography and dense terrain, the reach of national government in PNG was both tenuous and short. The foundling government had struggled to provide services to remote communities where most of the population continues to live. It was in this gaping lacuna where the churches and countless evangelical missionaries had strived—and indeed thrived—to provide much needed basic health care and schooling in the provinces. The reality is that the state needed the services of the church in order to survive. In exchange, souls were bought and territorialised between rival denominations to overlay local custom and traditions.

With odd bravado, Port Moresby enjoyed the dubious notoriety of being ranked the world's 'most dangerous city' by the *Economist* at that time. It bristled with high-rise apartments fenced with razor wire to repel the *raskol* gangs.[38] Far from being the romantic rogues that this word might evoke, Moresby's *raskol*s were widely perceived as drug-crazed thugs wielding machetes which they sometimes used with horrific brutality. Dismemberment was intended to prevent the souls of their enemies from entering the afterlife. The gut-wrenching violence of these events was not their sensationalism; it was the numbing ordinariness of their familiarity.

Law and order in PNG were often brutish and quite unregulated. Back in Mt. Hagen, I met a police inspector who boasted how his men had taught the perpetrators of a bank robbery 'a lesson' outside the township with their M16s, in a grisly display of being a 'big man' (traditional leader in *Tok Pisin*, or *Pidgin*, the lingua franca). Those that made it to court were sent to prison where they served their sentence in a blackhole of inhumanity and disease. Those prisons were rarely secure; in one outbreak, three hundred convicts escaped, many never to be recaptured.

The incidence of sexual and family violence, in particular, was pandemic in PNG estimated at twice the global benchmarks. One of our team was a very bright young intern, Abby McCloud, who went on to complete her doctoral fieldwork in the Highlands and is now a regionally respected expert advising police and aid agencies in this grimly challenging field.

Night after night in the long hours of the predawn, I would awake jolted from sleep by panic at the sheer enormity of PNG's law and justice problems. Only some of these were reported in the press. Two I would never forget:—

> *Horror Ordeal*—An elderly man was brutally murdered at the Tete Settlement in Port Moresby yesterday as he tried to prevent a band of armed criminals from raping his wife and daughters. The former employee of the National Broadcasting Commission, was shot several times and then chopped up by at least 10 armed men as his wife and teenage daughter watched in horror, before his body was burned with the house.[39]

> *Young Girl Pack-Raped on Bus as Driver and Crew Watched* - Last Wednesday, my neighbour and her small daughter were about to board a bus bound for the Gordon market. As she boarded the bus, to her horror, she saw there in the back seat a poor and lone Central Highland teenage girl being raped by four young men. The poor girl could not scream for help because her mouth had been gagged, and she was held down by the four men. My neighbour was terrified and hurriedly got out of the bus but did not report the matter for fear of reprisals.[40]

We did the best we could within the aid program that operated in a continuous cycle of four phases: research and analysis of problems and needs; design of a program to address selected priorities; implementation of activities over a 5-year period; and evaluation of effectiveness, before refining and repeating the cycle. This program, which was designed by a thoughtful and dedicated government lawyer Kirsten Bishop with whom I shared the path of fleeing private law practice, aimed to restore public safety by providing technical assistance and resources for a panoply of activities. These included refurbishing court houses, training magistrates, and supplying computers. The program promoted the rights of women, introduced protection orders, established family violence units in police stations, and supported the appointment of hundreds of women as magistrates and court officers in the Village Courts. It introduced a neighbourhood watch scheme that halved crime in Moresby's central business district, and a community supervision network that broke the chain of repeat-offending. It improved the efficiency of prosecutors and introduced legal aid. It funded the building and expansion of prisons because bureaucrats in Canberra favoured this kind of activity as 'quick spends' to display reassuringly visible results, unlike many other activities—such as promoting human rights that required longer lead times and were more difficult to measure. Most of this support was directed to the providers of law and justice services—such as the police, courts and the prisons—rather than directly to the communities whom they served, for example, the introduction of community policing in Moresby, which visibly reducing crime by reframing the policing role from punishment to social welfare focusing on avoidance and diverting juveniles at-risk.

On gaining independence, PNG had inherited Australia's rule of law and adversarial system of justice. In that system, barristers present a dispute before an independent, law-trained judge or magistrate who adjudicates like an umpire overseeing a sport. Ultimately, it is a trial of strength using rules set by law. This system provided foreign investors in mining and forestry businesses with what the World Bank called 'institutional security of property and title'—that is, their capital investments were secured and protected by a system of laws, courts and enforcement mechanisms that would presumably provide taxable revenues streams to the state in due course.

The major challenge that confounded us, however, was that this system varied markedly from the traditional means of maintaining social harmony and resolving disputes. Local people who had been living for millennia in remote communities across PNG now found themselves living on land which had suddenly become mining concessions or forests that were being logged for export. There might have been some measure of 'consultations' in the past, but it was unlikely that these were understood or agreed upon. Numerous disputes arose with traditional landholders who were bewildered and aggrieved by the expropriation of windfall mining profits, the lack of compensation for contaminated water supplies, and the destruction of their local eco-systems. These disputes, involving massive sums were heard in courts that were plagued by significant delays, astronomical expense, and arcane procedures. At the heart of these disputes were fundamentally divergent expectations of justice itself. The collision of traditional and neo-colonial systems was fraught, endemic and complex. On reflection, reform endeavours were too often oblivious to customary methods and expectations for settling disputes, seeing tradition as an obstacle in the way of progress and modernity rather than a local strength to be built upon to develop socially appropriate and sustainable institutions. It is sobering to observe that many of our endeavours were misdirected by a complex of lingering neo-colonial condescension and a lack of respect for the importance and sophistication of local custom and tradition. As a consequence, much of their benefits were captured by service provides within the court system rather that received by the beneficiaries they were charged to serve.

Witchcraft and sorcery for example still abound in PNG. Newspapers continue to report on women being drowned as witches. I soon realised that these customs and beliefs, however repugnant and anachronistic, should never be taken frivolously. One day, our secretary, Ella, a woman of 40 in apparently robust good health, was absent from her desk. In just one week, she withered and died in hospital.

'You would call it cancer,' her Australian-trained local surgeon explained. 'But, actually, an angry neighbour had cast a spell on her.'

The modern state's legal system did not acknowledge or address these customs and beliefs appropriately, yet they remained pervasive and traditionally accepted.

Stephen Mokis, from Manus Island, was CEO of the Ombudsman Commission, the body responsible for investigating misconduct in office under the government's Leadership Code. He educated me on *kastom* (traditional custom in *Tok Pisin*) with infinite patience. PNG is vibrant with local customs and tradition. *Kastom* is much more complex than the display of chewing betel nut, carrying a *bilum* bag of woven pandanus, or disporting a penis sheath for tourists. It rests on culturally embedded norms that have evolved over millennia. Moreover, *kastom* is alive, dynamic and continually adapting in the face of external change. He explained that outsiders, including the Australian civil servants administering the aid program, often misunderstood what they termed 'wantokism.' This was a label they applied to what they saw as being corruption, nepotism and theft among local politicians. But this behaviour is actually part of a feudalistic system of reciprocity, patronage, largesse and protection. This misunderstanding was highlighted when the ABCTV's flagship investigative program '*4 Corners*', broadcast its supposed coup of filming PNG's PM receiving a brown paper bag full of cash. Australian viewers were shocked by his brazen lack of shame, while he was proud to be displayed to local viewers as a Big Man dispensing largesse to his 'wantok.' Determining where to draw the line could often be very difficult—not only for Australian civil servants but also their PNG colleagues, Stephen explained. Some behaviour however clearly crossed the line into dishonesty. When it did, it was usually prosecuted by the Ombudsman Commission.

'*Wantok*' literally means one talk or one language in *Tok Pisin*. It centres on networks of association or relationality connecting individuals—shared language, land, family, clan, region and province—to describe the organisation of social identity which comprises the local community rather than the nation state. In *kastom*, a traditional leader or *big man* is duty-bound to distribute bounty among his kinship, tribal group or village. Usually, though not invariably, when politicians allocate resources to those for whom they are responsible, they are conforming to the tradition of distributing them to members of their own village, rather than to some recently imported notion of the state or national community.

Port Moresby, as the national capital, is home to the national parliament. But it is isolated from the rest of the country by the rugged Owen Stanley Range. Beyond the capital, there are 839 living language groups separated by mountains and forests, each with its own distinctive traditions, culture, kinship and affiliations which define daily life at the local level. Treating the PM's behaviour with the bag of cash as being corrupt revealed Australia's institutional blindness to and disrespect of *kastom*. But because Australia carries the purse-strings, Papua New Guineans routinely have to listen to condescending lectures about integrity and responsibility before patiently resuming their dealings according to *kastom*.

Another part of my job was to evaluate the effectiveness of ongoing reform efforts. This involved burrowing through lengthy reports of earlier activities. Reading these, I found that the Australian development program had generally contributed to improving the performance of PNG's law and justice agencies through providing improved systems and processes, training, better equipment and infrastructure. Many of these reports included elaborate datasets and displayed graphs that rated their outcomes as being 'highly efficient' and very cost-effective. But, in my research, I had also read meta-evaluations—that is evaluations of evaluations themselves—that painted a much less comforting picture about the lack of evidence of impact and attribution, and debates over the standards of methodological rigour. Indeed, I had often observed a mismatch between what I saw in the field and what I read in official reports. Evidently, these reports told only part of the story. They were often self-serving, being produced by contractors dependent on donors whose own future funding rested on demonstrating evidence of their success—in what Linn Hammergren, my colleague who was the most prolific and analytical political scientist at the World Bank, has termed the 'fireman's syndrome' of never standing on your own hose. Herein lay an underlying, even unavoidable, conflict of interests—at the least, an unspoken alignment of interests between the donor and its contractors—which, curiously, was not generally seen as being corrupt.[41]

I needed to step away from all the paperwork to look around me. Observing proceedings inside courtrooms, even the existence or absence of queues outside the courthouse, could tell a more nuanced story about access to justice and the performance of the courts. So, one day, I visited the market at Waigani, a district of Moresby, to mingle with shoppers and store-holders.

'How do you feel about all the improvements,' I asked?

'*What* improvements?' they volleyed.

Many of our collective endeavours were, at best, 'islands of achievement' which had yet to join up to make any discernible improvement to the lives of ordinary people[42]. Doubtless it was true that we needed more time for results to become visible. At the core of much reform ambition was the hope and even presumption for normative change which, at its roots, required an inter-generational change in social attitudes and values—for example, a respect for the new—though equally alien to *kastom*—notions of human rights to bring the attitudes and values to change the abusive sexual behaviours towards women. But would these behaviours change, and how long could everyone wait …?

I discussed our challenges—not just relating to change, but also to measuring it—with Stephen. He looked over our reports which contained an impressive framework of 165 indicators of performance against which data was being painstakingly collected. After some minutes, he gave a wonderful chuckle.

'You've missed one.'

'Oh, which one,' I asked incredulously?

'*The Ela Beach test!*' he replied, grinning with glee.

I digested the sagacity of his suggestion.

Stephen's eyes twinkled with the patience of a compassionate teacher commending a retarded student who was finally grasping the lesson. The success of our program would become evident, he explained, when families returned to Ela Beach, which was then a wasteland of rotting rubbish and opportunistic crime, to picnic and watch the sunset with their children.

'In fact, why don't you replace all of your other indicators with this single indicator of success,' he gently chided, before hurrying away to yet another donor meeting.

Returning after a five-year absence, I learned some interesting lessons about how well we had achieved our goals. The first lesson was that nothing is static; change has happened, even though it was much slower than expected or desired. The second lesson was that change is characteristically unpredictable, and definitely not uniformly linear in direction, however much we may try to steer it. The evidence showed that there are too many uncontrollable 'externalities' that could intervene and influence the direction of change. I found the 'sure bets', or what my American colleagues like to call 'low hanging fruit', had disappeared without any trace as soon as the funding had ceased. But equally, I found unexpected and undreamed-of outcomes had come into being. For example, in 2005, the PNG's Supreme Court exerted astonishing independence to expel Australia's federal police as part of Australian Prime Minister John Howard's 'Enhanced Cooperation Program'.[43] The ECP had the pretention to airlift Australian police officers into Port Moresby to administer law and order on the streets, with full immunity to any prosecution by the local authorities. The Supreme Court ruled that this was contrary to the Constitution of Papua New Guinea. Evidently, Australia's lawyers had failed to read it.

This was a hugely courageous judicial decision which sent the southerners packing with their tails ignominiously between their legs. It also displayed a remarkably skilled adaptation of their rule of law.

Looking back, I can now see that many of our endeavours were tainted by the hubris of neo-colonialism and misdirected to focus predominantly on supporting the formal court system, where it was captured by service providers, while ignoring customary processes for peace, harmony and justice. These endeavours had overlooked the Village Court magistrates who settled most disputes at community level and restored peace and harmony from day to day, and the communities which they served. Some improvements were certainly made, though invariably much more slowly than we had expected.

Promoting justice is an infinite road with many paths. Change is slow and unpredictable. Sometimes it is obstructed by vested interests, but more often by systemic inertia, path dependency and the complexity of numerous changing interdependent parts. Some years later, in 2012, the Australian Government invited me to provide a vision for their next 5-year program of support for law and justice in PNG. By then, I had learned to respect custom and tradition which had evolved and adapted over centuries as generally being the best fit for purpose in its local context, which should be built on. I had also completed my doctorate which advocated for justice to be promoted more centrally in development endeavours.

These were still early days. Our work, like *kastom,* continued to adapt however slowly. When I last visited in 2018, the crime rate was falling. Ela Beach had been cleared and was once again pristine. Australia had also started to support the Village Courts which administer a mix of customary and state justice at community level across the land. In hindsight, how simple the obvious can sometimes seem.

Cambodia: After Year Zero

Tuol Sleng Security Prison 21, or S-21, was once a high school in Phnom Penh. During its "reign of terror", the Khmer Rouge imprisoned, tortured and executed 17,000 people there. To save on the cost of bullets, they slaughtered most prisoners with pickaxes. Some were strapped to steel bedframes and electrocuted. At nearby Choeung Ek, the infamous "killing field", they shattered babies' skulls against trees by swinging them from their feet. Years later on a visit to Choeung Ek, I trod on bits of bone and clothing exposed in the mud by the monsoon rains. There were 196 killing fields across Cambodia.

On 15 April 1975, Pol Pot celebrated the beginning of '*Year Zero*' to signify the rebirth of '*Kampuchea*.' During the next 4 years, he led the Khmer Rouge to cause innumerable deaths through war, genocide, mass execution, slave labour, famine and disease. It is conservatively estimated that 2.5 million people—one quarter of the total population—died. Of these, the Khmer Rouge executed at least 1.5 million. Another million fled to the United States, Europe and Australia. Anyone connected to the previous government of King Sihanouk was exterminated. Professionals, intellectuals, artists, musicians and writers were executed for being privileged members of a decadent culture. Even those who wore glasses were targeted for being able to read. Yet Pol Pot had himself been educated in France and wore glasses.

But in October 1977, I did not yet know all this. I stood on the Mekong's banks looking across the Thai border into Cambodia. There was no discernible movement on the other side. Once the government was defeated, the borders were closed. News services had fallen silent, but rumours had already started to circulate that some very bad things were happening across those waters. I felt menace in the stillness.

After the borders reopened, I returned to Cambodia to work many times. My first three visits were during the mid-90 s on an American aid project. The civil war between the new government and the Khmer Rouge was still smouldering in the provinces. I saw Kalashnikov rifles for sale in the Russian Market. Naked girls doped on heroin sold refreshments and other services in the casino. Shops displayed

L. Armytage, *Confronting Injustice*,
https://doi.org/10.1007/978-981-95-3573-6_10

signs saying 'No Guns'. An Australian backpacker, David Wilson, had been kidnapped by the Khmer Rouge and left to die a grisly death, his Achilles tendons severed, when a ransom bid had failed. Our project was instructed never to stop on the highways, even if the people carried guns. The war finally spluttered to its end when amnesties for the KR cadre were granted.

I then returned again a decade later, in 2005, on two short visits to design a new approach for the Australian government to realign a dysfunctional project. By concentrating on procedural reforms of reducing delay, that project had helped the courts to conduct hearings more efficiently, but with the perverse effect of accelerating the unjust dispossession of the poor by the courts, which were captured by the elites, from their land.

Later that year, Miyako and I moved in Phnom Penh when I was hired by the UN as its senior counsel for judicial reform. We lived in an elegant colonial-era apartment overlooking the Mekong River swirling silently on its 5000-km journey from the Tibetan Himalayas, through the paddy fields of Asia to the South China Sea. Cooled by the breeze, we often enjoyed this view from our balcony in the evenings. Timber fishing boats drifted patiently for their catch, while laden barges ploughed their way upstream through the night. Every morning, the sun would rise precisely at 6.10, an orb of scorching golden light. Instantly the air would jump from humid to swelteringly hot. It was a deceptively charming city with lingering French accents in its architecture and food that few tourists bothered to explore before rushing upcountry to Angkor Wat.

Angkor was the ancient capital of the Khmer Kingdom which dominated Southeast Asia between the ninth and fifteenth centuries. Spreading over 400 km^2, dotted with scores of magnificent temples in both the Hindu and Buddhist traditions, it was for a time the world's largest city. How Angkor languished remains an archaeological mystery. It lay buried beneath dense jungle until being rediscovered in 1860 by Henri Mouhot, a French naturalist. Angkor Wat, literally meaning the "city of temples," was built in the twelfth century as a Hindu temple dedicated to the god Vishnu. Later it was sacked and transformed into a Buddhist shrine by King Jayavarman VII. The walls of its countless galleries are adorned with carvings of thousands of dancing *Apsaras*. These *Apsaras* are enchanting celestial maidens, or nymphs of the waters, in Hindu and Buddhist cultures. At Angkor Wat, the maidens' feet and breasts are often highly polished, their gleaming patinas attesting to the devotions of countless pilgrims over the centuries. When I first visited, it was still possible to ramble alone throughout these ancient ruins. But now it is increasingly difficult to find a quiet space in which to contemplate their serenity. The latest threat to the preservation of these fragile structures is the influx of mass tourists, with ever more visitors from China. Access is now restricted to crowded walkways.

Over the centuries, the roots of massive strangler figs have taken hold, twisting their way up through the stone framework of Ta Prohm, a temple dedicated to the mother of Jayavarman. This temple has an elaborate complex of towers, courtyards, cloisters and corridors over several acres. Many of its corridors are now impassable, clogged by fallen stone blocks dislodged by these invasive trees. Massive roots climb the walls and slither over the roofs of the central enclosure like giant bubble gum in an awesome display of the power of the towering jungle to subjugate even the grandest of monuments. After the restoration of peace in 1992, UNESCO inscribed Ta Prohm and other temples on the World Heritage Endangered List for their unique architectural, archaeological and artistic significance. Of these, Bayon is also distinctive. There are over 200 serene smiling faces on the four-sided 'face towers' that cluster around its central peak, surrounded by carvings of heroic tales and scenes of Khmer life. The similarity of these gigantic faces to other statues of the king has led scholars to conclude they are representations of Jayavarman himself, rather than of Lord Shiva or Buddha.

As I strolled among the ancient temples, now mostly stripped of their original colours, I would glimpse the Buddhist monks going about their devotions in amber, saffron and golden robes. While modern Cambodia might seem secular, Buddhism has existed here since the fifth century and has been the state religion ever since. Monks have played an important role in Khmer culture, serving as educators and healers, and sometimes also as activists. It is still normal for young men to serve as monks for two years before starting their careers and marrying. During the Khmer Rouge regime, however, monks were expelled from the wats and forced into manual labour. Thousands died. Most recently, monks have become politically active again, leading anti-government demonstrations on issues ranging from political and press freedom to garment-workers' wages, and protection of the environment.

These then are the postcard spectacles that the tourists come to see: the magnificent ruins of Angkor and the splendid flowing robes of the monks. Cambodia is a country of gentle people and postcard views draped in the equatorial colours of amber, saffron and gold. But this is *not* the full story of modern-day Cambodia, which was the hardest place in which I have ever worked.

Behind the postcard spectacles, Cambodia is struggling to recover from its past. The catastrophe of the genocide (1975–1979) is the defining event of modern Cambodian history. But it remains unresolved and excluded from school history books. While the country is now undergoing frenzied economic growth and reconstruction, it remains deeply traumatized behind its glossy facade. Its society is characterized by dictatorship in democratic drag, massive inequality of wealth, ruthless exploitation of workers and unrelenting dispossession of the poor. As I was soon to discover, all this was enforced by the corrupt police and the servile courts.

I was exploring Angkor early one morning to evade the tourist hordes and the furnace of the tropical sun, when I was stopped by a policeman. As an expat employed by the UN, I was generally exempt from extortion, but the ever-present lurking threat of something gone wrong was never pleasant. What happened next was totally unexpected, and took me some moments to understand. The policeman offered to sell me his badge. It was real, with his official number stamped on the back. He wanted US$10. Just $10. The police are the public face and hands of government. But being paid almost nothing, they are driven into corruption. I stumbled backwards, sickened by the pathetic sordidness of the encounter.

When I started as senior counsel with the UN, my job was to engage with the Royal Government to direct a law and justice reform program. On arrival, the government thanked me for coming but explained that what they had really wanted was my salary package to spend as they wanted, rather than my services. After a month of sitting dispirited in an empty office, it became impossible to delude myself that I had misunderstood. The government had no intention of engaging and did not want any help from another foreign expert. Somehow the UN had made a mistake. But back in Sydney, we'd already sold the car and closed our home. And the contract was generous. So, bemused, we stayed. Sitting at my empty desk, I had plenty of time to contemplate the Hobbesian '*brutishness of life in nature*' in the aftermath of the genocide, and how that had happened.

Since the mid-nineteenth century, the French had occupied and exploited the Kingdom of Cambodia as a colony it called Indochina. This kingdom was headed by King Sihanouk, a decadent but popular dilettante who—when not holidaying in Paris—occupied the Royal Palace during the Japanese occupation until the French withdrawal in 1953. He then claimed the mantle of 'Father of the Nation'. Caring little for the welfare of his people, however, his reign rapidly disintegrated into republican upheaval. Destabilized by the war in neighbouring Vietnam, Cambodia descended into civil war in 1967. Sihanouk then fled to China when he was ousted in a US-supported coup led by General Lon Nol which, after a series of epic miscalculations, was itself defeated by Pol Pot's Khmer Rouge.

Always opportunistic, however hapless, Sihanouk returned in 1975 as head of state for the Khmer Rouge. But once again, he hurriedly fled the country, again abandoning his people, when they imposed a radical Marxist-Leninist-style regime to transform *Kampuchea* into a rural, classless society. This was a hard-core full blown class revolution. Many left-wing western intellectuals cheered the Khmer Rouge—at least, until they emptied the hospitals and drove the sick and dying into the countryside on foot to be 'purified' through manual labour. The highways were littered with rotting corpses and discarded belongings. They abolished money, private property, religion and Khmer culture in a merciless effort to expunge the privilege and decadence of Sihanouk's reign.

Every Cambodian was affected by the horrors of the genocide that followed, either as victim or perpetrator. Half of the entire population was killed, enslaved or fled. Every family was torn apart, none was spared. In the 90 s, Yale University found evidence of trauma throughout the surviving population as severe as the Jewish Holocaust. Of those who survived, 80% remained traumatised. It was an unspeakable catastrophe that Cambodia is yet to reconcile, from which it is yet to recover.

Our cook, Dina, was 12 years old when the troubles began. Of her four sisters, she was the sole survivor. When peace was finally restored, the survivors of the extermination returned to live alongside the perpetrators in towns and villages across the country. Miyako became friends with Dina's family, and we helped with the schooling and medical expenses of their daughters. But when we talked with these children, they could not believe the atrocities that she had survived. Those were unimaginable, so could not exist. There was still no history taught in schools at that time. It was a blank space that was silently passed over.

Outwardly, there was no public anger or resentment. But how could that possibly be, I wondered? An answer may possibly be found in Buddhism. Buddhists believe in karma. Karma describes the law of cause and effect, where a person's actions influence their future experiences. In Buddhism, karma is not seen as any form of divine judgment or fate, but rather as a natural and impersonal law governing the ethical consequences of actions. Buddhists believe that actions have consequences and that bad actions in life may be redressed, perhaps in the next life. In the absence of any worldly justice, that belief might be the best but only redress that they had.

Pol Pot's reign was finally terminated when the Vietnamese invaded Cambodia in 1979 to protect its border against Khmer Rouge incursions and also to pre-empt encirclement by China. But nothing remained the same. The genocide had gutted Cambodian society of its human capital, culture, traditions, norms and values. The UN was mandated to restore democracy, but it did so in name alone. Hun Sen, a former Khmer Rouge fighter, became Prime Minister in 1985 and has held power ever since until recently passing it to his son. He ruled through barely disguised violence. The UN, ILO and Human Rights Watch have reported repeatedly on people murdered in the streets by 'unknown assailants' for opposing aspects of Hun Sen's government. In the '90 s, I remember a prominent political candidate was gunned down in broad daylight. It was hardly unusual. No one was prosecuted. Ever since, all but the most courageous or foolhardy have remained silent. Hun Sen imprisons or exiles his political opponents and suppresses the media. Each election has been hollower than the last. Under his rule, the legacy of Cambodia's history has metastasised. The institutions of government and the rule of law have been contaminated: the National Assembly is a rubber stamp, the police are corrupt, and the judiciary has been captured by Hun Sen and his cronies, as documented by Douglas North.[44] This descent into dictatorship was witnessed by the international community which had stepped in to help the destitute survivors. The government then harvested their aid in the order of US$ 500 million each year with venal promises of reform that were rarely honoured. This was to become a Faustian bargain from which donors like the World Bank retreated but then, in anguish over abandoning the needy, returned.

Only seven judges survived the genocide. Most had been executed by the Khmer Rouge. Just one judge ever returned to the bench. The courts, like most government institutions, were stripped of their expertise, organisational culture, and traditions. After the fall of Pol Pot's regime, the newly appointed judges scrimmaged to survive on an archaic stipend of $20 a month. Impoverished, they were susceptible to patronage and rapidly captured within Hun Sen's new order. Lacking any principled understanding of their role under the constitution to uphold laws independently and impartially, they soon acquiesced to the daily practice of receiving instructions from the government on the disposal of cases. In effect, they became Hun Sen's enforcer.

While I was endeavouring to work with these courts, I discovered that the going rate to procure a judgeship was then a princely US$60,000. The calculus of corruption was inescapable: incumbents borrowed heavily to make such a major investment against which they must then levy rents by soliciting payments from the parties for disposing their cases favourably. The courts became a business unconcerned with their constitutional mandate to administer justice by serving as a 'check and balance' against the abuse of power by holding the executive accountable to law, which is now entrenched as the new norm.

For a time, I worked with the judges' school designing curricula for teaching novice judges about the principles of judicial independence, integrity and fair trial. But it felt like I was drying my face with a tissue in the monsoon. They nodded and smirked. But however young, these novices already knew that to cross the government had career, indeed life, terminating consequences.

Over the decades since 'Year Zero', with its the abolition of property and money, a new middle class has emerged. But the distribution of wealth is tightly held by the coterie of Hun Sen's supporters. Cronyism is rife in this new order. Control of the economy is shared by a political elite which does not hesitate to use violence to preserve its control. The families of army officers drive expensive SUVs displaying military insignia to brazenly assert their immunity from any interference, even that of the police. Access to precious resources, notably land and food, is tightly guarded by them in a textbook example of a 'closed access order' society.[45] To retain his ascendency, Hun Sen then pits his most senior cronies, such as the ministers for defence and home affairs, against each other to very publicly purge anyone who dares to oppose him.

Those who have joined Hùn Sen's coterie—and most recently that of his West Point-educated son Hun Manet—enjoy the limitless fruits of this new order from which they pay their fealty. Amid the bustling traffic of tuk-tuks (3-wheel auto-rickshaw taxis), I have seen more Rolls Royce Phantoms jostle with late model Porsches for parking spots on the busy streets of Phnom Penh than in New York, Paris or London. The elite have amassed vast untaxed fortunes, often through illicit land grabbing and logging. Meanwhile, those who have not gained access to this new order are destined to exclusion and entrenched poverty. While the number of those living in poverty has notionally fallen to 20% of the population, poverty remains endemic. Those living in poverty would double to 40%—almost half the population—if they were to lose just 30¢ per day. There are few business or employment options for those excluded from this order.

Our tuk-tuk driver, Chan, who declined to pay fealty and voted against Hun Sen 20 years ago, remains trapped in a hand-to-mouth existence. For Chan, there is no ladder to climb up from driving his tuk-tuk, nor for his wife from the garment factory into a better life. Confronting unrelenting subsistence, there is now a weary grimness in his face where cheery smiles used to be. We first met Chan when he was a newly married young tuk-tuk driver and hired him regularly while we were living in Phnom Penh. We liked his honesty, his safe driving, and most of all for his cheery smiles. His wife, Pissey, had started a tailoring workshop with some neighbours in their home. But when we returned to Cambodia some years later, a certain grimness had replaced his smiles. The taxi was gone, as was Pissey's workshop. Their hopes now rest with their daughters marrying expats, as two already have, to start new lives abroad.

Towards the end of my annually renewable contract, I was taken aside by an intermediary of the government's law and justice reform unit with whom I had endeavoured to work. If I wanted to renew my contract, he explained quietly, I must reach 'an arrangement'. What arrangement? The price, apparently paid by others, was 15% of my contract to be passed by me to the government. I had read a lot about corruption from colleagues like Linn and Doug, but I had never before had I experienced it. Its slime had reached out to touch me. It felt like I had been infected by a virus. I had to leave the office. When I reported this approach to the UN's head of mission, he said nothing. Apparently, it was an unspoken cost of doing business. I was sickened. But worse, I felt so naïve at being shocked.

Anywhere must be better than here, I thought. To escape the purgatory of my empty government office, I went in search of doing more useful work elsewhere. Soon I was immersed in the lives of those on the lowest rungs of Cambodia's social hierarchy: the garment workers, the waste pickers, the dispossessed and others searching for justice through the courts.

First, I went to find out more about the lives of Cambodia's garment workers. In 2005, there were some 700 factories that produced clothing and shoes for global brands, which included Gap, Nike, Levi, Walmart, Calvin Klein and Tesco. These factories were Cambodia's largest employer, providing around 700,000 jobs for women to support their families. While Cambodia was a late entrant and relatively small supplier to the world market, this industry was extremely important, contributing 16.5% to GDP and making up 75% of its exports. The global market was massive, extremely competitive and highly mobile in its constant search for the lowest cost base. When production costs became uncompetitive, companies would abruptly close their factories and relocate to cheaper countries. Wages were a crucial component of those production costs.

The government suppressed labour costs by sanctioning a 'minimum wage' of US$45 per month, at that time. That wage was barely enough to meet their basic living expenses in Phnom Penh. The average hourly wage of garment factory workers was 24¢ in Bangladesh, 45¢ in Cambodia, 53¢ in Vietnam and $1.26 in China. To survive in this competitive global workplace, workers were obliged to work 6 days per week, with compulsory overtime, usually for 60 hours every week. For this, they could possibly earn up to $120 each month. While considerably more than the official minimum wage, it was systemic penury. Literally tens of thousands of women skimped by sharing food and accommodation in squalid dormitories without power or running water, in order to save $20 per month to send home to support their near-destitute families who were subsisting in the provinces.

To secure its place in this supply chain, the Cambodian government then mobilized riot police to brutally crush strikes by garment factory workers who sought any improvements in their wages and conditions. Several protesters, including women, were shot dead in broad daylight at a rally in front of the Independence Monument near our home in central Phnom Penh. To my horror, the newspapers then published photographs of their bodies left in pools of blood littering the boulevard. This use of violence was rarely concealed. Later, others were killed, and many more injured, when these police opened fire using live ammunition to disband another protest in the industrial quarter.

Over the following months, I worked with the International Labour Organisation to photograph and document the lives of these women working in the garment factories. They are the invisible human face in the massive global supply chain, working in a "race to the bottom" for miserly wages earned often in intolerable conditions.[46] Many suffered malnutrition causing them to faint in 40 °C heat on the factory floor.[47] Those unable to survive these conditions were replaced by other women queuing for their jobs outside the factories. This exploitation was exacerbated by debt bondage which required new workers to pay for their job in these factories usually costing weeks, even months, of their future earnings. While wages in the garment industry have nominally improved since then, much of this was eroded by inflation and predatory property owners immediately raising their rent.

Each evening, I witnessed the relief and release of suppressed excitement as these workers ended their shifts. Despite the harsh conditions and meagre pay, they were grinning and chatting excitedly as they were bodily frisked by guards at the gate.[48] But they had very little spare time, or energy, to socialize. Visiting their families in the provinces was expensive and reserved for special holidays, perhaps once or twice at best each year.

A few are self-employed, making a living from their homes. 'We must work for 60 hours, we have no choice to live,' Faeri, a garment worker, told me wearily from the window of her stall, while her young daughter watched-on from behind.[49]

Cambodian women on the lowest echelons of society have very few options. They can accept the exploitative conditions of the garment factories in return for the security of a regular wage however meagre. Their alternatives are to return to subsistence living with their families in the provinces from which they are trying to escape. Or they can scavenge for waste on the toxic dumps for uncertain earnings. Or they can become an '*entertainer*'.[50] At that time, young women might be paid US$60 each month as a 'beer girl' in a bar or restaurant, which she might double with tips. Those who opted to sleep with their customers could even earn $100 for a night but, if they did so, faced the risk of violence, STDs and shame. Whatever they choose, most are destined to poverty, poor health and a shortened life expectancy.

I photographed these unseen women in the garment factories to document their dignity, strength and resilience. The International Labour Organisation exhibited these images as part of their 'Better Factories' initiative which was opened by the Minister for Industry in Phnom Penh. Later, I published these portraits and told their stories in the book *Unseen Faces Unheard Voices, Portraits of Injustice*.[51] Now, whenever I buy new clothes, I find myself asking these questions: are these women better or worse off for having a job; is it the cure or the curse of their poverty; knowing what I now know, should I even be buying this garment and, finally, am I now complicit in this exploitation? These are confronting questions for each of us, as consumers, in considering our options on the notional High Street. Perhaps the best that most of us can do is to acknowledge this harsh provenance and ensure that it is not wasted.

I continued my photographic documentation of the most marginalised Cambodians by heading to Stung Meanchey, Phnom Penh's municipal rubbish dump. At that time, the city produced some 1600 tons of garbage each day, half of which would fester in the tropical heat on the streets, be tossed into the Mekong or picked up by children and the elderly who scrounge for any saleable rubbish like plastic bottles. The rest was dumped at Stung Meanchey.

At Stung Meanchey, I found a wasteland of garish plastic colours and swirling toxic vapours. The stench of burning chemicals swirling from the ground inflamed my eyes, stung my lungs and riled the gut.[52] Around me, waste pickers of all ages teemed across the surface gathering anything recyclable into nylon sacks. At that time, these pickers worked in the scorching sun for 12-hours to earn US$1–2 every day. The rewards were minuscule: to earn $1, a picker must collect about 20 kg, or about 1000 empty plastic bottles. Each day, they dig with their bare hands into the waste of human faeces, broken glass, industrial chemicals, heavy metals, soiled hospital bandages, used syringe needles, even discarded organs and amputated limbs in an effort to find rubbish that might earn them just a few cents. On some days they might find things to recycle, but on others nothing. Without physical protection, other than paper masks, they are constantly exposed to serious health and safety hazards. They suffer back and joint pain, vision and respiratory problems, parasite infestation, malnutrition and diseases including tuberculosis, bronchitis, pneumonia and dysentery. Many are covered in rashes, open sores, dog bites and puncture wounds. Once a family member becomes sick, their entire family is at risk of being plunged into dire straits. Health care is a luxury beyond their means and consequently many suffer substantially reduced life expectancy.

Waste pickers live in a space outside the state. They receive no government support, no industrial or social protection. I found scores of families eking out their living on the dump. Their homes were shanties erected from waste materials, without power or running water. Their children were growing up without adequate nutrition or any schooling, thus denied any prospects for a better life.[53]

'Of course, I don't want to work here,' Seng Sophea, an unemployed teacher, told me with resignation in English on the dump at Stung Meanchey.[54]

It was on one of my many trips to Stung Meanchey that I met Srey Lak (literally, 'Beautiful Girl'). She was clutching a bouquet of dead water lilies. She was feral and filthy. She was probably six years old, though we never knew her true age. Her birth had not been registered and she had no official identity. She was living on the dump with her mother in a single room shack with no electricity, water or sewerage. Her mother was alcoholic, drug-dependent and sick. Her father had absconded. She had never been to school and could neither read nor write. Like scores of other children, she scrounged for scraps to support herself and her mother. They were surviving as outcasts.[55]

For a day's work, she earned about 50 cents. The UN estimates that 10,000–20,000 children work on the streets, in Cambodia, collecting aluminium, glass and plastics. Between 10–25% of all children aged 7 or older are engaged in some form of labour. Many are trapped in human slavery, hazardous labour, drug trafficking and prostitution across the region. Despite rising global growth, social inequity in Cambodia is rising, embedding the cycle of poverty, malnutrition and neglect.

With her mother's permission, Miyako and I enrolled Srey Lak and her sister in a local school which provides world-class education and full board to children from destitute families. Here she rapidly excelled, topping her class and later travelled to Kathmandu to represent Cambodia at a regional youth conference. Some years later, when we visited her as a chirpy young teenager, we asked how she would like to spend the afternoon together.

'Pizza,' was her instant answer!

Later, I learned that children in Cambodia's many orphanages are acutely vulnerable to being trafficked across Cambodia and in neighbouring Thailand.[56] Sexual trafficking is the most lucrative among child labour. Almost one-third of sex workers are between the ages of 12 and 17. Despite slavery being illegal, there have never been any reported convictions for crimes of forced labour or trafficking.

In 2009, the city closed the Stung Meanchey dump after residents fell sick and it became an eyesore for the tourist industry. They moved it away to Choeung Ek, behind the killing fields and beyond public gaze.

Hun Sen's voracious appetite for wealth has destroyed the lives of countless Cambodians. His government routinely evicts citizens from their land to which they have rightful ownership. The land is then used to incentivise foreign investment, mainly from China. After the Khmer Rouge had destroyed all property records, a law was later introduced to provide land title to those who could prove they had possessed that land for 10 years. The poor however were usually unaware of their rights, or powerless to exercise them. They also had difficulty in proving the legitimacy of their land possession when contested by a wealthy interloper. The courts were then used by that interloper to evict the poor from their land and seize it with impunity. Needless to say, it was usual practice to pay bribes to the judges who in turn remitted kickbacks to the minister, who provided them protection for their fealty. In doing so, they betrayed their mandate, becoming the oppressor, not the protector, of the constitution. Instead of protecting the poor from dispossession, children from bondage, and garment workers from exploitation, Hun Sen's courts routinely enforce injustices such as this. It would be naïve to protest that this is not at his behest, because nothing can happen in Cambodia that does not reward him.

One day, I visited Andong Village. Shortly before, the government had mobilised military police to evict the residents of Sambok Chap to level the township as an intensive agricultural development for Chinese investors who had obtained a court order. The residents were trucked away to an empty field at Andong which was one of many such resettlements in isolated wastelands beyond the airport. There were no houses, electricity, sewerage, shops, schools or hospitals. The absence of public transport stripped the jobs from those who had them because the cost of commuting was higher than their wages. They erected plastic sheet shanties with the aid of civil society organisations who struggled to rehabilitate this slum. Each year, this village regularly flooded under the monsoon. Its waters mixed with human waste to create a breeding ground for mosquitos that spread dengue. I visited with Kong Rady, an NGO doctor who tended the most desperately needy. He worked fast, stoically, but with gentle hands.

'We do the best we can. But each week, there are always so many new patients,' he told me with a tired smile. The courts had legalised this destitution.[57]

After some months away from my empty office, the UN agreed to transfer me to the *Khmer Rouge Tribunal*. Hun Sen, himself a former KR officer, had obstructed the quest for justice for decades by claiming that amnesty was the price for peace.

Finally, in 2006, the government acceded with the UN to establish the 'Extraordinary Chambers of the Courts of Cambodia' (the ECCC, more commonly called the KR Tribunal) to provide justice to the victims of the Khmer Rouge. By then, Pol Pot, the KR leader, had however already died. Nonetheless the Tribunal had at last been established to prosecute the remaining leaders of the genocide and the other crimes against humanity. I was keen to assist in expediting any just reckoning of this catastrophe. My responsibilities were to induct the judges' panel, which was an eclectic mix of Cambodian and foreign judges from Australia, France, New Zealand, Poland and the US, in a process to determine the court's jurisprudence and how it would go about its work as a unique war crimes jurisdiction.

In 2020, after 15 years of proceedings and much obfuscation, the Tribunal finally convicted three senior officers of the Khmer Rouge of crimes against humanity: the commandant of S-21, Kaing Guek Eav, known as "Duch"; Nuon Chea, then aged 90, who had served as Pol Pot's right-hand man; and Khieu Samphan, the head of state. Each was sentenced to serve what was left of their lives in prison.

This trial delivered some measures of justice. It ended the impunity of these senior leaders and condemned a catastrophe that had had no name officially until that time. The lie that everything was normal was at last formally repudiated, and norms of right and wrong may now be restored in the new society. There are now some books in schools that document this history, and the grandchildren of both survivors and perpetrators are being taught their lessons. Buddhists can now celebrate the festival of *Pchum Ben*, which is linked to the ancient Ankorian tradition that the spirits of the deceased return to this world, to feed the hungry ghosts of those souls who remain trapped by having died violently or without proper funerary rites. This festival is deeply rooted in the belief that during these days, the gates of hell open, allowing the spirits of the dead to roam the earth. These spirits are said to suffer from hunger and thirst, and it is believed that they can only receive food and offerings from the living. At last, the healing of reconciliation can now begin. These are profound achievements in which I am proud to have contributed some small part.

The lure of Cambodia had been irresistible to me, as to others. I had been drawn to learn more about the genocide. I had come to contemplate the unspeakable horrors of that abyss. How could this have happened? The atrocity of Cambodia's genocide was not a remote artefact of ancient history committed by unknown people of some bygone era. How did a seemingly gentle and beautiful people literally destroy themselves and their society? Ultimately, I had to confront the shocking realisation that murderous inhumanity can lurk in any person's heart—perhaps even mine, for no one is exempt. Cambodia displays the horror that we can destroy each other, ourselves, our society and our civilisation, in just 4 years. Cambodia remains deeply damaged by the psychosis of this genocide, which eradicated all norms of its previous society. Greed and force have now become the prevailing new order. That damage will not be fixed in any single act, for example, by the Tribunal. It may take generations to purge this epigenetic trauma. Learning these truths was deeply affecting.

This was the most challenging year of my career. Perhaps I should have left at the start. But I hung in. That is what marathon runners train to do; to endure and push through. Thankfully, on reflection, I did. The catharsis of this ordeal spurred me to find other paths for seeking justice—in the garment factories, on the wastelands of Strung Meanchey and finally in the KRT. Miyako and I put Srey Lak with her sister into school and later started a charity to educate other destitute girls. I exhibited and published my first photographs showing their faces and telling their stories in the book '*Unseen Faces, Unheard Voices*.' And I found the inspiration and imperative to start my doctorate. Once done, two years later, the portrait of Srey Lak clasping those lilies has graced its cover.

Cambodia was the pivot for everything that would come later. From catharsis came epiphany then regeneration. It was painfully uncomfortable. But that discomfort impelled my passage. What I found eclipsed all that had gone before. Building on this understanding, I vowed to find a better way to make the world a fairer place.[58]

Nepal: Behind the Postcard

At 11.56 am on Saturday 25 April 2015, a massive 7.8-magnitude earthquake devastated Nepal, killing more than 9000 people. In the following moments, the village of Langtang was obliterated when some 40 million tons of rock and ice from a glacial lake came crashing down from the mountain above. The avalanche buried the village without a trace, instantly crushing 175 villagers, 27 guides and porters and, it is estimated from uncancelled visa records, some 15–30 foreign trekkers. The ensuing gale flattened every tree for 5 km down the valley. Only the rock walls of the valley remained.

The earthquake destroyed more than 600,000 buildings, including Nepal's most prized heritage structures around Durbar Square which is a UNESCO World Heritage site in the capital Kathmandu. In neighbouring Patan, many twelfth century Buddhist temples also collapsed into rubble. Hundreds of thousands of people were left homeless; many were the poorest people who were already least able to replace their dwellings, thousands of whom have remained so ever since.

Just one year before, I had trekked up to and stayed in Langtang village with my Nepali work colleague and friend, Prem Chandra Rai, a trail-blazing Indigenous lawyer researching much-needed military law with which to resolve the many atrocities of the recent 'People's war'.

We spent 5 days walking up the valley close to the Chinese border, savouring the pristine air which was a refreshing tonic after the acrid smog and funky waste of Kathmandu. Over these days, he told me about his childhood. His father had served as an officer in Britain's fabled Gurkha regiment. After retiring, he returned to his home village of Taplejung in the far Eastern hill district, bordering Tibet and Sikkim. Here, Prem grew up witnessing the extreme poverty faced by his fellow villagers.

'There was no shops or market to buy, sell or exchange goods in our village. There was zero opportunity for employment. Those households that managed to afford cooking salt, cooking oil, kerosene lamp for the whole year were considered as a rich family. Most villagers must wait until the annual Dashain festival to eat *dal baht* (rice with lentil curry) with meat,' he told me.

L. Armytage, *Confronting Injustice*,
https://doi.org/10.1007/978-981-95-3573-6_11

Prem's family was fortunate because his father had a small pension. But it was this poverty and ignorance of the outside world which motivated him to go to school. There was a primary school but no secondary school within a walking distance which was why his elder siblings had discontinued their education. So, Prem stayed with distant relatives far from his home to complete his schooling.

'This is why only foreigners enjoy trekking in Nepal to celebrate nature in the mountains and rivers. Nepali people already walk enough just to survive each day.' he explained with a wry smile.

Prem is the first member of the indigenous Janajati community who has graduated from university. He is now a practicing lawyer who teaches in a law college and writes textbooks to fill the many gaps on its library shelves for future students.

'I want to show others in my community they can follow my path,' he told me.

We walked through lush beech forests, along a bustling river carrying glacial melt coloured azure from the particles of ground rock, between the parapets of the Himalayan peaks. The clouds skittering above the valley seemed to scrape against our heads. On the fifth afternoon, we reached Langtang village, a remote small village, nestling beneath the towering south face of the eponymous 7234-metre peak at the top of the valley. Here we feasted on momos, a local delicacy of steamed dumplings served scalding hot in a broth of local spices and herbs, made by Ditya, a young mother who welcomed us to stay in her home.

All was still as beautiful as I remembered from my first visit to Nepal as a 26-year-old backpacker in 1978, when I had stepped away from practising law and was travelling to explore paths less trodden. Nepal is home to 8 of the world's highest peaks including Everest, Kanchenjunga and Annapurna which had enticed me with their beauty, might and proximity to the heavens.

Then I had walked mostly alone, stopping in mountain villages for tantalisingly sweet *chai masala* (Indian-style spiced tea) and endless *dal baht*. It was already winter, blusteringly cold even before the snows. Most villagers had already descended with their herds to the warmer lower pastures, and Langtang was deserted. I pitched my tent beside a shuttered monastery and spent my Christmas clambering around under the shadows of the mountain above me.

At Langtang, I had found a sanctuary in which to contemplate the world and my place in it. I discovered a love of solitude. I loved walking through the cathedral of nature, embarking in the cold crisp mornings listening to the crunch of pebbles underfoot and the daylong chatter of birds in the trees' canopy above me. I loved the silence, feeling the wind, then the stillness. Beneath the ever-changing sky, I loved the unpretentious beauty of the mountain villages I walked through; the exquisite craftsmanship and symmetry of the hand-quarried schist, layered grey rock, ideal for the drystone walls of dwellings and teahouses where I rested and drank scalding *chai* before walking on. Ahead, giant snow-capped peaks penetrated passing clouds breath-takingly magnificent above valleys dissolved in mist. Waterfalls; churning rivers, laden with ground glacial rock clouded light blue; forest glades. I loved the wellness of my body, walking for hours on end. As I stepped one foot ahead of the other, I let my thoughts cascade through the stadium of my mind. This was a space of reflection and revelations, awareness flitting like a bird through the branches of my memory. I loved this solitude that allowed these precious moments of contemplation, sheltered from any intrusion. I was alone, but not lonely. My world of legal practice was left far behind. This was what I had come for.[59]

In later years, I have extended this love for the serenity of trekking to the alpine vistas of Mont Blanc overlooking the plains of Europe that diminish into the mists below, to the crimson and golden splendours of the Japanese fall on the ancient Nakasendo trail, and the sparse more subtle beauty of Tasmania's overland trail. But I also loved it because of the company I have found along those paths. In the openness of the mountains and nature's wilderness, I could shed the constraints of normal life and find myself in the simplicity of the track. This could also happen to others, and when it does it is possible to show ourselves more openly and share the real experiences in our lives, trusting in the companionship of the trail. And for this reason, there is often a sadness in ending these walks before resuming the hurly burly of normality.

I have returned to Nepal often. In 2001, Miyako and I were strapped in a rickety De Havilland Twin Otter as its engines strained to climb 3000 meters around the shoulder of Annapurna. At 8091 metres above Pokhara, Annapurna is the tenth highest mountain in the world, rising with the breathtaking majesty of a goddess, into the clouds. From the ground, it had been impossible to gauge its size. Then the plane became just a speck flitting over treetops and rocky outcrops before disappearing around its lowest flanks. Inside the rattling cabin, the engines were deafening. It gave us little comfort to know that these aging craft often fell from the sky killing all on board. Over the past three decades, there had been 27 crashes due to the inclement weather, mountainous terrain and aging aircraft failure, most recently in the previous year. Greatly relieved when we landed at Jomsom, we started our walk along the Annapurna Circuit. At that time, there were still no roads or solar-powered showers. But occasionally we enjoyed the delight of fresh apple pies, a legacy of the German missionaries. That night, we sheltered in a cowshed and brushed our teeth in a stream in the dark.

This time, it was geopolitics that had brought us back to Nepal. We had been evacuated from Islamabad after the al-Qaeda attack on the World Trade Centre in New York on 11 September 2001. One month later, the US invaded Afghanistan. In between, massive grey transport planes transited Pakistani airfields at night without lights or identification markings. Suddenly, it felt dangerous for expats to be seen there. Armed guards were posted at our residences. Grenade screens were installed on our office windows. When we arrived in Kathmandu and stayed three months during which we resumed our joy for mountain walking. But it was to be another decade, in 2013, before my work on a human rights project would really expose me to the real lives of its people.

The tale of Nepal is a tale of two countries: the majestic mountain highlands that the climbers and trekkers see—wondrous as they truly are—and the lowlands of the Terai that the tourists never see. In between is the royal palace situated in the capital of this tiny Hindu kingdom.

Back on my first visit in 1978, I saw young King Birendra dashing past in his red Alfa Romeo coupe along the as yet uncluttered streets of Kathmandu. Much loved by his people as an avatar of Lord Vishnu, he needed no close protection. Educated at Eton and Harvard, he was eager to modernise his tiny kingdom through democracy and economic development, and maintain harmony with India and China who glared at each other from across his borders by delicately steering a policy of non-alignment. He had no inkling of the future that awaited him.

On 1 June 2001, it was reported that his son Prince Dipendra shot him, his mother the queen and six other relatives at a family gathering in the palace before committing suicide. Prem however confided that many Nepalis believed he was murdered by his brother Gyanedra to whom the throne then passed. Whatever happened, the government censored the assassination clumsily:

> The wildest reports have mentioned differences among members of the royal family to the point of some imagined shooting, a palace coup and such preposterous concoctions. The less said about these fabrications the better.

These events hastened the increasingly militant Maoist insurgency that had been fermenting for some years to overthrow the monarchy. A 'people's war' of internal armed conflict soon erupted and continued for over a decade in which thousands were killed, with numerous human rights atrocities on all sides. Gyanendra was authoritarian and deeply unpopular. Scandal-prone and ill-suited to the role, he was finally forced to abdicate. The civil war ended with the signing of the Comprehensive Peace Agreement between the Maoists and the government in 2006 which abolished the monarchy, dissolved the constitution and established a constituent assembly the following year.

Ever since, Nepal has experimented bumpily with parliamentary democracy. It has suffered wild political instability, often violent rioting and perpetually dysfunctional public services. The new parliamentary assembly was mired in learning how to function, starting with the daunting task of drafting a new constitution. Its members were unable or unwilling to reach compromise on any of its key issues. The process stalled dismally amid factional squabbles, obstructionist posturing, walk-outs and petulant power sharing. When finally formulated, it suffered violent birth-pangs, with scores dying in clashes over what they considered its defects. In some years, the assembly enacted no legislation whatsoever. Decision-making on even non-contentious matters became routinely logjammed. Everyone agreed on the need to widen the city's narrow streets to ease steadily worsening congestion, for example. But the government's road-widening program constantly stalled, because it required the demolition of homes, further obstructing traffic lanes with equipment standing idle for months on end. When I returned ten years later, to complete the Annapurna Circuit with friends in 2025, even this project had been orphaned by the next government, and I found myself snared in traffic that was ever-more congested.

Nepal is a fragmented and impoverished society. One fifth of its population of 30 million live in dire poverty. Among the poorest are the ethnic Madhesi, a minority who live a subsistence existence on the Terai—the lowlands along the southern border with India. When the Muslims of northern India rose up during the fourteenth century, Hindu and Buddhist Indians fled to this region to escape religious persecution. Ethnic Madhesi now make up 20% of the Nepali population. But they remained politically marginalized despite the new constitution guaranteeing equality, and among the most economically disadvantaged.

The Terai lies between the Himalayas to the north and the Indo-Ganges plain to the south. Occupying a quarter of Nepal, these fertile flatlands are the country's most agriculturally productive region and are the economic heart of Nepal. Major crops include rice, wheat, sugarcane, jute, tobacco, and maize. In addition to agriculture, there are also manufacturing industries producing jute, sugar, soap, cement, leather and some textiles. Living conditions are, however, extremely rudimentary, with most dwellings made of timber and clay with thatched roofs. Villagers often share their homes with livestock. In summer, temperatures can reach 40 °C; in the monsoon, there are increasingly frequent floods. The winters are brief but often harsh.

Abject poverty besets most of the people living on the Terai. Among the problems they confront are dismal living conditions and few opportunities to prosper, dysfunctional provision of even the most basic services such as clean water, primary school education and health care, social fragility and instability as the legacies of the civil war. These problems affect many, but for most Madhesis they are disproportionately worse.

Compounding the challenges of poverty and political instability, Nepali society is riven by schisms of patriarchy, as well as entrenched caste, class and ethnic divisions. The political situation remains unstable and volatile with simmering contention over 'federalism', leaving the inclusion of marginalised groups such as the Madhesis and Dalits unresolved. At the launch of the republic in 2008, the Madhesis called a general strike demanding political inclusion, which brought the economy to a complete standstill. Exasperated by their continuing exclusion, the Madhesis then staged violent closures and lock-outs—known as 'bandhs'—that crippled the economy and killed scores of people across the Terai.

Life is particularly grim for Madhesi Dalit women. They are the invisible and silent victims of daily injustices, notably physical and sexual violence both inside and outside their homes. In Madhesi society, it is culturally appropriate for women to be seen but not heard. They are generally uneducated and illiterate. They work all day in the fields, then prepare meals for their menfolk. There is no romanticism in their backbreaking work in the paddy fields. Their poverty is grim and unrelenting. Madhesi women, and Madhesi Dalit women in particular, are massively disadvantaged. Certainly, they are not alone in their disadvantage. But equally certainly, they are four times more vulnerable to physical and sexual violence than most people. Gender, ethnicity, caste and poverty conflate to embed their exclusion and systemic injustice.

Caste remains pervasive in Nepal, despite being formally outlawed in 1962. The caste system is arcane and extremely complex but, in essence, it is similar to that of India: the highest are *Brahmins*, and the lowest are *Dalits*, colloquially known as 'untouchables.' By privileging the language and culture of higher-caste Hindus, the modern state has marginalized non-Hindu and low-caste groups, with the result that they are ignorant of the law and their rights to protection.

Between 2010–2013, after completing the doctorate, I plunged back into practice in Nepal to apply what I had discovered and learned in reforming the courts better.

I returned many times to work in Nepal with the International Commission of Jurists, an INGO with an office in Kathmandu which was led by Frederick Rawski, a courageous quietly spoken human rights defender from New York with vast experience. I had been drawn by my admiration for ICJ's defenders working in the trenches of intense conflict, such as the Maoist insurgency where all sides were tainted by atrocities. In Nepal, the ICJ focused mainly on transitional justice and peacebuilding framed by the post-conflict situation. In addition to Prem, our team comprised some immensely impressive lawyers who spoke truth to power by calling out injustice. In later years, Hari Phuyal became Attorney General and is now a Supreme Court justice. Govinda 'Bandi' Sharma fearlessly investigated these atrocities and was later appointed minister for law. Bidhya Chapagain completed her doctorate exposing the lack of public trust in the impartiality and independence of the courts. And Satish Kharel continues his practice as an advocate leading public interest and class action litigation.

Besides stewarding this remarkable team, I watched Frederick being riven in his role to position the ICJ to privately build coalitions of change with the government, while simultaneously holding it to account publicly for its manifest shortcoming. Balancing both challenges, however much needed, demanded the perspicacity of Odysseus in navigating through the rocks of Scylla. More often, he resembled Saint Hippolytus whom, legend would have it, was dragged over the countryside by horses pulling in different directions until his flesh was torn by thistles and stones and finally pulled apart.

My own work, which was much less torturous, focused on improving access to justice for the Madhesi Dalits and other women of the Terai. They were unseen and unheard by government, the police or the courts, resulting in an abject justice gap for those who were unaware of their rights as citizens to protections under the law. My work was to undertake research of legal and political developments to redress them. Without this research, I would have remained blind to the realities of their disadvantage.

We aimed to improve the quality of justice for these marginalized women. Family and sexual violence is an unusually severe problem in Nepal. Our research revealed that 51% of Nepali women have suffered violence — emotional, physical, sexual and economic — in their lives, and 31% in the past year alone. This is almost double global benchmarks. Despite the prevalence of sexual violence, however, fewer than 10% of victims reported these crimes to the police for fear of bringing stigma. Deference to men is deeply imbedded in Nepali culture. For this reason, rape in marriage is still rarely penalized despite it being outlawed as a crime and, when it is, it is treated much more leniently than rape. Domestic violence continues to be widely seen as a private 'family' matter that would bring shame to both the victim and the family if made public. When victims do report, they are usually told to go home because it is domestic business. These crimes are also underreported to avoid aggravating the perpetrator to take revenge. Consequently, the perpetrators are rarely, if ever, prosecuted and even more rarely punished. The impunity for these crimes against women then remains embedded in culture and protected by patriarchy.[60]

Our work took us out of Kathmandu to remote communities in the foothills and on the plains of the Terai. We also brought women together from across the country. The benefits of these meetings were multi-directional education and sometimes lead to transformative change. On some visits, we were joined by judges from the supreme and appellate courts who were willing to address these meetings by explaining the law, the role of the courts, and the services available to protect them. Stepping out from their chambers to talk at public gathering required some courage. They encountered desperate needs beyond their awareness, often fundamental misunderstanding, and sometimes anger. These meetings also gave people a rare chance to have their voices heard, raise concerns and obtain solutions.

For girls growing up in this society, their future prospects are narrow. Over recent decades, the availability of education in Nepal has improved considerably, with massive tenfold growth in secondary schooling. But it is still severely limited. School attendance remains uneven. Most Madhesi Dalit girls living on the Terai, estimated at 76%, have never attended any school. While the national literacy rate has doubled since the 1980s, only 15% of children attend school on the Terai. Attendance is at its lowest among girls, and Dalit girls—in particular—are often reluctant to attend school for a number of reasons. They are expected to help their mothers in the home; they often cannot understand the dialect of instruction; there are very few toilets for them to use; and as they got older, they are embarrassed to use the fields to 'tend to their menstrual cycles'. In effect, they remain trapped in the generational exclusion of Madhesi women.

One hot afternoon on the Terai, I was attending village meetings around Mahottari near the Indian border. I was travelling with Mohan Kumar Karna a passionate younger lawyer working with the ICJ. We had stopped near his family home to get some refreshments and were shown to a small mud dwelling with a thatched roof. I had to bow down to enter the doorway. It was dark inside. The bare mud walls were blackened with soot, and there was no lighting other than that cast by the flames of the fire. A woman was squatting on the earth floor in the gloom brewing tea. For fuel, she was burning buffalo dung patties that had been dried on the walls outside. The smoke from the dung burned my eyes and throat, unsurprisingly, since it contained carbon monoxide, sulphur dioxide and other toxic pollutants. Prolonged exposure causes respiratory diseases, commonly for women and children. The furniture was sparse, comprising a single pallet for a bed, bench or table. Wordlessly, the woman made tea, which was scalding, sweet and delicious. Sitting behind her, I saw a teenage girl. She returned my smile and we talked with Mohan's help acting as interpreter.

Her name was Asma—'She who is exalted' in Maithali, a language similar to Hindi which is commonly spoken on the Terai. She was almost fifteen, and she was the only girl in the village who was going to school. When she told me she could read, her eyes gleamed with pride and hope in the light from the door. Some of her friends were already married and had children. They would stay in this village, Mohan explained tersely, and face a lifetime of backbreaking work in the paddies, cooking for their families, and choking in the dung smoke. After our fleeting meeting, I wished her well. I felt inadequate to dismantle the structural obstacles stacked so high around her, and hoped that she could venture farther and live a fuller life. But I will never know if she has.[61]

In Nepal, as also in Haiti, I witnessed and experienced what I had previously only read about in history books. Sometimes the massiveness of change—revolution, civil war, natural disaster and all the ensuing political turmoil—simply overwhelms the state, rendering it unable to operate. This is the current story of Nepal. The function of nascent democratic government crumbled like shale under the weight of the overwhelming needs. The resulting failure of the Nepali justice system to protect women and children from physical and sexual violence constitutes a colossal justice gap. The courts of Nepal, like most government institutions, are hopelessly underfunded. Our endeavours to improve access to justice were often eclipsed by transitional justice claims arising from the civil war. The government usually responded to Dalit women with indifference and rebuke, leaving their injustices unattended. But this could not be justified by the existential dangers of revolution, civil war, earthquake, dire economy or the country's faltering journey to democracy. While I found that the judges were generally ethically minded, most were enervated by the lack of resources to meet the needs that surrounded them. In practice, it was easier to turn a blind eye. Buck-passing by senior powerholders in the police, prosecution and judiciary revealed a deeply embedded vicious cycle which excluded the vulnerable and needy women and girls, particularly Madhesi Dalits, from the protections of the law.

Looking back at our work now, I understand that our ambition exceeded our budget and timeframe. Grasping at this opportunity, we had breathlessly attempted in just a 3-year project to take on what required normative and generational change. What we actually needed to bring change was 20 years of support. It took slow steady work to establish our presence, and then to build the demand for and the supply of improved court services—in communities and the judiciary respectively—to protect these people as normal citizens would insist on being treated. Did we eradicate domestic violence, exclusion or poverty? We did not. But we did provide ground-breaking training in human rights awareness; we supported women claiming their rights to protection in court; and we witnessed women's groups taking hold of their agenda, police starting to prosecute complaints, and judges starting to convict offenders. It had taken a lot of slow steady work.

These changes were exciting, even quietly transformational. Madhesi and other Dalit women living on the Nepali Terai do now know that they have legal rights to protection; the police do know they have a duty to enforce these rights; and the judges do know they have a responsibility to uphold and protect them. It is a start; we laid the foundations for substantive normative change. It now remains for the future to reveal what outcomes these changes will bring.

Langtang was obliterated by the earthquake, and I have never found out whether Ditya survived. But the village has now been rebuilt and relocated across what remains of the valley. Simultaneously, we laid some foundations of legal protection for Asma and her friends on the Terai for others who may follow to build upon.

Pacific: Doing No Harm

We had arrived on Pentecost on the weekly supply plane. Pentecost is one of the larger islands of Vanuatu. I was travelling with Wendy Raptigh, a tireless quietly spoken Ni-Vanuatu lawyer working in the courts who had volunteered as my guide. It was a relief to see the densely forested flank of its mountainous spine emerge over the horizon. We had flown from the picturesque capital, Port Vila, in a single engine plane which had been buffeted through clouds 1500 m above the churning ocean. Had its engine failed, we would surely have vanished as others had into the vast depths below, beyond any prospect of rescue. Thankfully, the plane glided across the radiant coral fringe, over the palm canopy, landing bumpily on the dirt runway.

There are few roads on Pentecost. From there, we visited remote communities by boat on waters that were so still in the lee of the mountain there was no knowing where they ended. There was no horizon to carry the sky, only the infinity ahead as we cleaved our spreading wake behind us. It was mesmerising.

The Pacific Ocean is a vast extraordinary expanse over which many of us have flown on our way to somewhere else. It is our largest ocean, covering more than the entire land area of the Earth and half of its total water surface. It is the deepest of all oceans, the Mariana Trench being one mile deeper than Mt. Everest is high. It extends from the Arctic to Antarctica, and from America to Asia. Within this breadth are literally thousands of islands of Micronesia, Melanesia and Polynesia, each unique in its culture and traditions. Some like Fiji and Samoa are mountainous and volcanic, while most are low-lying coral formations, like Kiribati and the Marshall Islands, acutely vulnerable to global warming and increasingly often becoming submerged by encroaching seas.

Over the centuries, the idea of the Pacific has lured philosophers, writers, artists and adventurers as a mythically romantic, unspoiled destination of pristine islands, laden palms, exotic fruits and spices, voluptuous dancing women and legions of missionaries in search of souls to save. All of which are true. Certainly, its cobalt waters are astonishingly beautiful. The philosopher Rousseau celebrated 'the noble savage', the artist Gauguin painted them, the writer Louis Stevenson set his

L. Armytage, *Confronting Injustice*,
https://doi.org/10.1007/978-981-95-3573-6_12

adventures of 'Treasure Island' among them, and I myself had often been garlanded by dancing women in welcoming ceremonies.

But the full reality is of course also more complex. The islands of the Pacific vary in traditions and religions from Indigenous animism to missionary Christianity. Traditional lifestyles and cultures remain vibrant, particularly on the more remote islands. Later, on our visit, we met a painted man in a loincloth practicing supernatural rites and other traditional rituals in a cave on the island of Espiritu Santo. But most islanders now wear shorts, ride mopeds and use mobile phones—digital technology being a significant force of connection and social transformation. Although many have limited contact with urban life, modernity is encompassing and unrelenting. Most children go to school, and some go on to university. But economic, environmental and political fragility are major challenges for the region. Older people may reminisce of a time when the climate was benign, they lived in pandanus huts and subsisted on fishing and coconuts—and many still do. But the seas are rising. Kiribati has an official policy to relocate its entire population to Fiji, in preparation for the approaching day when it is completely submerged by the ocean, as does Tuvalu with Australia. Samoa is a beautiful, mountainous country with fertile volcanic pastures overlooking the magnificent blue sea, but it must export its brightest youth to New Zealand in order to find work and eventually migrate. The economy of the Cook Islands rests on tourism, but others like Tonga remain afloat on foreign remittances alone. In picturesque Fiji, racial tensions simmer between the Indigenous inhabitants and indentured labourers trafficked by imperial Britain from India to work in the sugar plantations: there are deep fissures in society which have triggered four coups since its independence in 1970, and poverty is rampant after the demise of those plantations. The Solomon Islands descended into anarchy when it was recently overrun by armed ethnic militia necessitating a regional military intervention. And in PNG, a war of succession smoulders on Bougainville over the ownership of its vast minerals, and *raskol*s may still terrorise the streets.

I had first dreamed of working in the Pacific as a university student, lured by the romance of stuffing my degree in a backpack and adventuring into the great blue yonder to make the world a better place. But that had to wait for half my working lifetime until I had something useful to offer. That day came 25 years later when I was approached by Bryan Beaumont, a senior judge of the Federal Court of Australia. He had heard calls for help while sitting as a visiting judge on the region's appeal courts. Bryan had a devotion for the Pacific and understood the needs of its impoverished courts, which I respected and rapidly learned to share. He had garnered some seed funding from the UN which awarded me the job of mapping the needs of these courts and designing a program to help them.

In 1998, I relocated to the University of the South Pacific which occupies a glorious campus beside the glittering ocean in Suva, Fiji, where I was accommodated in the academic lodge situated in the botanical gardens. Each morning before dawn, I was startled awake by a truly astonishing cacophony of parrots and other wildlife.

Professor Mere Pulea, my counterpart and generous mentor, let me share her office. Here, I immersed myself in researching the region, discovering countries I'd previously hardly knew existed: the Cook Islands, Federated States of Micronesia, Kiribati, Marshall Islands, Nauru, Niue, Palau, Papua New Guinea, Samoa, Solomon Islands, Tokelau, Tonga, Tuvalu and Vanuatu. Most of the inhabitants of these islands were continuing to live traditional lives in small, remote communities, where they had little or no exposure and access to the courts. Their disputes were resolved, or not, using customary practices. My first excursion was to Kiribati, a newly independent nation with a population of 100,000 people living on 33 islands scattered across a breathtaking 3.5 million km^2 of ocean, which still takes weeks to traverse in a supply ship. At that time, a single expatriate judge and village chiefs administered its justice in the state and island courts respectively. My following weeks were an extraordinary adventure of discovery in encountering barriers to justice in distance, culture, knowledge, logistics and resources that I'd never before contemplated. After 3 mind-expanding months, I completed the plan and returned to Sydney in search of other work, which would take me farther afield from Azerbaijan, Haiti and Mongolia to all the places described in earlier chapters.

A decade later, in 2010, the Federal Court of Australia initiated the unique step of establishing its own development program and invited me to lead their bid to support the courts of the Pacific. This was an extraordinary opportunity to work on my earlier plan. In the meantime, a relay of donors had taken over from the UN—including the Asian Development Bank, British DFID and AusAID, each recognising the merit of supporting these courts. Now, the Government of New Zealand was soliciting a tender for further technical assistance.

I was drawn to the Federal Court, after working for some years with private firms contracting in the aid sector who didn't seem to really understand the role of the courts. Nor did they express much interest in finding out. For those businesses, or 'body shops,' justice was just another transactional commodity that needed to be streamlined, like urban transport or hospital bureaucracy. Their preoccupation with improving efficiency rather than justice was the anaemic service that resulted, lacking substantive outcomes for beneficiaries in terms of their quality of justice. Moreover, their profit-orientation usually led to cheap expedients. By then, I had also learned that the courts were uneasy in their dealings with governments and their commercial operators. The notion of judicial independence might seem esoteric to the public, but it is crucial in protecting the credibility of the justice system. Most chief justices believed that the community was more likely to trust the courts to give a fair decision when they are seen to stand separate from government and other interests. They understood the fragility of public trust which is non-existent in many countries like Cambodia or China where the courts conspicuously serve government as its enforcement arm, and the difficulties of restoring it.

I had experienced this reserve in Vincent Lunabek, Chief Justice of Vanuatu. He was a highly principled jurist, who had presided over many contentious cases involving his government, sometimes resulting in the jailing of its ministers. He was scrupulous about protecting the independence of the courts from interference. Some years ago, a disgruntled litigant had torched his courthouse, burning it to the ground. Ever since, the Supreme Court had been obliged to conduct its hearings in a converted residence, while funding could be found to rebuild it. After years of searching, the only funding available was offered by the PRC. China had been active over recent years in building its constituency of supporters across the region to consolidate its support at the UN over the 'Taiwan issue.' It had built government infrastructure—offices, stadiums, even courthouses—in several other Pacific Island Countries including the Cook Islands and Samoa. The Chief Justice has however steadfastly declined its offers to avoid creating any expectation of favours ever needing to be returned. In doing so, he has remained without a courthouse. Indeed, when I visited him on behalf of the Asian Development Bank, which is funded by all the governments from region including China, he declined to meet with me or even to respond to my emails. When I visited him on behalf of the Federal Court, however, he always greeted me effusively. French-educated, he is a charming man who speaks English with Gallic mannerisms, a twinkle in his eye and sometimes an occasional wink.

At the Federal Court, I was working with two other lawyers: Helen Burrows a quietly impressive woman who had set up the court's development program and earned the trust of its judges to steward what is the only court-run program in the world, and Lorenz Metzner a tirelessly resourceful man of meticulous thoroughness whose operational and financial oversight enabled me to sleep soundly at night. Together, we gathered our networks to build a world class team of professionals from the US, UK and the region. Over the following decade, we won a series of continuing contracts, which together became the longest and last assignment of my career.

I savoured this work, needing to think carefully about how best to support the courts in the Pacific owing to their distinctive cultural contexts, extraordinary diversity and dispersion across vast spaces. The region is often talked about in singular terms as 'the Pacific Islands' suggesting a homogenous union of states and peoples with shared features and needs. The reality is that it is a 'region' in name alone, with enormous variations within and between Melanesia, Polynesia and Melanesia. These embody diverse social and cultural endowments, colonial legacies, as well as past or continuing relationships with metropolitan powers. While we had what seemed a substantial budget of approximately AU$ 20 million, it was miniscule in addressing the size, volume and spectrum of needs. A single country, like PNG or the Solomons for example, could readily absorb that entire sum.

The vibrancy of tradition and culture across the region means that for most people the notion of justice remains customary or, at the very least, pluralistic and hybrid. Over the years, it has been convenient for outsiders to describe the delivery of justice as operating in two compartments, variously as the 'formal' or 'state' domain of law, and as the 'informal' or 'traditional' domain of customary law. This dichotomy has been convenient in enabling outsiders to differentiate between the two in order to focus on supporting the courts in administering state law. In reality, however, it is over-simplistic because it misconstrues how justice is usually dispensed. In many Pacific Island Countries, most 'judges' are non-law trained customary actors, like village elders and chiefs, who take on a variety of legal-cum-traditional roles under the aegis of the court. At times, they must grapple with the impact of the state's formal constitution on their traditional practices of corporal punishment and banishment. The notion of two distinct hemispheres is misleading because they overlap, sometimes leave gaps, and at other times compete or collide, most commonly in aspects of human rights. In effect, the chiefs cannot operate autonomously outside the constitution, just as the judges and magistrates cannot operate without custom and customary law. This co-dependency becomes particularly relevant when settling land disputes which are the most common form of disputes in the region. This pluralism, hybridity and fluidity in daily practices at the interface of customary and modern justice remains a vast though under-mapped vector of justice delivery across the region.

The nature of the relationship between the state and custom varies markedly from place to place. In some communities, social cohesion is strong, and the chiefs wield substantial authority; in others, traditional authority has been eroded and the police are expected to play a more active role. Chiefs sometimes complain that the police are diverting cases to the Magistrates Court to be resolved under state law when they should have been heard customarily in the Island or Village Court, thus eroding the community's respect in the chiefs' role and authority. Conversely, serious crimes such as murder and rape that formally fall within the exclusive mandate of the state's criminal law, are in practice sometimes dealt with more expeditiously at the local level owing to the non-availability of police and the remoteness of courts.

This complex of co-existence and co-dependency generally operates surprisingly smoothly. Broadly speaking, customary and court actors understand and act within their respective roles. While politicians, historians or anthropologists might argue about the march of modernity, this hybridity is stable, vibrant, fluid and surprisingly functional.

On Niue, I worked with Darren Tohovaka who was the Secretary to Justice and the court Registrar. Niue is a minuscule Pacific Island country with a population of some 11,124 people. There are three principal villages in Niue, and Darren also served as a chief of one of these villages. When he spoke of his village, I could feel his sense of identity, responsibility and pride.

'In my Village, we go fishing every day. Then I spend time with my boys teaching them our customs.' he told me.

Darren was a chief and had duties to perform for his family and community. The way he said 'my' village with such quiet pride connoted where he was grounded and belonged. This was the centre of his universe, and he was sharing it with me. In those moments, I realised the preciousness of his world, and envied his sense of community and belonging which has no equivalent in our modern cities.

The major reason for the prevalence of customary law is cultural. For most people, tradition and custom define their daily lives harmoniously. There are facets of customary justice, however, that are clearly broken. Notably, sexual crime is a major problem across the region where both customary and state justice generally fail the victims. The prevalence of family and sexual violence is almost twice the global benchmark in a number of countries, notably Kiribati, PNG and Vanuatu, on the best available data.

I sat in many community meetings with Wendy listening to the problems and needs of these local people. To begin with, we experienced the dead hand of patriarchy and taboo; everything was fine, we were assured in open meetings. That is, until we conducted our consultations by gender, listening to the experiences of the men and women separately. Very quickly, I learned to step back, sitting quietly in the shadows, while Wendy facilitated discussions in Bislama, the local language, translating important extracts as they arose. These were special experiences of considerable intimacy when women opened their hearts to speak of the unspeakable, telling often heartrending stories of hardship, violence and disempowerment.

Patriarchy, custom, tradition and ignorance of state-based law are all factors that inhibit the redress of justice. Social taboo and lack of education have embedded a tolerance for domestic crimes as being 'family business.' The victims of these often-violent crimes are usually women who rarely report them because they have little or no understanding of their rights and are generally afraid of the courts. When we interviewed some victims, they reported that they lived in constant fear and often felt most unsafe inside their own homes. They complained that they had nowhere else to go and had been forced to put up with abuse. Compounding this problem, their churches preached the Christian virtues of submission and forgiveness rather than offering to protect the victims or to chastise the perpetrators. Similarly, community chiefs do not usually intervene, and when they do, it is to encourage reconciliation. Police are rarely stationed in remote communities; in those communities where they are, victims often complain that they are too lenient, turn a blind eye or lack appropriate training. The predominantly male police, unsurprisingly, share many of the same social norms and values as the wider society, so are often indifferent or unsympathetic to imported notions of human rights and gender equality in societies characterised by communalism, patriarchy and often rigid forms of social hierarchy. Most communities do not have adequate information on the justice system or understanding of their legal rights. This situation is exacerbated by a shortage of lawyers and legal aid, which further restricts victim representation. Here we found a major justice gap where both customary and the law courts failed to redress injustices.

These problems are exacerbated by the existence of substantial barriers that obstruct claimants from seeking justice through the law courts. These barriers include geography, remoteness, cost, legal literacy and the availability of services such as lawyers and legal aid. Geography and distance in particular make it difficult, if not virtually impossible, for those living in remote communities to reach a court without extraordinary cost and delay. While courts do visit some bigger outlying islands, they do so occasionally and intermittently owing to cost, and all serious matters are relocated to the capital. Travel to the capital by boat is expensive and slow and can sometimes take many days; air travel is more rare and much more expensive. These cost factor affects both individuals in search of justice and the ability of the justice system to provide coverage to widely dispersed local populations, which are prohibitively expensive in the archipelagic countries like Kiribati, Solomon Islands and Vanuatu.

Many of the communities' needs stem from the fragility of traditional notions of peace and harmony. The limited reach of the state, unemployment, and the haemorrhaging of young people offshore combine to erode traditional social authority structures. These in turn jeopardise social stability and erode human security. When we consulted these communities, we found the levels of public confidence in courts and the police on whom they relied ranged from the moderate to the precarious. They shared their experiences and told us many stories which coalesced into three major problems access to justice, provision of substantive justice outcomes, and the efficient delivery of justice services.

Accordingly, we designed a wide-ranging program to address these needs with the goal to build the courts' capacity to deliver justice more accessibly, fairly and efficiently. This consisted of many activities to improve access to justice through legal empowerment, court outreach and community legal education. It also provided training to build competence and professionalism; promote human rights; improve efficiency and assist elders delivering customary justice. We provided a lot of training, particularly to local trainers to take over the training others. Wendy was one of these trainers; she was a natural who, in addition to working as a lawyer within the Supreme Court, took on responsibility for managing and delivering its training program.

We worked to rebalance the prevailing procedural approach which focused on improving court efficiency by reducing delay and backlog. While important, this approach was insufficient without also focusing on substantive aspects of justice such as equality and the ability to exercise human rights—for example, women's rights to physical and sexual security. Concentrating on procedural reforms is easier to implement and measure, but it can create perverse outcomes. In Cambodia, for example, I had earlier seen how Australian aid had supported the courts to conduct hearings more efficiently, that is faster, which had unwittingly accelerated the perverse outcome of dispossessing the poor from their land. To this end, we focused on improving the awareness of human rights by recruiting advisors like Dr. Carolyn Graydon, a staunch human rights defender who had forged her conviction and resilience in the refugee camps of Palestine and Syria.

A significant part of my own work was to improve access to justice by enabling unrepresented litigants to exercise their rights, that is, the majority of local people who routinely appeared before a court without a lawyer. Given the scarcity of lawyers in most communities, this involved travelling to and learning more about some of the most remote communities in the world. In conducting these consultations, I travelled far beyond the tourist path to distant atolls that resemble specks on the ocean from the window of a jetliner. I spent days in launches slicing through shimmering waters so still it was impossible to discern where the ocean ended and the sky began, and others through heaving swells between atolls. I spent further hours flying in single-engine aircraft across the vast ruffled ocean; still more bumping along corrugated tracks in the back of a 4 × 4; followed by nights sleeping beneath the limitless canopy of the heavens.

I am outward bound again, heading north into Asia or east into the Pacific, at 35,000 feet above the endless sparse hide of the Australian outback until the ocean's rim is reached. The constant display of patterns change below my window: cultivated paddocks rapidly giving way to the tendrils of dried riverbeds, and bleached flats of salt lakes that splash against the hillocks lining up in rows like sand dunes peppered with the speckle of scrub, who knows how thick, far below. Then passing through legions of clouds powdered and fluffed against the infinitely blue-black sky, blown relentlessly eastward tethered by their shadows across these landscapes. These ancient landscapes of reds, purples, ochres and tans untouched by any roof or road, fence or powerline. Is the distant skyline flat, or can I see the gentlest curve of the earth's orb? I cannot honestly tell, yet never cease to wonder. How I loved those many years of flying into Asia and the Pacific, passing through the monsoonal towers of turbulent clouds 8 miles high into limitless skies beyond that blend seamlessly with the ocean into infinity. These journeys gave me precious space to contemplate the present, reflect on the past, and dream of the future for hour on hour. How I savoured these moments of each journey that neither Aristotle nor Leonardo could ever experience. I am mesmerised in these spaces sheltered however temporarily from the rush and flurry of departure and arrival. And on each return, they are waiting to welcome me home. Every time.

These journeys took me to extraordinary places. On one visit to the island of Pohnpei in the Federated States of Micronesia, I discovered the mysterious ruins of Nan Madol. These little known ruins rival Easter Island for their outstanding archaeological significance in the Pacific. Sometimes also called 'the eighth wonder of the world', Nan Modal consists of 92 artificial islands spread over 200 acres abutting Pohnpei's mangrove-covered shore. Among the many remaining structures, the royal mortuary is the best-preserved. It is set within twin 8-meter walls built to repel the ocean and encloses an area the size of a football field. Its construction remains a mystery on a par with the Pyramids. It is estimated to have been erected in the twelfth century from massive blocks of black basalt weighing up to 50 tons each, taken from a volcano which is on the opposite side of the island. Many locals believe magic was used to build this megalith. As I clambered across the coral around this now deserted site, I wandered at the skilled and resilience of its engineering against the ocean elements over the centuries and was humbled by the mystery of its lost arts.

On another visit, I was staying with Miyako at Aggie Grey's in Apia, the capital of Samoa on Upolu, a volcanic cone, when a massive magnitude 8.1 earthquake struck. At this time, Aggie's was a genteel 3-storey colonial hotel with balconies overlooking the capital's quaint harbour. In earlier times, it had served as a brothel for US aircrews during WWII, hence the informality of its name. We were in the basement gym when the quake struck. It was early, and I was hefting weights on a bench before work, when I noticed to my fascination, then horror, the shadows moving as the concrete beams flexed in the ceiling above me and the entire building started to shake. Then the lights flickered. Rushing outside, we stood wobbling in astonishment on the roadway as the bitumen literally rippled backwards and forwards beneath our feet. Emergency sirens wailed across the township. Then flustered hotel staff rushed us with other guests to the upper floors. But when we saw from the balcony the harbour emptying before our eyes like a huge sink, we grabbed our passports and scarpered up the mountain. We were the lucky ones. On the other side on the southern coast, 189 tourists sleeping in their beachfront chalets were crushed against the coastal escarpment or swept out to sea by the tsunami, many without a trace. This toll was only finalised months later when their entry permits expired without an exit stamp.

Nature struck once again while I was visited Mangaia, a remote outlier of the Cook Islands inhabited by about 500 people living in three small villages. One Sunday morning, when all the locals were in church, I ventured to the shoreline and positioned myself on a coral outcrop to photograph the surging 7-meter ocean rollers. I was awed by their unrelenting force and the untiring procession of spearmint green waves that gleamed in the sun as they crested the reef. Each wave was then lacerated by the coral and finally collapsed on lesser outcrops some metres below me. I was captivated by the dance of these waves for over an hour, clambering from one outcrop to another for a better angle. As I was climbing to a higher vantage point, I sensed the surrounding sounds change. Turning, I saw the ocean surging higher than ever before. A rogue wave just meters away was charging me at chest-height. In that frozen moment, I dropped my prized camera to grasp for handholds in the coral. The wave slammed me hard, front-on, sweeping me off my feet and tossing me over. As I was churned around in the turbulence, the coral diced and sliced my shoulders, arms, hands and feet. But mercifully, my head was spared. Then it was gone, vanished as suddenly as it had come. Choking and dazed, I tried to stand, but couldn't. Was I alright? I was shaking all over. My teeth were chattering. I had to get out of the water, but I was now barefoot and could only crawl. It was agony. Somehow, I made it back to shore. Blood was dripping along the rocks. I saw a flipflop bouncing over the coral as it was sucked into the surging ocean. My camera was gone. I found half the telephoto-lens sheared from the body by the force of the wave. The camera, a professional Nikon weighing one kilogram, glinted through the water 20 meters out. It was electronic; destroyed. I left it and crawled up the slope where I slept. But I was soon woken by the pain of my lacerations stiffening.

When I finally got back to the village, it was mid-morning and deserted. The clinic was closed, but the nurse kindly came her home to clean my contusions. Two days later, they infected from the coral. I was so lucky; I had only fractured an elbow. It took me three nights before I fully realised how easily that wave could have brained me against the rocks and sucked my body straight out into the massive ocean without a single trace. Thankfully I was spared and able to return to Rarotonga on the main island, and then limp up to the hospital.

It is in remote communities, like these, that island or village court magistrates commonly presides over disputes on behalf of the state. Selected on the basis of their community's respect, they are usually untrained. Despite their formal knowledge of state law being elementary at best, and their grasp of principles of fair trial being intuitive, this arrangement has operated well over the years. There were however complaints about bias in small close-nit communities where the magistrate knows everyone and is related to many. These perceptions are difficult if not impossible to avoid, but they can undermine the credibility of the courts. Training is also needed in many fundamental aspects of substantive law and procedure, judging skills and ethics to improve their ability to administer justice in line with evolving social expectations.

To address these needs, we designed induction-level courses on law, justice and the role of the courts for island magistrates and courts officers which was delivered as part of a Certificate and Diploma of Justice by the University of the South Pacific, in which Wendy taught and Ingrid Kabua, who appears in the next chapter, and many others enrolled. The focus of these courses was on the particular needs of these magistrates. While the content of these courses was technically elementary, I was fascinated in writing the course that the task of reducing the complexity of the law into what is simple and clear can often be surprisingly challenging.

One afternoon on our travels through the islands, I sat quietly at the back of a community hall watching Wendy delivering a workshop. She was fashioning its lessons for a group of lay magistrates from neighbouring communities. I listened to the murmuring of their discussions in Bislama, *Nasonal lanwis blong Vanuatu*, (the national language) as she painstakingly clarified a principle of fair trial.

Mekem i Stret—'(As a magistrate) you must be fair,' she said.

'You cannot decide any case that involves your relative because it may be biased, or it may appear to be biased—at least, not without disclosing your relationship and getting the agreement of the other side,' she told them.

As she explained these concepts, one of the magistrates mouthed her words silently as she spoke. I saw flashes of recognition in their eyes at the same epiphanies of learning that I have experienced in my own postgraduate classrooms. It was enchanting to witness.

Hundreds of judges, magistrates and clerks have now completed these courses across the region. Establishing the Diploma has provided a stairway for the many motivated clerks and magistrates to qualify in law and in due course become eligible to serve as judges. This now provides a new stairway for the appointment of the first Indigenous Pacific island chief justice in the Pacific, which Ingrid and others are climbing.

Interest in this program was such that we then adapted segments for inclusion in the secondary school curricula of several Pacific island countries which has included Kiribati, Vanuatu, FSM and RMI to date. Adapting this program for schools extends the opportunity for learning much more broadly by laying the foundations for vastly improved community understanding of law and justice. It will help anyone who is needy to access the courts across the region. This work and its legacies are among the highlights on my path to building fairer societies.

Over this decade, we worked as best we could with the courts to help improve their delivery of justice and thereby the quality of human wellbeing across the Pacific. In doing so, we conducted hundreds of activities and trained hundreds of judicial and court officers on law and court efficiency and literally thousands of the public on human rights and family violence. We then consulted the communities in urban areas across the region on their levels of their satisfaction with the courts. While sampling was always statistically challenging, more than 80% of respondents reporting experiencing greater competence and reliability; three-quarters experiencing improvements in integrity and conduct, and more than two-thirds experiencing greater efficiency and accountability. It requires slow humbling work, comprising many incremental steps, to help build fairer societies.

During this final decade of my career, I had worked to apply my best understanding from all the experience and research gathered in some many countries along the way. In doing so, I had learned and also unlearned a huge amount. It is always challenging work, and altogether too easy for novices to oversimply the complexity of both the technical and ethical issues and thereby their solutions. I was endeavouring to promote a more just society by helping the courts to perform their functions effectively.

In doing so, I had started by seeing myself acting as an agent of change, which was always a challenging role; to improve without harming. I had now experienced that change was possible; indeed, changes certainly did happen. But they were incremental, often tangential and invariably much slower than expected. They were also characteristically unpredictable and uncontrollable. Observing this over extended periods of time working in many different places has caused me to understand my role differently now. Being an agent of change suffers a modernist conceit of presuming change is controllable and linear, which the evidence of practice repeatedly refutes. It further suffers a neo-colonial conceit of presuming that our vision of change is the best. I have relinquished any presumption of some God-given ethical right to direct and impose change from outside. Instead, I see my role as being an influence who, at my best, may share experience, disrupt statis and inspire the efforts of local champions to mediate the reallocation of their own interests.

My final advice to the New Zealand government was to reposition and develop future support to strengthen the role of the lowly 'hybrid actors'—that is, the thousands of village chiefs and island magistrates—who work from day to day at the interface of customary and state law to deliver justice across the Pacific. I am pleased this advice was accepted. I had learned to respect the age-old adage 'if it ain't broke, don't fix it'. In doing so, I had completed a circular journey to build fairer societies which had started by my presuming to improve through change and finished by my respecting the past and presuming to protect and preserve what was working well. It's a very delicate balance.

Marshall Islands: Whose Justice?

We were among the few passengers to disembark at Kwajalein.

It was a surreal experience. Stepping off the plane, despite being on official government business, we were interrogated by armed US soldiers before being confined in a razor wire enclosure. Was this what Guantanamo felt like, I wondered? But no, it was more bizarre. Through the mesh, we could see a golf course on which white people wearing Bermuda shorts were playing. Beyond were rows of spruce suburban cottages behind white picket fences and mowed lawns.

I had worked across the Pacific for almost 20 years before visiting the more remote parts of the Marshall Islands. I thought I knew its history, but I was still shocked by what I found.

In 1954, the United States detonated a 15-megaton thermo-nuclear bomb, called 'Bravo', on the Bikini Atoll in the Marshall Islands. It was 1000 times more powerful than the atomic bomb it dropped on Hiroshima at 8.15 on the summer's morning of 6 August 1945 which killed 120,000 civilians instantly. So powerful, it vaporized an entire island, carving a crater beneath the lagoon.

Since WWII, the US has tested 67 nuclear bombs in the Marshall Islands, over many of the islands in the Bikini and Enewetak Atolls. Some of these were lost in the ocean where they have been abandoned to degrade over time.

Then in 1977, the US built a concrete dome on Runit Island in the Enewetak Atoll, to bury a million cubic meters of radioactive soil, including Plutonium-239 which is the key isotope used to produce nuclear weapons. This was what remained of 30 megatons of nuclear waste generated in the Marshall Island tests and from others conducted on the American mainland, as well. This dome was called the 'tomb.' It was enormous with 45 cm-thick walls. The LA Times reported that US Army engineers had noted radioactive leakages even at the time of construction. Since the 1990s, its footings have degraded further, haemorrhaging nuclear waste into the waters of surrounding atolls. Columbia University also reported this waste was causing coral bleaching, extinction of marine life and damage to the islanders' health. The US government has however repeatedly denied responsibility. It has

L. Armytage, *Confronting Injustice*,
https://doi.org/10.1007/978-981-95-3573-6_13

asserted that the dome is safe. Even if there is any leakage, it is insignificant. And anyway, it's on Marshallese land, so it's their problem. The dome remains unguarded in the ocean.

When I visited in 2018, I was working with the Federal Court of Australia to support the courts across the Pacific to administer better justice. We were partnering with the courts of the Marshal Islands, and I was travelling with Ingrid Kabua who was the chief clerk of the courts. We had flown to the Kwajalein Atoll from Majuro, the capital, which is situated on an oval shaped narrow reef—like a massive nail clipping floating on the vast ocean from the windows of planes passing overhead—which is almost 50 km long. This reef encompasses a lagoon where visiting mother-ships from Asia drop anchor while sheltering to store the catches of their trawling fleets fishing nearby.

The Marshall Islands have a population of 42,000 people living on 1225 islands scattered across three-quarters of a million square miles of the Central Pacific. Most live on Majuro. During WWII, these islands were occupied by the Japanese, until they were 'liberated' by the Americans. In 1979, the United States granted these islands independence as a self-governing nation in an economic 'compact of free association' with the US.

The Kwajalein Atoll is an active US Army Garrison. Called 'Missile Alley' and the 'Missile Islands' in the press, this atoll has been used by the US for anti-ballistic missile testing and rocket launching from the Ronald Reagan Ballistic Missile Test Site since the late 1950s. It is a restricted military area from which even the Marshallese are prohibited without a permit. Each year, the US fires four intercontinental Minuteman 111 missiles from the Vandenberg Space Force Base in California 7000 km across the Pacific. Whenever it does, it closes all shipping lanes through the atoll to intercept the missiles, disrupting Marshallese fishing in their own waters for their livelihood.

After some delay, we were escorted by the soldiers out onto the jetty for Ebeye, some seven kilometres across the atoll, to stay overnight.

Ebeye is widely called the 'slum of the Pacific.' It is a small, densely populated island of 80 acres on which 13,000 people are squeezed. It serves as the dormitory for those lucky enough to have jobs as canteen workers or gardeners for the Americans on Kwajalein. Some 60% of the population of the Marshall Islands are unemployed. The American base is the largest employer in the region. Ebeye is also home for some of those evicted from their islands by nuclear contamination. Living conditions are cramped. Most live in a squalor of poverty and unending boredom. Unemployment is their main occupation. Elders lament the disruption of customary life from their traditional communities. There are high levels of substance abuse including among women; teen pregnancies among girls as young as 10 are commonplace; and the rates of suicides and depression are alarming. There is no space for even a single park or playground. The coastline and streets are littered with rusted machinery and festering rubbish. I was shamed to witness what the West has done, and relieved to hurry on the next morning.

After a lengthy ride on the official police launch, we arrived at the other end of the atoll. Life is much better here on Ebadon, a small coral island lush with palms and pristine white sands. It is home to a small community of some 100 people who live self-sufficiently on copra, pandanus and fishing. There is a primary school buzzing with chattering children. Remarkably, there are no police or government representatives, other than us. The elders or pastor mediate occasional land disputes, rowdy intoxication from moonshine and occasional fist fights. 'We're happy,' they assured us, describing their customary existence as being in equilibrium with 'the gospel.'

We already knew that most people in the Marshall Islands still enjoyed traditional lives under the protection of customary law. But at the same time, they had little idea about their legal rights under state law, or how to exercise them in a court of law. This lack of understanding constituted a critical barrier to justice—like others including distance, language, culture and cost. Without access, there can be no justice. This creates a 'justice gap' for Islanders when they ever confront having to deal with the formal system, usually in criminal matters, but also in land disputes when they are heard in state courts. To fill that gap, we were working to help traditional communities to know their legal rights and understand the role of the courts in protecting them. At the same time, the courts also needed to train their own staff, most of whom had no formal induction in the law. To address that parallel need, we had developed a new Diploma of Justice working with the University of the South Pacific to give court staff a career stairway of education that could lead ultimately to judicial appointment.

Across the strait, on the island of Mejato, we were greeted by a larger community who put on a lavish feast to honour our visit. But behind their smiles and the gay colours of the women's dresses was a grim story. They were the refugees and their descendants from Rongelap Atoll. Within hours of the Bravo detonation in 1954, 5 cm of fine white ash descended like snow to cover the island, its crops and their drinking water. It contaminated everything and everyone with radioactive nuclear fallout. The islanders suffered immediate radiation sicknesses inducing vomiting, diarrhea, skin burns and hair loss. After two days, the US evacuated everyone. After some time, many became homesick. When the US government ruled the island was again safe, it repatriated them. By the early 1960s, however, women started to suffer double the normal rates of miscarriages, stillbirths and thyroid tumours. By the mid 1970s, two-thirds of their children had thyroid tumours. But by then, their pleas for re-evacuation fell on deaf ears. Many Marshallese believe that the US was treating them as 'human guinea pigs' to study the continuing effects of radioactive fallout.

Finally, in 1985, the INGO Greenpeace intervened. It despatched its ship, the 'Rainbow Warrior,' to make four trips relocating 300 islanders with their possessions to Mejato some 180 km away. At the time, Mejato was a barren, unoccupied island with no infrastructure or community facilities. From there, some moved on to Ebeye in the hope of finding employment at the US base. But most have stayed on Mejato and continue to remain in limbo. Later, in 1985, the Rainbow Warrior was bombed and sunk by the French secret service in Auckland Harbour, killing one crew member, in a heinous display of imperial bile in retaliation for Greenpeace's successful activism to end France's atomic testing in the Pacific.

In 1988, the US belatedly established the Marshall Islands Nuclear Claims Tribunal to address the Marshallese's claims for compensation. Almost twenty years later, in 2007, this tribunal finally ruled to award these refugees more than US$1 billion in damages. As recently as in 2012, however, the Obama administration asserted that it had already adequately compensated the Rongelap victims and has refused to comply with its own Tribunal's ruling. The US has compensated each survivor with a stipend of $75.00 per quarter from a jointly managed trust fund of $70 million. But having by then exhausted its total allocated fund of $150 million for compensation, the Nuclear Claims Tribunal ceased to function and was dismantled.

When we met these Rongelap refugees 70 years after the 'Bravo' test, they remained incensed by their eviction, the inadequacy of compensation and the mistreatment that they were continuing to suffer. The outrage of their injustices is literally cancerous. Medical evidence supports the elders' account of the radiation cancers continuing from generation to generation. The impacts of nuclear testing within the Pacific Proving Grounds are clearly evident in the prevalence of radiogenic diseases. Increased incidences of heart disease, diabetes, and obesity are also associated with changes in dietary patterns and lifestyles imposed by forced evacuation from their homeland.

After the feasting when we had listened to their stories, I asked Ingrid how she felt about what we had heard.

'There is not a lot to dispute, add, or take away. It is sad, but it is the honest truth.'

Ingrid has the centred presence of a matriarch, even as a young mother, not easily given to histrionics or hyperbole.

'It makes some almost believe that the long arm of justice is short of reach of the looming shadows of the US's unthinkable crimes and blatant disregard to a society that it has forever maimed, mangled, and bungled up,' she added quietly.

An intense sense of the injustice of America's mistreatment pervades the Marshall Islands. Indeed, I find it impossible to overstate the nature and extent of these injustices: America asserted dominion over these islands; tested nuclear weapons that contaminated and killed their inhabitants; expelled them from their homes and exiled them to a barren outcrop; insulted them with derisory compensation; and then brushed aside the judgment of its own tribunal of their entitlements to just reparation. Then, the US ignored Marshallese's territoriality, jurisdiction and the primacy of its domestic law. These actions reveal a continuing and blatant disregard for the rule of law when it affects its own interests, and it asserts impunity in disregarding the determination of the Nuclear Claims Tribunal. At their core, these injustices arise from an abuse of American power which renders its conduct little less than coercive.

Every Marshallese whom I met felt abused and exploited. The extent of these injustices is starkly revealed in the question: would any American citizen accept $300 per year ($75 × 4) as fair and adequate compensation for the contemptible treatment which they have endured? Certainly not. A single American litigant could possibly exhaust the entire fund of $150 million in a US court before a jury of her peers. But there is a massive power imbalance that inhibits the Marshallese from finding a fairer process and solution. Political disempowerment and economic dependence on the perpetrators of these injustices continue to gag the Marshallese from publicly expressing their outrage.

American—western—concepts of justice have failed. Clearly, there is a mismatch in norms and expectations for justice in the plight of the Marshall Islands. So how could this mess have been handled better, I wondered? Could these injustices be resolved using local custom?

For the peoples of the Pacific generally, and the Marshall Islands in particular, most conduct is governed by custom and disputes are resolved through customary law. Customary law is that body of traditional rules and practices that enables community members to distinguish between acceptable and unacceptable behaviour, and to take action accordingly. It embodies the norms, conventions and practices that a community depends on to resolve its disputes. These norms may vary from community to community. In most communities both customary law and state law play accepted social roles. There is some overlap between customary law and state law: for example, in serious criminal matters and major commercial disputes. Generally speaking, however, state law has limited relevance in most traditional communities, such as Rongelap, which continue to resolve their problems according to local customary law.

A distinctive element of customary law in the Pacific, including the Marshall Islands, is the notion of restorative justice. In many communities across the region, restorative justice is much more important than any adversarial contest in the formal system. While this traditional path to dispute resolution may vary from country to country, even from village to village, there are some unifying characteristics. These are primarily concerned with assisting victims and restoring community harmony. The quality of the justice outcome is intrinsically inclusive, with all affected people being satisfied that they have had a real opportunity to participate, be heard and redressed. All parties, including victims, offenders and interested members of the community are encouraged to collaborate and reintegrate. At its heart, it sees a dispute as a disturbance or injury to human relationships in which the victims and the community are central to the resolution process. Reaching a final resolution in this way may involve protracted discussions, negotiations, bargaining and compromise. It is a holistic approach to peacemaking and reconciliation which aims for mutually acceptable 'win/win' outcomes. A successful resolution is celebrated with ceremonies, exchanges of gifts or payment of appropriate reparations, thus re-establishing a stable relationship between the disputants.

Restorative justice differs profoundly from state justice which emphasises concerns such as uniformity, predictability and certainty. Indeed, in state justice, criminal behaviour is determined through an adversarial process prosecuted by the state that excludes the victim and focuses on guilt, retribution and punishment by the state on a '*win/lose*' basis. These differences are sometimes summed up by describing state notions of justice generally focusing on '*law and order*' and customary notions focusing on '*peace and harmony.*'

Ingrid suggested that a better description for customary justice might sometimes, however, be '*harmony over truth*.' While local custom is unique and still strong, it can sometimes also act as a double-edged sword in repressing open discussion about injustices. She explained that the Marshallese people are culturally non-confrontational, meaning that they are hesitant to disagree with those in power. Indeed, she sees a weakness of customary law in situations of power-imbalance where the cultural tendency towards consensus-making may create outcomes that favour what the stronger party is willing to tolerate. She sees another weakness in the tendency to maintain and embed the social hierarchies of the leaders, including often strongly patriarchal norms, even in places with matrilineal land inheritance systems. In some Pacific communities, for example, women are not allowed to be present or speak during certain customary processes, even when the case concerns them. On such occasions, customary law principally benefits those sitting in the circle. Justice is not always served to those who have no voice, or victims who are pressured by society or religion to forgive their perpetrators, allowing them to repeat their wrongs. Hence some caution is needed to avoid over-romanticising the idea of customary law as a panacea for all problems.

We then took a big-game fishing launch from Majuro to the island of Arno for further consultations, some 40 km across surging ocean of the most intense sapphire blue colour I have ever seen. On the return voyage, the skipper trailed a deep-water line in the boiling wake as the launch ploughed through the waves like a tireless horse. A cry from the bridge broke my reverie. Some distance behind, a marlin's silvery flank flashed in the sun as it leapt five metres clear into the air fighting the line. Again, then again, it leapt, fighting the thrust of triple outboards. It was a massive creature, sharp as a spear yet thick as the trunk of a tree, and equal to the full power of the launch. But slowly it tired. When it was finally hefted aboard, its bill thrashed and slashed to each side, then it reared one last time as its tail crashed against the desk. Get back, yelled the skipper. In its last moments, electric streaks of iridescent blue pulsed silently along its flanks. Awed beyond words, I was rendered speechless by the taking of such a majestic life, which is allowed in Marshallese culture provided that it is shared among the whole community.

As we pounded our way back through the waves, Ingrid come across to sit beside me.

'So, do you think I should do that Diploma of Justice course, then?'

'Absolutely,' I urged her, 'you'll ace it!'

And she has, becoming the first graduate to complete the diploma and then upgrade to enrol in the law degree. This is the entry qualification for judges. I am hoping that one day she may also be appointed as the first Indigenous woman to serve as Chief Justice of these Islands.

Later, I was reminded of America's continuing presence and power, when we returned to Majuro. We were travelling aboard the official police launch again across the shimmering ultramarine waters of the 'middle corridor' when the skipper abruptly changed course. Why? I asked Ingrid. We were approaching the islands of Meck, she explained. These islands were 'restricted', even to the government. Meck was a ribbon of coral facing towards China. It was part of the Ronald Reagan Ballistic Missile Defence Testing Site and the base for US anti-ballistic Sprint and Spartan missiles. Most recently, Meck has been used to launch missiles, including the menacing '*Exoatmospheric kill vehicle*,' to intercept ballistic missiles with a 'hit-to-kill' capability. I could see the flat profile of this coral outlay broken by the hulks of military silos, radars and other infrastructure across the still waters of the atoll. Despite our official governmental status, I could feel the skipper skittering across these waters as quickly as possible. No question: this felt like the real-life lair of James Bond's villain Dr. No.

But it's not just on RMI. The wreckage of other people's wars litter many of the islands of Micronesia, Melanesia and Polynesia. Abandoned but unexploded WW11 ordnance and other munitions continue to kill and maim countless islanders every year which, even after eighty years, the perpetrators remain ever tardier to clean up.

On Rongelap, justice has yet to be delivered. The injustices which the Marshallese have suffered under the hand of America are visible in plain sight across the Pacific. These injustices can be seen in the context of the ongoing geopolitical competition between China and the US, which is currently playing out across the Pacific, echoing earlier geopolitical struggles between imperial powers who carved up and appropriated these pristine islands over the past two centuries. They go some way to explaining China's current welcome in parts of the region.

For all that, Western approaches have evidently failed to resolve legitimate and substantial grievances of the Rongelap and other communities. Customary approaches to conflict resolution in the Marshall Islands provide other ways to resolve injustices. Not only are these approaches more familiar to local claimants, but they remain vibrant and are continually adaptive. They may well be better fit for purpose. But reform endeavours have too often been blind to and even disrespectful of the many strengths of customary justice that cohere stable communities. We have much to learn from the Pacific islanders' concepts of restorative justice, and this learning begins by respecting the subtleties of their evolution over millennia.

Making Sense

Voice: Journey to Fairness

To make better sense of my journey, I undertook two research degrees along the way to find my voice. The first of these was in the '90s on the education of judges (Cht 4) and the second, fifteen years later, was on reforming the courts more generally to deliver better justice. Both served to transform me.

In Australia, we are fortunate to have honest courts and competent judges—which is unlike most of the places where I have worked. But even in Australia, most ordinary people cannot afford to exercise their rights owing to the cost of lawyers, the unfairness of the adversarial justice system where the wealthy monopolise the best counsel, and the inordinate delays.

Having crossed the razorback described in the chapter "Crossroads and Catharsis", I resigned from the Judicial Commission and returned to private practice, this time as a consultant. The imperative to survive and support my family provided massive incentives to build a viable consultancy. It was both terrifying and exhilarating. I had planned to apply what I had learned to improve the performance of the court system. But I soon found that opportunities to work with the courts in Australia were scarce. So, I adapted this plan and began advising major law firms, government and other legal service providers. After working with the Aboriginal Legal Service (Cht 5 "Unequal Australia"), I had the revelation about injustices surrounding me and the need to support the courts to deliver better justice wherever opportunity might arise. I then embarked working on many overseas aid programs beginning in Palestine (Cht 6 "Conflicting Histories"), then Pakistan (Cht 7 "Chaos and Charm") and PNG (Cht 8 "Colliding with the Present"), among many others across Asia, until most recently the Pacific (Chts 13 "Doing no Harm" and 14 "Whose Justice?'). Along the way, my role grew quite rapidly building from educating judges into reforming the courts within which they were often mired.

Over the following 15 years, I was swept off my feet, working in more than 50 countries, from Azerbaijan to Haiti, and from Mongolia to Myanmar in what became the most rewarding work of my career as a specialist in justice reform. Here, at last,

L. Armytage, *Confronting Injustice*,
https://doi.org/10.1007/978-981-95-3573-6_14

I had found my vocation to build a fairer world by helping the courts to administer better justice.

In many countries, I witnessed that most people routinely went without justice because the court process for delivering justice was often broken. In Australia, my own country, the Aboriginal Legal Service is dismally under-resourced, and the prisons are disproportionately filled by the churn of Indigenous people, with little visible prospect of breaking that vicious cycle. In Port Moresby, Papua New Guinea, my colleagues' physical safety was threatened on a daily basis by extremely violent crime which regularly fell beyond the control of the justice system. In Ramallah, on the West Bank, I worked with court staff so poorly paid that they openly procured illicit commissions. In Multan, Pakistan, I met litigants whose grandparents' disputes remained entangled in the courts for 60 years. In Panjshir, Afghanistan, I worked with judges who were untrained in even the basics of secular law. In Ulaanbaatar, Mongolia, I worked with judges who were transitioning from the former Soviet system to the free market, and who were totally unfamiliar with even the most fundamental notions of property rights and the enforcement of contracts. In Dhaka, Bangladesh, I worked in courthouses without electricity or any wherewithal to keep records. And in the Pacific, I worked with judges who had never been trained in state law. How could justice be administered under such circumstances?

In Phnom Penh, I worked with judges who knew that challenging the government for stealing land from customary owners had career—even life—terminating consequences. That year of struggling to engage with government leaders who were only interesting in harvesting foreign aid to fill their pockets was one of my most challenging professional experiences. I was filled with a deepening sense of despair at the corruption and betrayal of government through elite capture; by the acceptance of abuse of power; by the yawning chasm between the rich and the poor but, mostly, by my own futility in remedying these realities. From the overwhelming disappointment of these experiences arose my mounting misgivings about the prevailing approach of the World Bank and other agencies to development efforts that were preoccupied with economic growth rather than the pursuit of justice.

Indeed, the ideals of justice are routinely subverted in most countries. I remembered the lack of fairness, the massive cost and protracted delays that I had first experienced while practising law in the Australian courts, which had spurred me to entering this endeavour. Once again, John Hudzik patiently reminded me of the adage: 'The rich get a fine and the poor get time.' This applied not only in the US but also in my own country, particularly for Indigenous people.

Citizens, usually the powerless poor, are denied justice through impunity, corruption, abuse of power and the denial of rights. Over the past fifty years, development agencies have spent billions of dollars grappling with the challenge of improving 'the rule of law' through improving economic growth and good governance. But the results had often been underwhelming and, on occasion, dismal.

Promoting justice is self-evidently important to alleviate the privation and sufferings of injustice. But my experience of practice showed that it was fraught with a range of philosophic, conceptual, technical and operational challenges.

Why is promoting justice so difficult? I now found myself asking. There are several reasons, the main being explained, I believe, by the nature of justice itself and the process of change. Justice, which I will argue at its most simple is fairness, is a universal public good. The concept of justice is both normative and contextual. By this I mean that it rests on values or norms embedded in a society, which may vary comparatively depending on their context. Any change in the status quo to promote more or better justice for members of that society will affect the allocation of interests of its members. Indeed, a just outcome in one society may vary from that in another, provided it is fair—that is, it has been dispensed evenly between those members.

In practice, many of the injustices that I have encountered and endeavoured to redress over the years have required some measure of change in those norms, for example: to promote fairer societies where everyone—including the marginalised poor—can exercise their legal rights equally. Another topical example is to improve women's rights of physical and sexual safety from violence. Changes like these are complex because they rest on and affect attitudes and values which are deeply embedded in social structures and practices. These changes require long term integrated strategies including for example, cognitive change through awareness-raising and educational activities, like seminars, which are necessary but in themselves insufficient. Unfortunately, in practice, most project-based reform initiatives usually lack the opportunity, resources and timeframes to support more complex longer-term changes. Hence their results are often incomplete, provoking the usual lament that more time and resources are needed. Additionally, the 'political will' of governments and the continuity of donor agendas are often fragmented and disrupted by changing administrations, ideologies and priorities. Happily, this has not been the case in Australia's support for justice in its closest neighbour PNG over the past thirty years. But this continuous support, which in my experience is exceptional, acknowledges the iterative nature of the change process and the lengthy timeframes required.

Sometimes the challenges of promoting justice can be better understood in terms of political economy. Political economy is a branch of the social sciences that focuses on the interrelationships among individuals, governments and public policy, and more specifically seeks to explain how political institutions and economic systems influence societies in making public decisions. Simply put, it posits that powerholders retain a vested interest in the status quo because it favours their interests, and accordingly they resist change. This view builds on 'zero-sum' thinking which frames life as a battle over finite goods and resources where gains for one mean losses for another. It sees these resources as being in limited supply that requires cut-throat competition resulting in a winner taking all in a win/lose approach that increases inequality. The alternate to seeing these goods differently is 'positive-sum' thinking to share collective benefits on a win/win approach through cooperation and collaboration. The recent failure of Australia's referendum for an Aboriginal voice of parliament in 2023 can perhaps be best understood as displaying the prevalence of zero-sum rather than positive-sum thinking.

Justice is in its very nature contested, but it would be excessively cynical to claim that promoting justice is invariably or usually obstructed. While all parents sadly know that we must teach our children that there are wicked people in the world, it is my experience that human nature is only rarely malevolent. It is more appropriate to explain these difficulties arising from the existence of diverse interests in any society which often differ, usually coexist, but occasionally collide. The usual consequence of these phenomena is stasis, inertia and what social scientists call path dependency. This asserts that history matters: what has occurred in the past persists essentially through momentum and resistance to any change that tends towards a deviation.

The difficulties facing justice reform also have a perceptual dimension. Justice is in its nature intangible, difficult to see, and most commonly noticed in its denial. Measuring more just societies can certainly be undertaken for example in terms of statistics reducing the time of delays to trial, and others increasing the numbers of prosecutions and convictions of crimes and rights violations. But human rights and women's safety are usually invisible to the eye, unlike bricks and mortar infrastructure where a donor's new bridge, school or hospital is immediately clear for all to see. Its results are characteristically more difficult to discern, and then inferentially through proxies. When justice reforms work, no one notices the decline of injustices, but until then those injustices remain in sight.

Surely, there must be a better way! I now told myself. My choices were stark: I should either leave the development field before I—like too many others—became a cynical drunk, or I must confront these challenges by mustering everything that I could to find a better way. At its heart, this was the choice of optimism over pessimism, hope over despair, in seeing my work as being a glass half full rather than half empty. Once so framed, my path became clear. I drafted my doctoral proposal which was a critical evaluation of the global practice of justice reform, and an argument for an improved approach. It was accepted. I then declined the poisoned solicitation to extend my UN contract in Phnom Penh, outlined in Cht 10 "After Year Zero", and returned back to the academy for find solutions to the problems I had encountered.

I began by returning to my earliest work in PNG by framing these questions:—

> Night after night, in the long hours of the pre-dawn, I awake in Port Moresby, jolted by panic at the enormity of the justice problems, and what at those hours seems the almost laughable insufficiency of $100 million to address them. Why is this? What is wrong? What can I do to help fix them?[62]

To find answers, I immersed myself once again in researching the literature. Moving beyond the comfort of the familiar was daunting. I was filled with uncertainties. I was initially confounded by the narrowness of my knowledge and humbled by my bottomless ignorance. The more I knew, the more I discovered how little I knew. But I was hugely encouraged by my supervisor, David Kinley, whose stewardship was the best support any candidate could hope for. Soon, this journey became intriguing, then exhilarating, as I discovered the joy of ideas, marvelling at their beauty and astonishing power to make sense of the world.

My research of these ideas rapidly revealed that justice has been recognised as being core to the good life, good government and good society since antiquity. All human societies have institutionalised structures that embody varying renditions of justice. A society without justice denies human well-being. A government without justice is tyranny. The impunity of the powerful, and corruption among those charged to protect citizens and mandated to deliver justice, stifle both equality and fair treatment. I became preoccupied by the contest of interests which can deprive citizens of their rights to happiness. This is the core challenge of promoting justice. In recognising this, I understood the centrality of the contest that I was now grappling with. And, more so, I was enthralled that each generation since Aristotle has evidently confronted this contest.[63]

Aristotle explained the functions of society and the role of government to promote wellbeing, which he had called happiness, in a voice which was as relevant to me now as it evidently was to the Greeks in 328 BC. The Enlightenment thinking of Hobbes, Locke and Rousseau had then ignited revolutions which toppled despots and popes.[64] Discovering the multi-disciplinary dimensions of this research—whether in law and justice, philosophy, economics or political science—was hugely enriching. I revelled in the joys of interdisciplinary study, discovering how differently philosophers, political scientists and economists framed problems and thereby solved shared solutions. In watching these disciplines working to apply themselves to solve any particular social problem, I was intrigued to see that lawyers 'pull' to avoid undesirable behaviours through punishment, for example, while the economists 'push' to incentivise desired behaviours through rewards.

So, what is justice? I had already discovered in my work that there are many paths to justice around the world. Concepts of justice are culturally defined and bound. Some of the major traditions include the Western, Islamic, Confucian, Hindu and indigenous traditions. Each of these is distinctive, having different purposes and forms.

Justice embodies values which societies institutionalise through their laws and courts that administer those laws. All societies comprise some basic structure of institutions that embody renditions of justice, whether formal or informal. These renditions may be political (focusing on governance, social affairs and the allocation of interests), economic (focusing on opportunities for livelihood), social (focusing on civic order and safety) or humanistic (focusing on fundamental individual rights). There are numerous expressions of the purpose or teleology of justice. Justice may be primarily utilitarian—concerned with maximising social outcomes; egalitarian—concerned with equality of opportunity, individual rights and freedoms; distributive—concerned with allocating interests in wealth, power or privilege; retributive—concerned with punishing wrongdoing; or restorative—concerned with restoring social harmony. These expressions of justice may also be variously seen in terms of equality, need, reciprocity or deserts. Justice is sometimes distinguished from social justice. Potentially tautological, social justice is an evocative but no less amorphous concept that is usually invoked in lay contexts to emphasise the primacy of principles of equality and human rights to advocate for more egalitarian opportunities and outcomes which are similar to the distributive expression above.

As an Australian lawyer, I had been trained in the Western tradition, which was grounded in the thinking of Greek philosophers, like Aristotle, who emphasized the role of virtue and the state. It then built on Roman principles of law, and Christian values of morality and ethics that emphasized mercy, forgiveness, and the dignity of the individual. These foundations were then overlaid by the Enlightenment thinking of Locke and Mill to embody ideas of natural rights, utilitarianism, the social contract and concepts of liberalism highlighting the primacy of the individual and their rights.[65]

Consequently, I understood justice as being the notion of fairness and moral rightness in the treatment of individuals and the allocation of resources in a society. On this rendering, I saw my pursuit of justice as steering towards the ultimate goals of promoting fairness, ensuring equality and protecting individual rights, and thereby fostering social harmony and the common good. I saw a good justice system as being one that resolves disputes fairly and maintained social order upholding principles of liberty, equality, fairness, and respect for human dignity.

I focused my research on helping the courts to deliver better justice. I had worked with the courts all of my career, and was already familiar with their strengths and shortcomings. But more important, while many injustices are perpetrated politically, that is in the allocation and misallocation of interests by the executive government in any society, it is the judicial arm of government rather than the executive that is constitutionally mandated to independently administer justice according to law. Hence, my thesis focused on reforming justice in terms of rights that have been allocated in law; that is, in the juridical sense, rather than in the executive sense, of allocating political interests[66]. I wanted to help the judicial arm of the state—being the courts, judges and related personnel—to adjudicate the law and administer justice better.

In my work, this understanding was then enriched by being exposed to other conceptions of justice. I was fascinated to experience and explore the diverse notions of justice and the foundational values that they variously upheld. In Vietnam, Phong had taught me about justice based on the primacy of the citizen's duty to the communal interest trumping the individual's rights and freedoms. Here, I encountered Confucianism ideals originating in China, emphasizing values of public order, social harmony, the importance of hierarchical relationships and adherence to laws. My work with Samdani and Shafi'sbs and Dr. Rai in Pakistan and other Muslim countries like Afghanistan, had exposed me to Islamic notions of Sharia, derived from the Quran and Hadith, which emphasizes both divine law and human legal traditions. My work across the Indian sub-continent particularly in Nepal with Prem and Bidhya, had exposed me to Hindu influences of dharma encompassing duty and righteousness to guide personal and social conduct, including notions of karma and cosmic order, overlaid by British colonial 'common law'. Sometimes these notions of justice, for example in Cambodia, were influenced by Buddhism which emphasizes concepts of karma and compassion, where justice is viewed in terms of destiny and the order of natural consequences, ethical behaviour and the pursuit of enlightenment. In transitional Mongolia, I experienced the Soviet centralised command model of justice undergoing adaptation to the American free market model by replacing the inquisitorial process of adjudication with the capitalistic adversarial model of trial. In PNG, Stephen taught me about the Ela Beach test and the importance of staying focusing on people, the beneficiaries of justice. In the Pacific, more broadly, Ingrid and Wendy taught me about vibrant customs and traditions of restorative justice that was primarily concerned with a focus on the victim and the restoration of social harmony—which could usefully fill significant gaps in our own justice systems, should we simply respect them sufficiently to see. In doing so, I witnessed that each system is constantly evolving, hybridising and adapting—for nothing is static.

Each of these conceptions of justice is foundationally diverse, normatively plural and socially contextualised. Political scientists, like my friend John Hudzik, argue that justice is however subjectively perceived, being nothing more than what each of us might want it to be in any given distribution. Yet this hasn't stopped philosophers from trying to understand justice by defining it objectively. The challenge this attempt confronts is that notions like 'justice' are arguably humanistic concepts that exist in a system of thought that centres on the rational, autonomous self but ignores the conditioned nature of the individual. If that is so, then any understanding of justice may ultimately be personal, though is no less worthy of our consideration. For all that, I considered it necessary to push forward.

Reforming justice systems and processes—however defined and conceptualised—exists within a complex, dynamic and multidimensional global marketplace of international aid donors. These donors face vociferous demands for aid for the most desperate needs across the poverty spectrum of the Sustainable Development Goals: clean water, health, education, shelter, infrastructure. Within the cacophony of this bustling marketplace, justice is a minor though no less important voice capturing about 2% of the global aid budget.[67] Observers like Carothers have commented on what he describes as the '*rule of law revival*' from the fall of the Berlin Wall in 1989 through to the Noughties, which overlapped much of the period of my working involvement.[68] This period was also described as having 'three moments' (of state managed economic growth, the neo-liberal era of the small state and free markets, and then the enabling state),[69] and as being the zeitgeist of the 'theatre' of the rule of law.[70] Its focus on promoting the 'rule of law' was evolving organically responding to the ever-shifting ideologies, agendas and budgetary priorities of donor bodies around the world.

While donors broadly promoted the 'rule of law' during this period, their interests varied, reflecting a spectrum of rationale for reform spanning economic, political, human and social objectives, which was described as looking 'like the proverbial blind man's elephant—a trunk to one person, a tail to another'.[71] At the multilateral level of international aid agencies, the World Bank was confined by its mandate to promote an economistic—rather than a political—approach to supporting reform of the law courts. It did this as the means to encourage investment by building the courts capacity to secure property title and commercial contracts, guided by the thinking of Nobel laurate Douglas North on 'institutions'.[72] The Asian Development

Bank had an engineering-focused approach on urban and social development, building infrastructure, irrigation and transport systems; while the United Nations framed much of its support on developing human rights. At the bilateral level of donor countries, USAID (then) as the largest donor supported both political and economic goals of democracy and the courts as institutions supporting free markets; the UK supported good governance and the courts to uphold transparent and accountable government; Australia tended to cram its development pizza with 'the lot' but, when pushed, preferred public safety through 'cops and prisons' supporting law enforcement including the courts; while the PRC built government offices and court houses across Africa and the Pacific as part of its broader focus on infrastructure. Out on the scattered playing fields of the development world, each donor jostled for influence, space, position and prestige with their local counterparts and domestic constituencies, respectively.

I now saw most donors' prescriptions of justice reform for economistic, political or social rationale as necessary but no longer sufficient, in effect, as being anaemic in building substantively fairer societies. I found myself arguing that the prevailing focus on primarily promoting aggregate economic growth had put the cart before the horse. By emphasising utilitarian notions of efficiency, it had shown a distributive indifference to notions of equality and a neglect of rights. The prevailing rationale for economic development, in particular, could not sensibly be treated as an end in itself; markets are instrumental in providing social opportunity for transactions. But the pursuit of growth or wealth cannot be the goal of development. It seemed to me inescapable that development must provide the means to enhance the lives of people and improve civic wellbeing. But left untended, injustice obstructed that. There was a need to realign the reform approach. I now saw that justice itself must lie at the heart of reform endeavour, as a distinct goal rather than as an instrumental means of attaining another.

Justice is a complex, multifaceted and pluralistic concept which is embedded at the heart of every society. Each society builds on its own unique cultural, philosophical, religious and political values in its system of justice. Hence there can be no single system of justice that is perfect or even superior to any other. Given this diversity, how then could I avoid the dangers of being neo-colonial or hegemonic?

These dangers are exposed in the central debate of human rights between universalism and relativism which revolves around the applicability of human rights across different cultures and societies. On the one hand, the universalist position advocates that human rights are universal and should apply to all humans regardless of culture, religion, or nationality. This position is based on two precepts: the first of moral absolutism that there are fundamental moral principles that are universally valid; and secondly on the principle of equality that all people have the same rights. Its critics argue that universalism can impose Western or 'northern' values on non-Western societies, disrespecting the cultural, social and political contexts of other societies. On the other hand, the relativist position advocates that human rights should be interpreted in the context of local cultures and societies whatever they may be. This position is based on three precepts: the first, human rights norms should embody the diversity of different societies. Secondly, notions of morality and rights are culturally dependent and should not be imposed from outside; and thirdly, each society has the right to determine its human rights based on its own values and traditions. Its critics argue that relativism can however be used to shield human rights abuses under the guise of cultural practices, and fragments the underpinning notion of human rights having fundamental principles.[73]

For me, this was an esoteric debate of theoreticians, however important, but not of practitioners. I had resolved this debate in my own work by accepting the principles of human rights as being fundamental on the basis that the Universal Declaration of Human Rights—which declared these principles—was adopted by the United Nations General Assembly in 1948, and that the International Covenant on Civil and Political Rights (ICCPR)—which operationalises these principles—was adopted by the General Assembly in 1966 and has been ratified by 173 countries.[74] These principles had already been formally endorsed by 90% of all countries in the world. I saw no need to obfuscate further in discussion about whether they were applicable. In the real world of practice, the existence of injustice is usually starkly clear; I felt the imperative to move beyond that debate from talking to doing.

In doing so, I addressed two separate dimensions of justice, both of which are essential for just decision-making. Substantive justice is concerned with what is decided and focuses on the fairness of the outcomes having regard to notions of morality, equity, equality and fair distribution. Procedural justice is concerned with how decisions are made and focuses on the fairness of the processes used to make decisions, having regard to fair process, participation, consistency and accountability. While it may not be possible to satisfy all parties to a dispute over the substantive justice of any specific outcome decision, ensuring adherence to procedural justice provides a bridge for most to cross in ensuring they find the process to have been fair.

We lawyers call this bridge the rules of 'natural justice.' These rules are fundamental to procedural fairness and ensure that the process leading to just decision-making is itself fair. They include the rule against bias which ensures that decision-makers are impartial, and the right to a fair hearing. These rules and rights are embodied in Article 14 of the ICCPR. Natural justice, which is also called procedural fairness, is a fundamental concept which is included in legal systems around the world in one form or another to ensure that decisions are made fairly.

In practice, my work has often started by focusing on implementing Article 14 of the ICCPR which proclaims the rights to a fair trial. These rights, which are seen as both fundamental and universal, specify that all persons shall be equal before the courts. Everyone is entitled to a fair and public hearing by a competent, independent, and impartial tribunal established by law. Everyone charged with a criminal offense shall have the right to be presumed innocent until proven guilty according to law. Everyone charged with a criminal offence shall have the rights to be informed of the charges, adequate time and facilities to prepare their defence, to be tried without undue delay, to be tried in their presence, to defend themselves in person or through legal assistance, to have an interpreter, to cross-examine witnesses, and the right to appeal any conviction.[75]

In my experience, the existence of these rights has never been contentious. While I avoided using the label 'human rights' which could trigger ideological baggage, I promoted the application of these rights in the context of each situation. I hybridised my approach by applying these universal rights on a localised basis. Doing this was altogether challenging enough to implement. In doing so, I have never been implicated by others in any hubris of neo-colonial superiority or in any invader's folly of pursuing hegemony.

Appreciating the infinite diversity of different paths to justice, it was my intention to help the courts to improve their delivery of justice within their respective contexts by redressing specific problems and barriers which obstructed them. These problems most commonly included unfairness, cost and delay. My quest was to promote justice as fairness, building as it inescapably does on principles of equality, because I understand and believe that fairness is fundamentally embedded in every society and culture and system of justice. Indeed, it is impossible for me to accept it is ethical or moral to proceed on any other basis. In doing so, I embraced my own ethical responsibility to acknowledge my values, understanding that these may not always be shared by others. Otherwise, I have no choice but to opt-out, which I chose not to do.

While there may be no universal definition of justice, justice is universally identified in its absence.

'But it's *not* fair!' she cried.

I have used the allegory of the 4-year-old child to identify the denial of justice—unfairness, which is anathema to human wellbeing. This child serves as my heuristic device to provide much-needed certainty in the dusty laneways of war-torn Kabul, or under the shading palms of a Pacific coral island. It is quite clear. We have all experienced unfairness during our lives, and in that experience we each know the absence of justice. This understanding is neither ideological nor intellectual; it is visceral and, in that sense, both ontological and universal.

This 4-year-old child is also an analogue of the turtle standing on the back on another turtle all the way down. These turtles are the philosophers' adage that refers to the idea that any explanation always requires a further explanation, which is also known as the regress argument in epistemology that any proposition requires a justification. Any proposition whatsoever can be infinitely questioned. So, it was here that I chose to draw my line in the sand to argue the foundational nature of fairness as the precept of justice—irrespective of society, culture or history. We all *know* when fairness is denied. So, I argued that justice is most readily understood as fairness. Fairness rests on the notions of equality, even treatment and equity. What fairness looks like will depend on its context of social norms and values. Fairness applies to all in each differing context. How that injustice is redressed is however contextual and local. Where unfairness exists, I built on the thinking of John Rawls, another philosopher, who sees justice as being fairness. He argues that fairness rests on equity to require that even treatment preferences the disadvantaged and is not equal, or same, treatment.[76]

I was then illuminated by the clarity and power of Amartya Sen's thinking which argues that justice is ultimately concerned with the enhancement of human freedoms. Sen was awarded the Nobel Prize in Economics in 1998 for his work on the measures of poverty, inequality, and the development of human capabilities which has had a significant impact on the field of development economics.[77] His vision builds on Aristotelian notions of distributional equality, where wellbeing is a function of how fully individuals can exercise their human capabilities having regard to notions of equality and rights. Hence justice reform should aim to enhance people's capability—their freedom—to exercise their legal rights and entitlements.[78]

Sen explores the idea of justice through an enchantingly simple riddle of three children squabbling over a flute that they had found near their village. He asks each of us to decide to whom it should be given: the child who carved it, the child who could play it or the child who had the fewest toys. Our answers reveal whether we are libertarian (rewarding entitlement), utilitarian (maximising benefit), or egalitarian (promoting fairness).[79] Each has its own distinctive merits. In contemplating this riddle, I recognised my own understanding of justice is for promoting fairness. I also realised that my knowing this truth was a priori, that is, an intuition which preceded either proof or ideology. Having done so, I then advocated for justice to be repositioned more centrally in evolving notions of equitable development.

Contrary to American scholars who laud 'newness' as a cardinal virtue of scholarship, I found myself heartened to return to Aristotle who gave me great comfort in the perpetuity of certain truths:

> Man, when perfected, is the best of animals; but if he is isolated from law and justice, he is the worst of all .... Justice which is his salvation belongs to the polis (state); for justice, which is the determination of what is just, is an ordering of the political association ... Justice and equity are neither absolutely identical nor generically different. .... This is the essential nature of equity; it is a rectification of law in so far as the law is defective on account of its generality.... It is now clear what equity is, and that it is just, and superior to one kind of justice.[80]

When the thesis was done, I was so fatigued I could no longer tell whether I had said anything or not. I remained that child who was birched repeatedly for stupidity. I held my breath until the doctorate was awarded. When it was, I was hugely relieved. I was ecstatic though incredulous when it was then accepted for publication by Cambridge University Press.[81] I edited the manuscript in an attic apartment overlooking ancient Perugia, with its swooping swallows over the lovely Umbrian valley, starting each day in the silent stillness of San Lorenzo Cathedral. Miyako and I then shared some celebratory months on a fellowship at the University of Cambridge (which was the alma mater of my never-met grandfather and don Geoffrey Grant Morris) before the launch, where we listened spellbound as the choirs sang evensong that soared to the vaulted domes of the college chapels as the daylight dimmed around us. I then presented these arguments at Oxford, Harvard and Berkeley, and designed courses in the graduate programs of the University of Sydney and the Australian National University which I presented to students over the following decade.

Writing these books has felt photosynthetic to me in the sense of transforming and making sense of all I had learned along my journey. In doing so, I again felt that presence of my grandfather standing at my shoulder silently guiding my step. As he does now. I wanted to map the terrain I had crossed to help myself understand and also to share with others who might follow. This has somehow felt like sending prayers to heaven. When they were published and cited by others, it has felt they are being taken further by those who do follow.

Once done, I returned from the academy back into the 'real' world of practice, as narrated in the middle part of this book, to apply and refine these ideas into my ongoing quest to build fairer societies by helping the courts to deliver better justice.

Sight: Beauty in Unexpected Places

Startled, the child turns in the smouldering wasteland of coloured plastic, medical waste and toxic vapours. She is clutching a bunch of wilted water lilies still tied with pink ribbon. She looks straight at me, frozen in total bewilderment.

I take the shot head-on.

She lived and worked on the rubbish dump earning 50¢ cents on a good day, under the scorching sun. Like hundreds of other kids. Maybe she was 8. There were no records. No schooling. No help. Her name was *Srey Lak*—literally, Beautiful Girl.[82]

Five years later, I was preparing my doctorate for publication. I needed permission to use her portrait on the cover of '*Reforming Justice*'.[83] Somehow everything about her standing with those dead flowers in that garish landscape of urban rubbish framed the whole story better than any words. By some miracle, we were able to find her again. She was still living on that dump. But now her mother had died, she was feral and almost unrecognisable. We put her and her sister through school from the royalties. Here she got fed regularly and slept safely. She learned to read and write, to speak English, and topping her class. Another miracle!

As a child, I was filled with wonder at the magic of photographs that captured moments of life on paper. My camera taught me to see. Through the viewfinder, I learned to find beauty in the simplest things: the finest filaments of fallen leaves, the ellipse of pebbles on a beach rounded through millennia by the pounding waves, the ever-moving sheer perfection of symmetry in a raindrop on water. I was awed to capture their beauty with fidelity. I would peer into the lens, with its glistening eye reflecting my inversion, searching for clues of its power and mystery. As a teenager, armed with my Panasonic, and later an old Rolleiflex, I went hunting for images to capture. I would marvel at the photograph emerging through the gloomy miasma of our bathroom sink which served as my dark room. I was mesmerised as I looked through the lens, chose a subject, composed its position, and waited for my eye to find the perfect moment. The more I looked, the more I could see. My eyes searched for beauty, which I soon learned to find in unexpected places. This was a joyful space where time melted, and I hummed in contentment.

L. Armytage, *Confronting Injustice*,
https://doi.org/10.1007/978-981-95-3573-6_15

How I feasted on the masters of this craft: the lustrous textures of Edward Weston's nudes, the frozen moments of Cartier-Bresson's scampering children, the peerless authority of Ansel Adam's landscapes, the haunting rebuke of Sebastião Salgado's portraits of poverty, and the exuberance of Steve McCurry's exotica.

Photography is a contemplation of light. As I write, now, the view from my window overlooking Sydney is a panorama of our famous harbour. Each day, sometimes several times a day, I photograph this view. My position is fixed, so the cityscape is always identical. Yet every image is different, from the tentative hints of dawn with its first tints of crimson, purple, orange and gold; to an emerging silhouette of the skyline; the radiant announcement of sunrise; then the arc of the sun blazing overhead, descending and dissolving in fading light; the city towers rise shimmering against the darkening indigo sky; the moon arcing through the blackness; and finally, the canopy of stars blinking silently overhead.

Each day, the sun emerges from behind different buildings, traversing from the Centrepoint spire to travel north over the Harbour Bridge until summer's peak, then back. Long ago, I had thought that clear skies gave the best view. But the more I looked, the more I saw beauty in the clouds silently forming and dissolving in a constantly moving display, never still. I became transfixed by the might of storms, flinging wind in my face, rain on the lens with splashes of lightening to reveal, however momentarily, the mighty contests of the elements above. It is always the same view, yet never the same light. As the years passed, the more I looked, the more I could see that this view is never-ending.

And this fascination has caused me to reflect on how our minds work to process visual information. As a lawyer, I have always used words to communicate throughout my career. But as a person, I have more often expressed sentiments through photographs. I have enjoyed working with the precision, clarity and descriptive power of words, and delighted in examining dictionaries for the subtleties of nuanced meanings. Yet, I had also noticed their limitations in affecting audiences. Sometimes my verbal messages just don't get through. When working with judges, celebrated for their mental capacity, I've been interested in noticing how often the pages of reports that I have given them, carefully drafted and replete with detailed footnotes, were open at the pages with images, whether photographs, tables or other graphics. Even the most cerebral readers, like judges, evidently need a mix and balance in how they receive information—adopting in the adage, 'a picture is worth 1000 words.' This extends to storing our mental information. I have found that my memory for places is often stored in images of a view which evokes that place, while those of Miyako are more likely stored the flavours she recalls of the food. When recalling a pleasant travel experience, I will retrieve the scenery, while she'll recall the food—and our memories converge when recalling a restaurant with a view.

These processes have some grounding in science. Neuroscientists have ascertained that certain cognitive functions are localized in one or other hemispheres of the brain. In relation to senses and actions, each hemisphere processes different information. The left is understood to process logic-based skills such as learning a language and mathematics, while the right processes creative tasks such as art, as well as emotion. Hence the school of neurolinguistic programming (NLP) advocates that the left hemisphere engages the analytical, logically ordered, rational and verbal processing of the brain; while the right hemisphere engages with and conveys intuitive, emotional, impulsive and creative expressions.

Once, years ago while working at the Judicial Commission, I was talking with another presenter, who was a senior detective, at one of our workshops. I was wondering whether NLF functioning was primarily a neurological or a metaphorical phenomenon. He responded that it might not matter.

'It explains why we train our new detectives that way we do,' he replied.

'How come?'

'Well, over the years, we've learned to train them to monitor the eye movements of suspects during interrogation. We've found from practical experience that when a suspect looks up to the right, they're probably telling the truth. But when they look up to the left, we've learned they're probably lying. Now I understand why,' he replied with a smile of revelation.

It was partly for such reasons that I was drawn towards photography as a means of improving my ability to communicate. I have spent much of my life using words as a lawyer and educator seeking to influence, persuade and change the ways people think and behave. I could usually communicate effectively using words, but I have found that sometimes I can communicate better using images. As a photographer, I could engage my audience's senses, intuitions and emotions, rather than their thinking and reasoning, which offers an alternative and additional pathway to their cognitive functioning. So it was that I began bringing my camera on my work travels.

As the years passed, I used the camera to portray realities that could affect the viewer in ways that words couldn't. My work took me far beyond the tourist path to spectacular places in many countries with exotic people. My photographs documented what I saw—both beautiful and ugly—for the viewer to contemplate. My challenge was to capture these realities with clarity and integrity. I wanted my photographs not only to attract the viewer but also to prompt and inspire their reflection.

In my first published book of photographs '*Unseen Faces, Unheard Voices*', which I co-authored with Miyako, I wanted to bear witness to the lives of the people I'd met and worked with in Afghanistan, Cambodia, Nepal and Pakistan, most of whom were excluded from the protection of the courts.[84] Those countries are among the world's poorest and often the least just. Afghanistan remains a 'failed state' trapped for two generations in war. Cambodia and Nepal have each collapsed in living memory: one under genocide; and the other in civil war and revolution. Pakistan regularly teeters on the brink of disaster and chaos in the turmoil of terrorism and the corrosion of corruption. These realities are largely the legacies of history in which the present grapples to clean up the unfinished business of the past. The courts in all of those countries too often fail to deliver any promise of justice to the poor and needy. Citizens, usually the powerless poor, routinely suffer injustices as a result of the impunity and corruption of the powerful and inefficiency of justice delivery.

In this collection of photographs, I took the viewer beyond the picturesque saffron robes of the monks, behind the walls of Angkor Wat, and away from the towering beauty of the Himalayas, to tell the stories of those people who go unseen by foreign tourists. These are the garment workers of Phnom Penh, the Madhesi women of the Nepali Terai, the Kuchi nomads of the Hindu Kush, and others with whom I'd worked.

These people are among the poorest of the world's poor. They are survivors of war and genocide; refugees; the dispossessed and homeless; victims of sexual violence and trafficking; slum-dwellers, waste pickers and outcasts. They live outside the state, without any of the services that should be provided to them as citizens. They have little or no access to adequate nutrition, education, health care, employment security or personal safety. Many—if not most—lack any official identity. The law, police or the courts rarely protect them and more often oppress them. For most viewers of this book, theirs is an alien existence; but for them this is their lived experience. They live in diverse societies and traditions — some are Hindu, others Muslim, Buddhist or Christian—but all are victims of injustice.

Many of these subjects are women. Despite their diversity, the disadvantage of their gender is universal. Women are invariably the poorest of the poor, the most marginalized of the disadvantaged. They are most likely to suffer the deepest physical, sexual or economic deprivations, exploitation and injustice. Some are bonded, others trafficked, even enslaved. Life for them is harsh. There is nothing romantic here; the grimness of their poverty is ugly. And yet, there is also a remarkable beauty in the dignity of their strength. Perseverance and stoic resilience. The book bears witness to those injustices and casts a light on their plight.

In the photographs, I wanted to show these unseen people. I wanted to portray the ugliness of their unjust circumstances counter-balanced by this beauty. My challenge as a photographer was to portray them with fidelity. While the people in my photographs may seem exotic, 'their' worlds and 'our' worlds are inter-connected. Only accidents of birth and arbitrary good fortune separate us. We are more implicated in their lives and their plight than we might ever know. Most readers may not be aware that all of our clothes are stitched by these invisible garment workers in Phnom Penh, and elsewhere, who work for 12 hours every day to earn just $28.80 a week—half the living wage. By exposing the hardship of their lives, I am posing a question to each viewer: seeing and understanding the injustices of this world, what can each of us do to build a fairer society?

I use my camera as a documentary tool. The photographs in this book portray a reality that affects the feelings of the viewer in ways that words cannot. Some images are joyful: the impish grin of a curb side seamstress's daughter; and the gleaming vitality and optimism of the dalit schoolgirl. But others are confronting and disturbing: the desolation in Rania's eyes in the Jalozai refugee camp,[85] and the sadness of the orphan child with a balloon.[86]

I also use my camera as a tool for protest and advocacy. I want these photographs to attract but then to disturb the viewer to stir compassion and finally to inspire reflections about justice, good society and our participation in it. Ultimately, my message is to advocate for the transformative power of education to provide opportunity—particularly for girls—and to encourage the viewer to participate in improving the lives of the less fortunate.

In my second book of photographs, '*Homeless*', I wanted the images to do all the heavy lifting.[87] This time, I focused on injustice nearer to home—'here', not somewhere 'over there'. I chose to document the homeless in my home city of Sydney, and I sought to find a better way to connect with them. I was uncomfortable in my encounters with the homeless on the street, feeling guilty at turning away or shy about intruding into their space. I was also conscious of sometimes making judgments about whether or not someone was worthy of a donation, which I wished I hadn't. I was torn between ignoring the homeless because of concerns that they may squander my donation on alcohol or drugs, and my feelings of compassion for the less fortunate. This was my problem, and I realised I needed to fix it.

So, I started on a journey to learn about homelessness. Once I'd decided, it became easier. When I approached someone sitting on the street, I suspended all judgment and reached out as one human being to another. When they understood I genuinely wanted to hear and then tell their stories in a book, they were always happy to talk. Rather than standing looking down, I sat beside them and listened to their stories. Talking is a form of human contact which I soon learned they often longed for. Once we got talking, I'd reach out to touch a hand, arm or shoulder to cross the gap that separated us. The first thing I heard—every time—was that they felt alone and lonely. They were invisible, hidden in plain sight. I was devastated when I realised how often my own discomfort in turning away had exacerbated that. Many told me about being trapped in a churn of subsistence survival on the streets for years, even a decade. None wanted to live that way. Anyone who thinks that they are 'dole bludgers' choosing to scam the system has no idea about the overwhelming depletion of their choices.[88]

So, instead of turning away and walking past, I now stopped to talk.

'Hello. How's your day going?'

'It's hell living under a park shelter. We all hate it,' Matthew told me in Martin Place.

'I feel judged. They make me feel like a failure. But they don't understand. All that separates them from us is about two pay packets,' Scott said, holding a paper cup with a few coins in it. He'd spent his life as a builder's labourer, until he had to stop to get an operation for varicose veins.[89]

As I talked with the homeless, I learned that there are many paths to destitution.

'I'm homeless 'cos dad passed away, and mum left me,' Chloe aged 20 told me.

'But I'm lucky,' said Ross, 'I'm on disability.'[90]

'I had a messy childhood,' said Matty from a doorway at Kings Cross.[91]

'I had to sell my flat after my wife died, then my Mother,' said Matthew on the Pitt Street Mall.[92]

'My dad gave me my habit,' explained Sharon on King Street, Newtown.[93]

'I'm not ill, I just over-medicated a few times,' Ashley explained.[94]

'You can photograph the sign "I fled domestic violence," but please don't show my face,' she pleaded.[95]

Everyone on the street has their own story. Child abuse, severe injury and psychosis are common. Some have PhD's, others had run successful businesses—until a reversal upset their lives. Almost all have had homes and families in their past.

There is often substance abuse, though it is usually a symptom, rarely the cause of homelessness. There is always poverty, followed by trauma—a car crash, retrenchment or divorce. There are so many causes. One bad knock too many, and a life's balance can be shattered, and they suddenly found themselves alone in the crowded city crowd. It's a terrifying prospect.

These encounters triggered a long-buried memory from my early childhood. Returning home one day after visiting my grandmother, from our car window I'd seen an elderly woman sheltering under a bridge from the pouring rain with all her possessions piled in bags around her. What on earth was she doing there? She could have been my Granny. It was many decades later before I realised that she was a Hungarian refugee fleeing from the Soviet invasion of 1956. Thereafter, I'd been haunted by the horror of such inexplicable misfortune. I have been fortunate in my life, but deep down I have always dreaded the possibly of such misfortune.

While compiling photographs for this book, I tried 'sleeping rough' on the streets for two nights to experience what it felt like. It was hard, *really* hard. People whom I would normally consider my peers walked past me without blinking. Others looked down with a mixture of pity and disgust. I felt judged and shunned. After just 24 hours, I'd had a gut full. During those challenging hours, I developed a new respect for the homeless for their resilience, courage and forbearance.

'I'm here, but I'm invisible,' Jay told me on George Street, Sydney. 'They see me but then they don't and continue walking past.'[96]

A bit later, I went out on one of the night trains leaving Sydney around midnight to disgorge the last revellers to their far-flung beds before idling in remote stations until returning with the early risers before 5 am the next day. Here I found a separate society of weary men and women using the trains' warm dry benches as a benign albeit temporary respite from the wintery streets.[97]

Beyond bearing witness, I was advocating compassion for these people who I now understood could so easily be me under other circumstances. I wanted to show their lives with humanity and dignity, having recoiled from the work of other photographers which rendered the homeless as harrowed cast members of *Les Misérables*. So, with their permission, I named each person beneath their portrait to affirm their identity and give voice to their story. Most of my images gave direct eye contact with the viewer. By doing so, I wanted to connect the viewer with the homeless, what they were thinking and feeling. I wanted this connection to enable the viewer to see the homeless with fresh eyes and be affected by what they saw. Building an ethical approach that did not demonise or stereotype the homeless became an important part of my journey. I am indebted to these people who generously gave me their trust, and hope that I have kept my promise to present them with respect.

When I'd finally published '*Homeless*', I discovered it was important for me to find those I'd photographed in order to return their portraits and to express my gratitude to them. Many I found, but others I couldn't. Had they found a home at last, moved to another corner, or finally over-medicated? These questions linger.

In both books, I deliberated at length over my motives, shrinking from political correctness, virtue signalling or poverty porn. I was endeavouring to engage the empathy and the compassion of the viewer. By empathy, I was endeavouring to put the viewer in the shoes of the subject to care and share the emotional dimensions of the subject's situation. By compassion, I was wanting to go further to motivate the viewer to consider improving that situation by taking some action.

Photography has taught me to find beauty in many unexpected places, from the swirling clouds gliding silently and unnoticed overhead, to the stoic dignity of the poor and the resilience of the homeless around me. Do we see them, or have we chosen not to look? I realise that I had turned away earlier from what I didn't want to see because I was uncomfortable. I now understand that it is not them who are the failures; it is us. It is our inhumanity that is on display.

The homeless, the unseen and the unheard reveal how we chose to see our community, and in doing so they also show us our own humanity.

Teaching: Completing the Loop

Think about the last time you bought a new electrical appliance—maybe the latest smartphone, a TV with 'intelligent' programming or earbuds. How did you get it to work? You have four choices. Did you: (a) press all the buttons until it worked; (b) press all the buttons until you got stuck and then asked for help? (c) ask the salesperson to set it up and show you, or (d) read the manual from cover to cover before opening the box?

When I first took this exercise, I did the obvious. Then I asked Miyako to do it, as well. She did the same thing. Except, what we each did was different. I had pressed all the buttons, then asked for help, discovering that I am a 'pragmatic' learner, (b) above. She had read the manual, discovering that she is a 'theoretical' learner, (d) above. I have never read manuals because they are incomprehensible, at least to me.

This exercise taught me a lot about my own learning preferences, and how to meet those of others.

I was instantly drawn to the work of David Kolb on experiential learning.[98] He argues that we all have a continuous cycle of experiencing, reflecting, conceptualizing and experimenting that ultimately leads to effective learning. Each learner exhibits a preferred style of learning based on this cycle. There are four main learning types: the 'activist' who mainly learns by doing; the 'theorist' who learns by reading, the 'reflector' who learns by imitating; and the 'pragmatist' who learns by experimenting and questioning. Most people apply a combination of these four learning styles, but are not usually conscious of their own preferences. We invariably presume that our learning style is normal and that it is shared by everyone until, that is, we do that exercise above and recognise the different learning preferences of others. What all this means for the 'teacher' is the need to address the learning preferences of their 'students' through explaining, demonstrating, exercising or responding to address their learning preferences—that is, to use a combination of lecturing, researching, practicing and interacting.

L. Armytage, *Confronting Injustice*,
https://doi.org/10.1007/978-981-95-3573-6_16

While researching '*Educating Judges,*' discussed earlier in the chapter "Voice: Journey to Fairness", my interest in teaching had deepened. I was drawn to teaching because I was intrigued by the mystery of learning and wanted to learn more. I had suffered learning difficulties as a child and developed techniques to overcome those difficulties. Later as an adult, I discovered a fascination in facilitating the learning of others, initially in teaching legal skills, like negotiation, to punctuate the intensity of practicing law. I started teaching by doing, acquiring a mix of practical experience in different settings on the job and in classrooms. I explored what was then known about learning. It was a captivating exercise. I had to rethink my own learning to order to explain it clearly to others, and soon I discovered myself being more engaged when communicating as an educator than as an advocate.

Working with the judiciary, I spent a lot of time thinking about how best to promote judges' learning. I found judges to be a cohort of intensely autonomous and highly successful professionals who are distinctive as adult learners. As such, I found I performed much better as a facilitator of their learning than as a trainer steering their learning. I saw my role as being to inspire learning, to enable the learner to discover what had remained up until that moment a secret to their understanding of their work, life and their place within it. My challenge was to prompt and guide the learner—whether a law student, lawyer, judge or other professional—along the path of discovering and exploring what they still needed to find out. I would watch their eyes, monitoring their interest and adapting my presentation to their curiosity, confusion, challenge or fatigue, drawing them ever closer to the mystery of what they didn't yet know. I also enjoyed sharing the strengths and elegance of good ideas that enabled others to understand and think with greater clarity. I saw their excitement grow as they discovered these ideas—like finding jewels in the sand—and realised their revelatory power. I loved to see their eyes light up in that epiphany of understanding, and I marvelled as they grappled to apply their learning to solve new problems. This was an exciting role with many of the same challenges and responsibilities of a parent, and it was also a privileged space in which to win their trust and respect.

I also found the work of Benjamin Bloom helpful in categorising educational activities into three domains of knowledge, skills and attitudes.[99] I had found this distinction useful in distinguishing which technique to use for what purpose. As judges are already generally proficient in 'knowing the law,' the transfer and acquisition of information, that is teaching for knowledge, is not as essential as teaching to develop skills. Accordingly, conducting lectures conveying knowledge was rarely useful. Altogether different facilitation techniques are required in teaching judges to develop the distinctive skills of judging, such as writing a clear and succinct judgment, for example, problem-solving exercises and simulations using a four-step model of explanation, demonstration, practice and feedback. Similarly, promoting critical reflection of appropriate attitudes and values of judging, such as ethics, fair treatment and leadership requires other training modalities, for example, pitting peers in debates with their peers to explain and justify their attitudes towards a moderated consensus.

Other theorists advocated the virtues of active and participatory learning. The Socratic method, for instance, is a classic form of inquiry-based learning that focuses on active participation and engagement in the exploration of ideas, as distinct from the more receptive or passive modes of didactic teaching more commonly used with children. This method uses questioning as a means of stimulating critical thinking and acquiring new knowledge. It encourages challenging assumptions, examining evidence, critically evaluating arguments, and exploring different perspectives. Roleplay, problem-solving simulation exercises, and question-and-answer panels are also aspects of the Socratic method. Debating can then be introduced once the learner becomes familiar with the general issues.

I had applied and experimented with these learning theories when I worked with judges in Australia, and then further afield in many different legal and education systems overseas. In doing so, I was intrigued to discover that human beings learned in broadly the same way irrespective of the diversity of their cultural contexts and pedagogic traditions. In workshops that I conducted in Hanoi, for example, for Vietnamese judges deeply imbued with Buddhist respect, and also in Kabul, for Afghan judges, schooled in the rigid orthodoxy of Muslim madrasas, I observed them bounding with little hesitation from their practice of mechanically scribing every word into participatory and experiential learning activities, as comfortably as their Australian counterparts.

My own learning was by no means theoretical. My understanding of facilitating others to learn evolved with my experience which I continued to refine through these experiences. There is theoretical learning through books and instruction, and there is also practical learning through experience. Much of my more important learning about injustice took place unexpectedly while I was living and working in some extraordinarily diverse countries.

I have already remarked on Stephen's scolding me for our unsustainably technocratic reform approach in Port Moresby, and his offering me the far superior 'Ela Beach' test for measuring success in crime reduction. I have also mentioned Laima's rebuke of my misunderstanding of Afghan women's use of the burqa.[100]

In Port-au-Prince, for another example, I learned that even in dire poverty, the human spirit cannot be suppressed. Haiti was the first slave economy to rebel and eject its French masters in 1791. For that transgression, it has been punished economically by imperial powers ever since. When I witnessed a woman squatting chastely to pee in the streets between parked cars, I realised that poverty is so widespread that private toilets are a rarity. Despite, or perhaps because of, this poverty, local culture has great vitality. People speak loudly, sing with little encouragement, and wear brightly coloured clothing. One Sunday I was walking in the mountains when I was enchanted by the splendour of the churchgoers in pristine pressed white smocks walking for miles along paths along the hilltops to fill their churches. But sadly, it was here too that I also learned I could not dance. Watching me shift arrhythmically from one foot to the other, blighted by my Anglo self-consciousness, my Haitian colleague and companion pityingly observed that my body was like a block of wood. Her movements were however as fluid as rippling water.

In Dhaka, I worked with Sayedur Rahman who was a retired District & Session Judge. He was a gentle man who was quietly insightful on the many problems and needs of the Bangladeshi judiciary, as well as the quirks of its hierarchy. While addressing meetings in my role as the foreign expert, I was required to provide the Chief Justice with solutions to the many problems besetting his courts. This was often challenging because, as a visitor, I was on many reckonings the least knowledgeable of anyone in the room. Sayedur was not however permitted to speak directly to the Chief Justice who was his lofty superior. So, before each meeting, Sayedur would painstakingly brief me on the dilapidation of the court houses, the chaos of the court records on the sagging shelves of the decaying storerooms, the gaps in the court reporting system, the shortage of computers, or whatever else was to be discussed. I would then perform the solemn pantomime of reciting this litany to which the Chief Justice would nod sagely and accept our advice.

'But, why on earth is this arcane ritual required?' I asked after the meeting.

Sayedur chuckled.

He explained that my esteemed role was essentially ritualistic. Had he spoken directly, he would have been seen to disrespect and subvert the hierarchy and would have been disregarded. When I recited what he had told me, however, this hierarchy was enhanced by my status not only as an 'expert' but, more importantly, as a transient who was not a protagonist and had no personal agendas to push that might need to be resisted.

In Apia, I worked with Aumua Ming Leung Wai between 2007/2009 in devising Samoa's law and justice reform strategy. Ming was a successful lawyer who had surrendered his lucrative legal practice to discharge his chiefly responsibilities by serving as the Attorney-General. As the months passed, we developed a close friendship. On Wednesday afternoons, he would play golf on the lushly grassed volcanic slopes of the main island Opulu. Even though I couldn't play, I would join him. On the first two to three holes, I would swing the club casually and, to our shared disbelief, often hit my ball to soar weightlessly through the air a couple of hundred meters. Occasionally, I might even win. But after several holes, as soon as I started to try, my shots veered wildly, ploughing divots of turf from the ground or missing altogether. As the weeks passed, we discovered that we enjoyed this routine, however amateur, for another reason. In the sanctuary of the golf course overlooking the infinite Pacific Ocean around us, we were freed from the interruption of meetings and phone calls. It was also entirely private. As we walked, we talked. Soon we found ourselves exploring the issues, opportunities and options freed from our respective official roles.

'My government wants you to do this', I once heard myself say to our shared astonishment, 'but my advice to you is not to - for the following reasons …'.

He would then reciprocate by confiding his misgivings and disclosing his own constraints, from where we could then explore a more sensible course of action which often diverged from the plan but was better and genuinely theirs's to implement. It was here, on the mountain side overlooking the glittering ocean, that we developed a mutual trust that I cherished and have searched to replicate elsewhere.

The harvest of these discussions, and other consultations with civil society in remote communities, was the design of a 5-year plan that offered unforeseen insights. Not only did it address the usual concerns about juvenile crime but, more importantly, it illuminated for the first time a spectrum of connected but otherwise disparate problems fermenting at the interface of customary and contemporary societies. These included the erosion of local authority and respect for traditional elders—the *pulenu'u*—in the overlap, gaps and collisions of these social authority structures. In particular, they sheltered endemic domestic and family violence behind the shadows of custom, social taboo and the churches' insistence on victims' forgiveness for—rather than protection from—serial perpetrators. We agreed that the coexistence of customary culture and modern law and justice processes remains a significantly underdefined space in all or most Pacific island societies warranting further research.

But such collaborations were not always possible. In Phnom Penh, I had already learned about corruption and intrigue from the government itself, when my local assistant informed me that if I wanted a contract extension, I would need to reach an 'arrangement' with the head of its justice reform unit. This solicitation, which was discussed in the chapter 10 "Cambodia - after Year Zero," had been so brazen it was clear I would not be the first to accept such an offer. I then learned that this corruption was tacitly tolerated as a cost of doing business by those at the highest level of the UN.

I soon learned that corruption is all-pervasive. In Islamabad, Miyako needed to obtain a police certificate to progress her application for a resident visa to Australia. An inspector of police, quite senior in overseeing teams of other officers, had offered to come to the house to supply her with one. He arrived while she was at work, and asked our cook: "So, what's she worth?" We recoiled, and reported it to our office who told me they would handle it. But it wasn't until he had received a 'gratuity' of US$100 from our office that she was finally handed the soiled certificate. No society is immune from this sickness. Learning to see corruption in foreign places then taught me to see what I had previously accepted as being 'normal practice' to reveal this blight operating in plain sight at the highest levels of government in my own country.

In Baku, I learned about dictatorship. Azerbaijan is an oil-rich nation which was the original target of Hitler's invasion of Russia in 1942 before becoming mortally distracted at Stalingrad. Its streets are adorned with massive posters of the 'father of the nation', communist ruler Heydar Aliyev, proclaiming his paternalistic devotion for the citizens. Since the end of the Cold War Azerbaijan has masqueraded as a new democracy 'in drag'. While I was working there in 2010, a respected journalist who had been critical of the regime was imprisoned, tortured and died under 'mysterious' circumstances. My client, the World Bank, had funded the highway from Baku to the airport at a cost of around US$1 billion. In a footnote to its report, it quietly attached a cost scale for highway construction around the globe. This revealed, for those who chose to look, that the Baku highway had cost three times the global norm. Most of this plunder, having passed through many hands, reached the purse of the current ruler, Ilham Aliyev, proud Heydar's son.

One day in our office at the Ministry of Justice in Baku, my phlegmatic colleague, Sulaiman, pointed silently but urgently to the ceiling as I was talking with him.

'Let's have lunch,' he interrupted.

Once outside, he explained that I was under constant surveillance. From then on, we shared many walks in engrossing discussions about how things really worked in Azerbaijan. When the job ended, he warned me that he could never continue our honest and open discussions by email or text. He never has, because he too is continuously being monitored[101].

I soon learned that Big Brother monitors foreigners and citizens alike, wherever they are. In Male, capital of the Maldives which are a delightful honeymoon destination of romantic islands for affluent tourists, my predecessor had been deported—without notice—the day after he sent a confidential email to our office at the Asian Development Bank. In his email, he had foolishly described how the president siphoned foreign aid to his own businesses.

Before leaving the Maldives, I also learned about the fruits of elite plunder, the likes of which I'd already witnessed in Cambodia and Azerbaijan. Miyako and I were invited to a fabulous Maldivian island resort as a farewell gesture. Its beachside villas boasted chilled air conditioning, spacious sun decks and over-water immersion pools with sting rays and reef sharks gliding silently across the coral below. Even 25 years ago, in 2000, these villas cost US$1200 per night, an extravagance that only film stars like Tom Cruise, evading the paparazzi, could afford. And, of course, Russian oligarchs having looted the assets of the Soviet state, whom I witnessed tipping bell boys and porters in freshly minted US$100 bills from rolls of cash as thick as pork sausages.

In Mongolia, I learned about the disruption and follies of revolutionary chaos during the mid-90 s, which was a time of extraordinary change. The fall of the Berlin Wall had presaged the emergence of many post-Soviet states into the capitalist global economy with its so-called 'free market.' This had spurred what Tom Carothers termed the 'rule of law revival' which was driven by the triumphalist zeal of American-style capitalism and democracy.[102] It was also supposedly the moment of the ending of history.[103] I flew from Beijing for hours north over the Great Wall of China, across vast frozen expanses of the Gobi-Manchurian steppe to the capital, Ulan Bator. It was so cold here in winter that I saw ice cream being sold directly from the icy pavements. No refrigeration was needed. Walking outside, at −40c, the hairs in my nose froze brittle and my throat burned when I inhaled too quickly. The cityscape was strangely bare and colourless without any of the clutter of advertising hoardings. The State Bank, not yet reorientated to 'free market' transactions, had just sent the economy into freefall. By failing to secure its loan funds to enforceable securities, it had flung all of its capital assets to the artic winds. It went bust.

Here, I found myself training the judges on the most basic principles of contract law and property title, which had never before been needed in the command economy. It was here too that a witless American advisor had advocated that the courts depart from their inquisitorial model of hearings to adopt America's adversarial model. This folly mired the legislature for decades in rewiring the entire procedural apparatus of the judiciary for no discernible benefit beyond reflecting what that advisor had been familiar with back in Maddison County USA. More than anything else, this debacle displayed the hegemonic role of aid trumping its development goals.

In Hanoi, I learned about the camouflage of competing ideologies. The Vietnamese enjoy a hard-earned self-assurance after having defeated much bigger enemies in the form of the Chinese, French and most recently American invaders. I worked with Cao Xuan Phong, a bright young lawyer attached to the Politburo, who spoke excellent English. Here I conducted a workshop on judges' role to uphold the law, which I thought had gone far better than I had expected. The judges had participated enthusiastically in discussions and exercises, rather than scribbling head down every word I'd uttered which is their respectful custom. Afterwards, however, I learned a lesson.

'In the Socialist Republic, our focus is on the citizen's duties not on their rights,' Phong chided me.

I had of course read about that, and immediately felt foolish. But later, I recalled JFK's famous homily:

'Ask not what your country can do for you—ask what you can do for your country.'

Surely, I reflected, these sentiments were essentially identical. But if this is so, then this would indicate that the 'American war,' as the Vietnamese call it, was actually not a conflict of competing ideologies and values at all, since they preached the same messages. This insight coincided with a parallel revelation. In my doctoral research, I had been astonished to find that the Gini-Coefficient, which is the economic measure of the distribution of wealth across a population, had for many years been almost identical in both China and the US, despite their profound divergence of political and economic ideologies which they asserted. If, then, the measurement of social wellbeing, wealth and opportunity are almost indistinguishable in their effects, what purpose do such ideologies really serve, other than the self-interests of their respective elites, I have long since wondered ….

Later, a number of these Vietnam judges visited Sydney on a study tour, where I was hosting their visit to inform and educate them on the modernity and other virtues of our system. I had scheduled a program of intensive meetings with our judges and observations of the courts. The visitors—all judges in the Socialist Republic of Vietnam must be active members of the Communist Party—were diligently attentive. After each session they asked numerous questions. By day 3, I started to notice a pattern.

'What do barristers charge?

'How do you deal with unrepresented litigants?

'Do you have legal aid? What does it cover?

'How long are your court lists?

Politely, but quite systematically, I realised that they were probing differences in our system. Clearly there are many. I listened more closely to my own answers to their questions, and then to the answers of other presenters. No problem, we all answered openly, also proudly. Doubtless they would be better informed and could make some improvements when they returned to Hanoi, I supposed. Or not. But then I replayed my answers and the others again. The more I listened, the more I found myself questioning their sufficiency. Slowly, but surely, I found myself being gently but resolutely steered to defects in our system that were there for all to see, but which I no longer consciously noticed: the delays, the costs, the unfairness of the adversarial process wherever there is an imbalance of resources between the parties. Our visitors remained scrupulously polite. But by the end of their visit, I realised that I was not just their teacher but also their student learning to see the familiar through the eyes of the stranger. This was a profound lesson which has caused me to look with fresh more questioning eyes at many aspects of Australia, western values and 'our' way of doing things. I can now see, for example, corruption comfortably ensconced in plain sight as being 'just the way we always do things' that riddles our public offices at the highest levels yet remains sheltered by political parties who are complicit in their spoils.

After learning from these experiences in the course of my work practice, I moved on to teaching postgraduate students back in Australia. After my doctorate, the University of Sydney had appointed me as an adjunct professor and invited me to design a course on my research for the postgraduate program which focused on building fairer societies by helping the courts to administer justice better. While my thesis had dealt mainly with overseas aid, I wanted this course to grapple with the bigger questions that surrounded my practice, namely: what is a fair society, how can it be improved, and what can each of us do to help that happen? These are not only questions to be asked about somewhere 'over there'. They are also important, but too often overlooked 'here' in our own community.

After I launched this course, some of my students described me as being passionate, which surprised me. While listing some of the injustices I'd encountered, I suppose I must have involuntarily dropped the dreaded 'f-bomb'. I recalled seeing a startled eyebrow raised. Each year thereafter, before starting the class, I would resolve never to drop that bomb again. Each year, while discussing the likes of Hun Sen in Cambodia or Ilham Aliyev in Azerbaijan, I would teeter searching for the best words to express their misuse of public power, pathological corruption, insatiable greed, repression and impunity. But as I did so, a fuse would hiss in my head as I struggled to find a better word. Time after time again, my outrage would boil over, and that expletive would slither unstoppably through my teeth.

Reading my students' essays was like conducting an endoscopy to probe the neural passageways of their minds. Their answers revealed how they interpreted the questions, stored knowledge and framed their thinking to address any given task. There was often something quite intimate in reading their responses to a question however many had already answered before them. But while expecting to hear familiar tropes from most essays, there were sometimes fascinating—and occasionally bewildering—excursions being taken in the way each student has framed the question and thereby their answers.

When assessing their learning, I found that it was generally a straightforward matter to measure the acquisition of knowledge—however predictable. It was much less simple to assess other aspects of their learning which ultimately rested on making a more subjective assessment. Like appraising art, an instructor uses criteria to weigh the quality of each student's answer, but grading those criteria remains unavoidably impressionistic. Ultimately, I came to believe that each person's own learning is relational to the context of their life, rather than the content, values or opinions of their instructor. So, I now approach each essay by asking the student (in my head) to '*show me what you've got.*' I am interested to discover what has enriched and developed them as cognitive beings. It is in their grasp to sweep me off my feet and when occasionally they do, I am filled with wonder at the application of their learning, its uniqueness and creativity.

Georgia was the brightest student that I've ever had the privilege to teach. It was during the Covid lockdown and her class was conducted remotely. Her eyes glittered from the screen as she watched me regearing to keep up with her questions. Later, while reading the students' essays, submitted anonymously, I was gobsmacked by the restrained elegance and prodigious assurance of one. It could only have been hers' in its ability to express complex but nuanced ideas. It was already of publishable quality. In discussing Marta Nussbaum's capabilities approach to human rights, she argued:

> (This) provides a comprehensive and equitable justification for development work, as well as providing measurable performance indicators. It retains mechanisms to ensure that procedural conceptions of the rule of law are deployed, that institutions are robust and good governance is achieved. However, this is *merely a lattice* upon which the capabilities flourish. The procedural goes hand in hand with the substantive, and it is this substantive concept of justice, dignity, and the rule of law which is necessary to address the inequity that has resulted from a *formal, procedural, institutional and economic myopia* that treats the individual as a means, rather than an end (italics added).

When the course was done, I invited her for coffee and career advice. She was gangly, socially awkward, and wearing daggy outsized clothes. Yet I felt humbled in proximity to this 20-year-old, less than one third my age, oblivious to her own brilliance. In a decade, should she choose, she could comfortably be lecturing at Harvard.

It is of course difficult to gauge the learning of students who do not participate in class. It is altogether too easy however to confuse extroverted participation with intelligence, as much as their opposites. At the start of teaching, I found myself presuming that students who asked interesting questions, led discussions and were visibly engaged, were the students more likely to be learning the most. But, when I read their essays, I was often disappointed to discover that their expression of ideas was ordinary, even banal. Then, to my surprise, I would find that a quiet student who had sat unresponsive in the back row was often capable of submitting a more perceptive essay, replete with innovative research and inventive ideas. I was now discovering that I had inadvertently correlated extroversion with intelligence, even though extroversion was little more than a socially endorsed expressive trait respected in certain cultures. I now look past the gesticulations of those cheerleaders in search of insights from more reticent students who would otherwise be eclipsed.

Recently, I read the journal of Mei, a visiting Chinese student, who had spoken only rarely in class, then only when answering questions directed to her. In discussing her understanding of '*closed access order*' societies which privilege the elite's access to economic opportunity through the use of state-sanctioned violence (discussed in Chapter 10 "Cambodia - after Year Zero"), she observed that:—.

> China has made significant progress in transitioning from a feudal system to its current political structure. In some respects, the country meets the criteria of an open society. *However, in terms of thought education and control over the people, China seems to be reverting to a more closed-off approach reminiscent of historical periods such as the Qing Dynasty's isolation era (locking its doors against the world).* [italics added].

Mei's courage and confidence, and as much as her ability, to critique and apply complex new concepts to her own lived experience greatly cheered me.

While teaching in the graduate program, I was simultaneously working at the pre-entry level with the University of the South Pacific. Despite the width of the academic gap between these programs, I have found the mysteries and wonders of learning are universal to both, which continues to intrigue me. These mysteries are as elusive to me now as those capitals of Europe were to me as an 8-year-old, like wriggly tadpoles slithering around the page however hard I tried to pin them down, and still do.

And then, I marvel in wonder as the gleam of revelation brightens their eyes.

Ela Beach

In this book, I have been rummaging through the archive of my memories to share these stories about finding my way from law to justice. It's been an engrossing journey to exotic and fascinating places to work with hugely impressive people in often desperate spaces far beyond the tourist path. In striving to make the world a fairer place, I have passed through war, genocide, coups and dictatorship to confront the legacies of history, empire, atomic testing and natural disaster.

In some ways, my work has been framed by the end of WWII and the decline of European empire; living with all the uncertainties and confusion that hallmark our secular postmodern generation. The rule of law 'moment', as it was sometimes called, extended for over thirty years from the Cold War to fill the space apparently vacated by the demise of Soviet communism—broadly between 1989–2020. Much of this work was in clearing up the refuse of those empires. That moment, with its various opportunities and challenges has now passed. In its place, a emergent Trumpian new order of virulent nationalism is closing both hearts and borders, and transferring aid budgets into rearmament. As I write, geopolitics stand at an inflection point of uncertainty. Meantime, injustices proliferate.

Promoting justice is important, but it's also challenging. Many years back, when I started working to build fairer societies, I suppose that I believed deep down that all it would take was for me to work hard enough and smart enough. Driven by my childhood fear of failure, I balanced sometimes three separate projects at once—in Cambodia, Afghanistan and the Maldives, or the Pacific, Bangladesh and Nepal—to attain my maximum potential. I needed this drive and the energy of inexperience to frontally confront the world as I found it. But now, I understand things differently. I have acquired the lived experience to know that change is complex, slow, non-linear and often uncontrollable—however well it may be planned and implemented. It is in the very nature of life that in reconciling competing interests the pursuit of justice will be perpetual and forever incomplete. I now see the pursuit of justice as an unending quest. In our post -colonial era, I have now jettisoned any pretention of righteousness that asserts an entitlement to direct change from outside. Instead, the

L. Armytage, *Confronting Injustice*,
https://doi.org/10.1007/978-981-95-3573-6_17

best that I can aim to do is to displace the statis of injustice and to inspire and enable our partners to realign their interests in line with those evolving norms that we share. It is a delicate balance of ethical responsibility to engage without harming while avoiding abdicating by just watching.

The injustices of the poor with whom I have worked are both fraught and distressing. I feel a shame in not sharing their hardship, even voyeuristic in witnessing them. I am incensed by the unfairness that is perpetrated through an abuse of power. Is this quixotic or evangelical? Hardly. It's a smouldering incandescent disturbance, a visceral disgust, that erupts inside me.

There are many injustices in our world. Knowing what I now do, seeing what I have, there is little choice. I could not turn away, nor could I stand back. I have been driven by our mutual opportunity to leave this world a little bit better than we found it. I have little assurance of rightness, but must give it my best shot.

Could I have done better? No doubt. Sometimes the wind was at my back, at others—as in Afghanistan—it was not. But even there, I was always consoled by the irrepressibility of the human spirit. So, I must wait for those winds to change. Most often, change is slower than expected. My insistence in persevering in the face of endless challenges might be blindness or hubris. Or, it might be courage and defiance, or both. I don't rightly know. While a part of our lives as human beings may be spent in a search for certainty, sense and meaning, the best I have usually found is equilibrium. Pursuing justice might seem a Sisyphean, at least elusive, quest of battling to redress never-ending unfairness; but I see its destination in finding some equilibrium in that contest. For there is a contentment, peace and even beauty, to be found in that equilibrium. It remains for the future, and others, to reveal how well we have fared.

Over these years, I have of course thought about how justice reform could be undertaken more effectively, both in my own research and in my work for the United Nations, World Bank, Australian and other governments. This has impelled me to provide many advices with recommendations—most though rarely all of which have been adopted—from fine adjustments to fundamental restructuring of approach. This memoir is not however the place for reciting granular strategic and technical analysis, some of which is bound by confidentiality, though much has already been separately published in books and is readily accessible.[104]

In narrating many of the stories in this memoir, which is the prequel to those more academic and technical books, I am looking back in gratitude. I have made a more personal journey to reflect on what I have learned about the many wonders and mysteries of life, the human spirit, justice and my endeavours to make the world a fairer place. I wanted to make some sense of my life, and to share what I had learned for those who may follow. While each of our paths is unique, we each share a universal journey to find our places in this world.

So, here is what I've learned; this is what I know. Justice is core to human dignity and fundamental to our wellbeing. There are many paths to justice, and we can learn much from each other, for example, from customary concepts of restorative justice. Yet, at its essence, justice is all about fairness. In finding my own path from law to justice, I have confronted crises which are cathartic but also lead to transformation.

In doing so, I have learned to trust my inner voice, listen to those fears that warn of dangers to be avoided, and value mistakes that have taught me. The more I have learned, the more I understand how little I know. I have also chosen to live with hope rather than despair, for life is full of wonder and mystery, and gives us many opportunities to attain our potential. Just as the beauty of the cherry blossom exists in its transience before the spring winds, so I have learned to seize these moments which have been so much better than ever expected. We can each make a difference. This is how history builds its path behind each of our steps, however small they might sometimes seem to be.

Did we eradicate injustice, domestic violence, exclusion or poverty? Certainly not. I am humbled by how small my steps are and how long they take. So much more remains to be done for Australia's Indigenous people, women and girls in Kabul, Palestinians in Gaza and the West Bank, and the exiles of Rongelap. It is a perpetual journey to justice whichever path we may take.

But did we make a difference? Is the world now more just, even a little bit fairer? Absolutely, yes. Working with so many others, I have helped the courts to deliver on their promise to deliver justice more fairly. In each place, this has meant something different. In Australia, judges are now so much better trained, and the over-representation of Indigenous people in our prisons is slowly but iteratively falling. In post-genocidal Cambodia, the rule of impunity of the Khmer Rouge has ended and reconciliation can begin. In Port Moresby, we loosened the *raskols'* grip of the night and crime is falling. In Pakistan, the cases are moving forward again. We dislodged the backlog that choked the courts and introduced continuous improvements that have done me out of my job. On the Nepali terai, we laid foundations to eradicate domestic violence, and women can now exercise their rights to physical and sexual security. On Rongelap, I learned that customary concepts of restorative justice offer us all much of value to respect and adopt. In the Pacific, the chiefs are resolving disputes more fairly. We have built curricula in schools for children to understand their rights, and a stairway of learning for magistrates to climb and preside in their own courts. These are slow, incremental steps. Each is measurably contributing to improving justice and human wellbeing. Some are conclusive, while others are the foundations for fairer societies as our gifts to the future for others to build on. Collectively, these legacies are achievements of which I am quietly proud to have contributed some small part.

Injustice outrages us all. But often we are helpless to redress it, and we must endure its afflictions. But after many years of searching, I was fortunate to find that I could harness this outrage as my engine to promote justice. This engine has driven my direction in the world giving purpose and value to my work ever since for which I am deeply grateful.

Should I have spent my time better, more enjoyably, more usefully? Working in the torrid operating spaces of war-torn Afghanistan, crime-riven Port Moresby or post-genocide Cambodia, I have found solace from these endless questions and lingering self-doubts by engaging with the challenges as best I could. I loved confronting these challenges which have stimulated and fulfilled me for the best years of my career. The unrelenting pragmatism of what is feasible in the opportunity available moderates the pretensions of any design, however neo-colonial, condescending or hegemonic. This reality is a great leveller. Knowing all that I now do, there is some grace in having given it my best shot.

We are each unique, and how we see our own lives changes. Earlier, my life was a journey to reach a destination—to make partner by 30; or to complete a PhD. Later, it became a devotion to express and fulfil my potential; and a grand adventure giving much enrichment. These were ways of seeing and knowing myself.

In my mind, it's nearing evening now, and there's not so much time left before the sun goes down. These moments are precious. Sometimes I'm back on Ela Beach with Miyako and my friend Stephen's family watching the sunset. Our children and grandchildren are playing in the water which glitters around them. It's so much better than I had ever expected.

Testimonials

"This book is a terrific read; it is engaging, eye-opening, entertaining and beautifully written. At the book's core is a cornucopia of the author's experiences of reforming the law courts to deliver better justice in some of the most dangerous places on Earth. The author's reflections built on deep foundations of practical experience that are what make this book such an education as well as a pleasure to read. Livingston delights us with turns of phrase that arrest us as much by their poignancy as by their insight."

—Professor David Kinley, *Chair of Human Rights Law, Sydney Law School*

"Very gutsy, these truths should come out"

—Dr Linn Hammergren, *Senior Political Scientist, World Bank*

"A torrid story - emotionally charged, tough and passionate"

—Dr Doug J Porter, *Adviser, Justice for the Poor Program, World Bank*

"This is amazing work, beautifully written, I love it. It is a rare author that can weave together personal narrative and professional reflection as effectively as Dr. Armytage does here."

—Frederick Rawski, *Former Asia Director, Int'l Commission of Jurists*

"This is a travelogue, a philosophy, a socio-political study, an idea of justice, and a beautiful literary work"

—Prem Chandra Rai, *Law Reformer, Kathmandu*

* All **royalties** from this book go to charities supporting education of disadvantaged girls.

L. Armytage, *Confronting Injustice*, https://doi.org/10.1007/978-981-95-3573-6

Endnotes

[1] Armytage, L&M. 2018, '*Unseen Faces, Unheard Voices,*' IBC, Tokyo, 171.

[2] Those working in international development are prone to be characterised as one of three stereotypes: missionaries, mercenaries or madmen. I will let you, the reader, decide which am I …

[3] Armytage, L. 2007, 'Justice in Afghanistan – Rebuilding Judicial Competence after the Generation of War,' *Heidelberg Journal of International Law*, HJIL/ZaöRV 67/1: 185–210.

[4] The 'difference principle,' see Rawls, J. 1971, *A Theory of Justice*, revised edn (1999), Oxford University Press, 13.

[5] Article 14, UN's *International Covenant on Civil & Political Rights* (ICCPR, 1966), ratified by 172 countries.

[6] Skadden, Arps, Slate, Meagher & Flom LLP.

[7] 1978/9.

[8] Schon, DA. 1987, *Educating the Reflective Practitioner*, Jossey-Bass, San Francisco.

[9] Armytage, L. 1996, *Educating Judges: Towards a New Model of Continuing Learning,* The Hague: Kluwer Law Int./Brill.

[10] Knowles, MS. 1984, *The Adult Learner: A Neglected Species* (3rd Ed.), Houston: Gulf.

[11] Cross, KP. 1981, *Adults as Learners*, San Francisco: Jossey-Bass.

[12] Kolb, D. 1984, *Experiential Learning: Experience as the Source of Learning and Development*, New York: Prentice Hall; & Herrmann, N. 1989, *The Creative Brain*, Lake Lure, N. Carolina: Ned Herrmann Brain Books.

[13] Another unmet ancestor, my maternal Great Grandfather Arthur Sedgwick, born in 1854, a don at Trinity College, Cambridge, addressed a letter to his Grandchildren and Great Grandchildren in May 1901 that he instructed be opened in 2000, in which he said: -*'I sincerely wish I could be alive to witness the opening of this box and to make the acquaintance of my great grandchildren. But this is impossible. Long before the year 2000 I shall have passed into the Ewigkeit*

L. Armytage, *Confronting Injustice*, https://doi.org/10.1007/978-981-95-3573-6

*(eternity) whither you, young and lusty as you may be now will follow me. Farewell. You have heard the voice of one who has long been silent and who now passes into everlasting silence."*It is in the spirit of that missive that I have dedicated this book to my own grandchildren.

[14] Samuels, G, (Judge of Appeal), "Judicial Competency: How It Can Be Maintained," *Australian Law Journal*, 1980, 54, 581–587, 585.

[15] https://shop.nfsa.gov.au/who-killed-malcolm-smith.

[16] Royal Commission into Aboriginal Deaths in Custody, 1991. *Royal Commission into Aboriginal Deaths in Custody: National report.* Vols. 1–5. Canberra: Australian Government Publishing Service; and see Chapter 6 'Unequal Australia'.

[17] I had been drawn to believe in secular humanism for its respect of reason, science, ethics and compassion, and for its rejection of institutionalised religion. Yet I also knew myself to have a spiritual awareness. My experience of god was profound but also mysterious, beyond my ability to understand or express. As a cognitive being, I am tantalised to live in the presence of this mystery. In this space, belief is not certainty but a way of being, and I have found my way to live in wonder and acceptance of the unknowable.

[18] Royal Commission into Aboriginal Deaths in Custody, 1991. *Royal Commission into Aboriginal Deaths in Custody: National report.* Vols. 1–5. Canberra: Australian Government Publishing Service.

[19] https://www.bangarra.com.au.

[20] https://iview.abc.net.au/show/boyer-lecture-2022-noel-pearson.

[21] Pascoe, B. 2014, *Dark Emu*, Magabala Books.

[22] Grant, S. 2016, *Talking to my Country,* HarperCollins.

[23] Perkins, R. (Director). (2022). *The Australian Wars* [TV documentary series]. Blackfella Films; SBS. https://www.sbs.com.au/ondemand/tv-series/the-australian-wars.

[24] *Mabo v Queensland (No 2)* (1992) 175 CLR 1.

[25] http://www.austlii.edu.au/au/special/rsjproject/rsjlibrary/hreoc/stolen/.

[26] https://nla.gov.au/nla.obj-2820865195/view.

[27] Email of Daniel Gudasić, 9 May 2024, National Centre for Crime and Justice Statistics, Australian Bureau of Statistics, www.abs.gov.au.

[28] Roy S. 2016, *The Gaza Strip: The Political Economy of De-development*, 3rd ed., Institute for Palestine Studies; Pappé, I. 2014. "Israel's incremental genocide in the Gaza ghetto." The Electronic Intifada. Retrieved from electronicintifada.net; Weizman E 2014, "Humanitarian Violence in Gaza." Democracy Now! democracynow.org; Warschawski M 2004, Toward an Open Tomb: The Crisis of Israeli Society (Monthly Review Press.

[29] UNGA Resolution 181, 1947.

[30] Smotrich B, 2025. "We are erasing the Palestinian state," he declared, "first in action and then officially." Israeli Finance Minister, reported by Beaumont P, *The Guardian Weekly*, 15/8/25, p 11.

[31] United Nations Independent International Commission of Inquiry. (2025, September 16). *Report on the situation in Gaza*, https://www.ohchr.org/en/press-releases/2025/09/israel-has-committed-genocide-gaza-strip-un-commission-finds.

[32] Armytage, L. diary, Islamabad, 2002.

[33] Samdani, KM. https://watandost.blogspot.com/2006/10/autobiography-of-honorable-pakistani.html.

[34] https://www.milligazette.com/news/1-community-news/6956-justice-samdani-pakistan-lost-one-of-its-great-treasures/.

[35] Chemin, M. 2009, 'The Impact of the Judiciary on Entrepreneurship: Evaluation of Pakistan's "Access to Justice Programme"', *Journal of Public Economics*, 93, 1: 114–25.

[36] https://en.wikipedia.org/wiki/Sandline_affair.

[37] Scott, J. 1998, *Seeing like a State*, Yale.

[38] '*Raskol'* is a derivative of rascal or criminal in *Tok Pisin*.

[39] *PNG Weekend National*, Friday 7 November 2003, 1.

[40] Bruce, M. 'Viewpoint', *Papua New Guinea Post Courier,* Wednesday 24 June 2004, 7.

[41] Hammergren, L. 2007, *Envisioning Reform: Improving Judicial Performance in Latin America*, Pennsylvania State University Press, 309; this is a quite delicate ethnomethodological issue - see: Armytage, L. 2012, 307–311.

[42] PNG-Australia Law & Justice Partnership (PALJP), AidWorks Initiative Number: INI194, Independent Progress Report; https://www.centreforjudicialstudies.com/wpcontent/uploads/paljp-progress-report.pdf, and https://www.dfat.gov.au/sites/default/files/paljp-management-response.pdf

[43] https://www.abc.net.au/news/2005-05-13/png-court-overturns-aust-police-immunity/1570088.

[44] North, D., Wallis, J., Webb, S., and Weingast, B. 2007, 'Limited Access Orders in the Developing World: A New Approach to the Problems of Development', *IEG Working Paper no 4359*, World Bank, Washington, DC.

[45] North, D., Wallis, J, & Weingast, B., 2009, *Violence and Social Orders*, Cambridge University Press.

[46] Armytage, L&M. 2018, 62–78.

[47] Armytage, L&M. 2018, 66.

[48] Armytage, L&M. 2018, 77.

[49] Armytage, L&M. 2018, 78.

[50] Prostitute.

[51] Armytage, L&M. 2018.

[52] Armytage, L&M. 2018, 40.

[53] Armytage, L&M. 2018, 46.

[54] Armytage, L&M. 2018, 49.

[55] Armytage, L&M. 2018, 18.

[56] Armytage, L&M. 2018, 104.

[57] Armytage, L&M. 2018, 57.

[58] The findings of this research are outlined in Cht 14 "Voice - Journey to Fairness".

[59] Armytage, L&M. 2018, 110–1.

[60] Armytage, L&M. 2018, 128–132.

[61] Armytage, L&M. 2018, 122.

[62] Armytage, L. 2102, '*Reforming Justice, a Journey to Fairness*,' Cambridge University Press, 1.

[63] Aristotle 1955, *Nicomachean Ethics*, trans. J. Thomson (revised 2004), London: Penguin; and Aristotle 1958, *Politics*, ed. E. Barker, Oxford University Press.

[64] Hobbes, T. 1651, *Leviathan*, ed. J. Plamenatz, 1962, Glasgow: Collins; Locke, J. 1690, *The Second Treatise of Government*, ed. T.P. Peardon (1952), New York: Liberal Arts Press; and Rousseau, J.J. 1762, *The Social Contract and Discourses*, trans. G. Cole (1973), revised edn, London: Dent.

[65] Mill, JS. 1859, *On Liberty* (2006) Filiquarian Publishing LLC.

[66] My colleague Linn Hammergren, a governance specialist at the World Bank, however sees justice as being primarily a political commodity, and only secondarily juridical.

[67] Armytage, L. 2102, 30; estimated using OECD data.

[68] Carothers, T. (ed.) 2006, *Promoting the Rule of Law Abroad: In Search of Knowledge*, Carnegie Endowment for International Peace, Washington, DC, 7; and Carothers, T. 1998, 'The Rule of Law Revival', *Foreign Affairs*, 77, 3: 95–106.

[69] Trubek, D. and Santos, A. (eds.) 2006, *The New Law and Economic Development: A Critical Appraisal*, Cambridge University Press, 7.

[70] Humphreys, S. 2010, *Theatre of the Rule of Law: Transnational Legal Intervention in Theory and Practice*, Cambridge University Press.

[71] Kleinfeld-Belton, R. 2005, 'Competing Definitions of the Rule of Law: Implications for Practitioners', *Working Paper no 55*, Carnegie Endowment for International Peace, Washington, DC., 5–6.

[72] Institutions are the humanly devised constraints that structure political, economic and social interaction. In this context, they are not organisations. North, D. 1990, *Institutions, Institutional Change, and Economic Performance*, Cambridge University Press; and North, D. 1991, 'Institutions', *Journal of Economic Perspectives*, 5, 1: 97–112, 97.

[73] Armytage, L. 2012, 77+.

[74] International Covenant on Civil and Political Rights (ICCPR) - adopted 16 December 1966, entered into force 23 March 1976; 999 UNTS 171.

[75] ICCPR, Art 14.

[76] This is explained in what Rawls calls 'the difference principle,' which is framed much more simply by my friend Justice Clarence Vui Nelson of the Samoan Supreme Court: 'It's all about fairness." Rawls, J. 1971, 13.

[77] https://www.nobelprize.org/prizes/economic-sciences/1998/press-release/.

[78] In particular, Sen, A. 1999, *Development as Freedom*, New York: Random House; and Sen, A. 2009, *The Idea of Justice*, London: Penguin.

[79] Sen, A. 2009, 12.

[80] Aristotle 1958 (1253a15), 7; and Aristotle 1955 (1137a35) and (1137b25–35),141.

[81] Armytage, L. 2012.

[82] See Chapter 10 "Cambodia - after Year Zero"; also, Armytage L&M, 2018, 77.

[83] A note about photographs: they are referenced to their earlier publication in these endnotes.

[84] Armytage, L&M. 2018.

[85] Armytage, L&M. 2018, 171, cited above.

[86] Armytage, L&M. 2018, 104, cited above.

[87] Armytage, L. 2022, *Homeless: Hidden in Plain Sight*, Chatwin, Seattle.

[88] Australian slang for a lazy person living on social security.

[89] Armytage, L. 2022, 47.

[90] Armytage, L. 2022, 45.

[91] Armytage, L. 2022, 20–1.

[92] Armytage, L. 2022, 36–7.

[93] Armytage, L. 2022, 24–7.

[94] Armytage, L. 2022, 79.

[95] Armytage, L. 2022, 81.

[96] Armytage, L. 2022, 10.

[97] Armytage, L. 2022, 82.

[98] Kolb, D. 1984, *Experiential Learning: Experience as the Source of Learning and Development*, New York: Prentice Hall.

[99] Bloom, BS. 1956, *Taxonomy of Educational Objectives*, London: Longmans, Green and Co.

[100] See Chapter 9 "Colliding with the Present" and Chapter 1 "Prologue: Afghanistan 1978", respectively.

[101] Name changed for confidentiality.

[102] Carothers, T. 1998, 'The Rule of Law Revival', *Foreign Affairs*, 77, 3: 95–106.

[103] Fukuyama F, 1992, *The End of History and the Last Man Standing*, Free Press.

[104] See, for example: Armytage, L. and Metzner, L. (eds) '*Searching for Success in Judicial Reform*,' Oxford University Press 2009; and Armytage L 2012, among others.

MIX
Papier aus verantwortungsvollen Quellen
Paper from responsible sources
FSC® C105338
www.fsc.org

If you have any concerns about our products,
you can contact us on
ProductSafety@springernature.com

In case Publisher is established outside the EU,
the EU authorized representative is:
Springer Nature Customer Service Center GmbH
Europaplatz 3, 69115 Heidelberg, Germany

Printed by Libri Plureos GmbH
in Hamburg, Germany